THE SWEEPING WIND

THE SWEEPING

WIND *A MEMOIR BY*

PAUL DE KRUIF

HARCOURT, BRACE & WORLD, INC. New York

To KEN PAYNE

Nature, with equal mind,
Sees all her sons at play;
Sees man control the wind,
The wind sweep man away . . .

Is it so small a thing
To have enjoy'd the sun,
To have lived light in the spring,
To have loved, to have thought, to have done;
To have advanced true friends, and beat down baffling foes—

—Matthew Arnold, *Empedocles on Etna*

December 11, 1957. On this blizzardy day I must begin again even though the sands of my hourglass are running low. Thirty-five years ago this day, Rhea held my hand as the sun peeped out of the gray for a moment and shone on the bride, and we laughed and believed the old superstition that this meant we were going to be happy. Some of our friends could not believe me to be a fit man for this good girl with the honest, wide-apart gray eyes. Rhea herself knew they had reasons for their doubts; like van Gogh's mysterious young Arlésienne, La Mousmée, her eyes often looked with just a touch of sadness into the inscrutable future. But there was this about Rhea: she was brave.

She stuck to the rugged task—the taming of a turbulent man—till at last our days became not only halcyon but happy. That was her victory. Ahead of us surely lay a long life's late golden afternoon. We were strong for our ages and I was confident of knowing tricks to keep us so. We worked together closer year by year; it was as if we were tossing passes in life's rough game without having to look where the other one was.

Then when Rhea's eyes closed in her last sleep at exactly two in the morning of July 9, 1957, after a terrible two weeks' fight to keep breathing, suddenly, nothing was the same for me any more. In these past months everything has changed. From a full life that seemed too good to be true, it has become an existence so torn, so mutilated that it does not seem to matter whether it goes on one more day.

I must now with this book begin again a search that first began in lost times. Yet this book will be the record of events bright in my memory, for it will attempt the reconstruction of two lives.

THE SWEEPING WIND

Wʜᴏ's that girl in the light-blue dress, the one with the wide-apart gray eyes?" I asked George Lutz, the laboratory dispenser. "Just a country girl from up North. Honest. A hard worker. They don't get gay with her."

This was my first day in mufti after almost two years at the war and I had swaggered into the lab in a trench coat, carrying a big trench stick, quite a dog, making a spectacular return to the bacteriology lab of the University of Michigan medical school. In those brave 1919 days I felt myself as one of the vanguard of the lost generation, one of those who have seen it all and had it all and could not give a damn. Or so I pretended.

"What's her name?" I persisted, despite George's warning. "Miss Barbarin," he said. "Rhea Elizabeth Barbarin. Some kind of French."

Well, I'd try my newly acquired war French on this striking Rhea; not college French but the argot learned from the *poilus* and the Paris taxi drivers and the *midinettes*. Without pretending to be a combat hero, I was vain enough to hint at having been a hero of the night.

But during the next days in the lab it turned out that this strange girl awed me. She'd walk past me on some lab errand looking at me and right through me, not flicking an eyelash or batting an eye.

It was rather as if this self-esteemed Paul de Kruif did not exist. Who do you think you are? her blank look said; and it made me wonder who indeed I thought I was.

It was many days before either of us acknowledged each other's existence and yet among the sixty-odd workers in the lab she was all I had eyes for and when she was not there the lab was empty. George Lutz watched me and smiled. Secretly I inspected Rhea as she deftly plated out cultures of microbes in a row of Petri dishes. What hands . . . Too bad she wasn't a man. What a microbe hunter she might get to be.

Then one day the ice melted. I walked into my private research lab and there was Rhea, sterilizing instruments in the water bath. "Doctor de Kruif, I'd like some advice from you," she said. "A friend of mine writes telling me there's a chance for a technician's job for me in the Philippines. Do you think that's a good place to work?"

What did I know about the Philippines? Only that it was a place where Admiral Dewey had said quietly, "You may fire when ready, Gridley." My ignorance didn't prevent me from advising her. "The trouble with the tropics is they're supposed to be bad for young women's health," I said. "The climate's supposed to play hob with your menstrual cycle." These bold and foolish words didn't shock her at all. It was between us right then as if we old friends, as if brother and sister, as if we could talk about anything. I had already conveyed, somehow, my feeling that I didn't want her to go.

But why? I was a mixed-up young microbe hunter. I already had too many responsibilities, being married and the father of two little boys, and as poor as a church mouse. I was caught up in a research on the blood-dissolving poison of the hemolytic streptococcus, preparing new experiments mornings; teaching advanced bacteriology afternoons; working late into the night over blood-agar plates dotted with colonies of streptococci and their mysterious halos of hemolysis, then going home far past midnight, my head swarming with ideas for tomorrow's experiments—and forbidden thoughts of this girl.

In the late spring I posted a notice calling for applicants to the summer school course in serology with an announcement that men only need apply. A miserable strategy, a cat-and-mouse game, and it worked. Rhea applied for the course and I did not refuse her.

That 1919 summer comes back to me as a whirl, of coaxing my streptococci to pour out more and more streptolysin that made bigger and more beautiful clear halos around their microbe colonies. It was that, deep into the night. And the magic of Rhea in the lab in the day; and inside my head the mixed-up madness of loving her and a moral feeling against this despicable lust. On the surface all seemed calm. Toward her my conduct was correct. Toward me she was not coy but worked at her experiments with a dexterity and economy of effort that entranced me. Yes, what hands, and what a clear head, so strange to find in a girl who had a following of swains. Then came a disturbing event that belied her serene interest in learning to bleed guinea pigs and setting up complement-fixation tests for the Wassermann reaction.

This event took place on a moonlight night on a bridge by the Old Mill Stream. That day Rhea had gone to Grand Rapids to be interviewed for a lab job at Blodgett Hospital. I'd recommended her for the position with the mixed motives of appearing a big-hearted Otis and gaining her gratitude. That night, on her return, we made a clandestine rendezvous and as we cruised in the tender July moonlight in the old Dodge phaeton she reported on her conference with the hospital authorities. What blocked her getting the job was her lack of training in blood chemistry and urinalysis. This roused my pity and she felt that, and snuggled a little closer as we drove slow through the white evening.

Now on the bridge by the waterfall of the millstream we came to a stop, stirred, both of us, by the silver and the sound of the cascading water, and then we were leaning on the bridge rail, close together, and then for the first time we kissed, long and tight together, and it was—for me—passion mixed with a solicitude never before experienced. This girl, I may not, must not harm her. With voice low and thick in my throat I said: "I love you, Rhea." She looked down and said nothing. This July 12, 1919, for me was our betrothal—irregular, impermissible, and unforgettable to this day.

"Now take me home," she said. There were two roads back to Ann Arbor and which should we take? "The longest way round is the sweetest way home," she said. We drove home, enchanted. "Thanks for the ride, Paul," she said at parting. "We mustn't see each other like this again. I've got to get away from Ann Arbor."

It was solemnly pledged that we would not see each other at all any more. Rhea got away from Ann Arbor, and her A grade in serology and her loveliness with its aura of reliability got her a good job in the biological laboratories of Parke Davis and Company in Detroit. I plunged back into the streptolysin research and it was thrilling how those deadly microbes made spectacular, clear halos on their blood-agar plates when grown on a special medium, horse serum mixed with sheep red-blood cells. It seemed that the bigger the hemolytic halos made by a given strain of streptococcus, the higher the virulence, the deadliness. So it seemed. That was my hunch. I had something here. My microbe-hunter master, Dr. Frederick G. Novy, grunted approval and told me the work might be presented at the coming meetings of the Society for Experimental Biology. That excited my vanity. The forlorn wanting of Rhea began to fade. A future of scientific celibacy bid fair to replace frustrated passion, and then, in the autumn, came a letter from Rhea.

It was a matter-of-fact little note saying only that she was enjoying her work at Parke Davis very much and thanks for everything. The next week we faced each other at lunch at the old Hotel Pontchartrain in Detroit and for both of us it was enchantment. "Will you lend me a nickel, Paul?" she asked, as I put her on the streetcar back to the laboratory. "I forgot my purse." She apologized as she smiled down at me from the car step. Would I lend her a nickel? I'd give her my life.

This day was momentous because it began the wreck of what seemed the promising career of a microbe hunter. It revealed an inner feeling of devil take all. A mad plan formed in my head that day, to make a new life, to make enough money to take care of my family responsibilities and at the same time to kick free to marry the unattainable Rhea. It was crazy and wild. How did I know she would be so foolish and brave as to marry me even if it were possible?

But that day in October, 1919, I went back to the Pontchartrain and in the writing room wrote a letter to Henry L. Mencken— never having met him, he never having heard of me—telling him my admiration of the clear way he described the phenomenon of catalysis, asking his advice as to whether a young scientific man should dare to try popular writing on the side. In four days the first of many years of sharp, gay, brilliant, often obscene notes came back from Mencken telling me certainly it was worth while to try it.

Now, somewhat neglecting my blood-dissolving streptococci, I worked into the night on a sketch—satirical in a style deriving from Mencken—examining the scientific pretenses of an eminent professor. How lucky for me that my new mentor didn't think it good enough for his *Smart Set*. Its sarcasm was not too funny and could only have hurt an old man who had indeed been kind to me. But, having been asked to contrubutute to a highbrow magazine, I thought I was a writer. To tough-faced Tom Le Blanc, my lab assistant, a sailor veteran of the war, I confided that I was going to add writing to microbe hunting. His sneering reply was memorable. "You—a writer?" he asked. "Ha—that's just as if you'd announce to me you were going to be a capitalist. What would you use for money, kiddo?"

On the train to Cincinnati to read my streptococcus paper, under Professor Novy's sponsorship, I awoke in the morning in a stuffy upper berth hearing—was it the piccolos?—singing in the coda of Beethoven's Fifth Symphony, clear and soaring and telling me to make Professor Novy and Rhea proud of me this day of the reading of my first scientific paper. Beethoven was in my head awake and dreaming these days. Again and again the first bar with its four opening notes—"thus fate knocks at the door"— sounded in my head at this time when Rhea was remote and seemed forever unattainable and lost to me.

After the scientific meeting in Cincinnati in December, 1918, I went to New York. There was the chance of a job at the great Rockefeller Institute for Medical Research. At the suggestion of Dr. Donald D. van Slyke, who sponsored me, and through the kindness of its director, Dr. Simon Flexner, I landed it. I tried to call Rhea long-distance to give her the exciting news but her phone didn't answer and that brought a spasm of jealousy—who was courting her now?

But far more thrilling to me than to be appointed an associate in the Rockefeller Institute—and in Dr. Flexner's own department —was my first meeting with Henry Mencken. He was a gusty, friendly, ribald, profane savant with his hair parted in the middle over a face like a jolly, jeering full moon with jug ears. He obviously sized me up as a small-town hick from the Dutch bible belt, with my fur cap and short belted overcoat made over from an ulster of my father's. In a letter he had promised me a drink "to make my hair curl" but it was not forthcoming. Timidly, I invited him to lunch, but he was up to his ears putting an issue of the *Smart Set* to bed. Just the same he talked to me almost an hour with incandescent brilliance seasoned with glorious obscenity. While there was no chance to consult him about a possible market for my callow writings, yet it thrilled me to be able to write Rhea I'd met Mencken. To this letter there was no answer.

Yet that day began a friendship between Mencken and me which was soon to be joined by Rhea, who cooked German dinners for us and drank beer with us, seidel for seidel, without leaving the table before we had to. Because Rhea was a small girl, this aroused Menck's respect.

My return from New York to Ann Arbor was anticlimactic. First, I had to tell Professor Novy—my growling, kindly chief— that I was leaving Michigan for the Rockefeller Institute in the autumn. It was tough to tell him for a curious reason. It was not so much that he would be sorry to lose me—my turbulence had at times been a source of embarrassment to him. It was hard to say I was leaving him for the Rockefeller because Dr. Novy took a dim view of Rockefellerian bacteriology.

Novy was the Nestor of American microbe hunters. He was the world's authority on the spirochetes of relapsing fever; one of these corkscrew microbes bears his name. He was the first person to cultivate artificially the trypanosome of deadly Nagana. How could I ever have thought of deserting him for the toy science of the Rockefeller? He had got his science working under Robert Koch in Berlin and Emile Roux at the Institut Pasteur in Paris. These shrines of science were far different from the Rockefeller, whose fame was marked by such sad scientific mistakes as that of declaring globoid bodies to be the cause of infantile paralysis.

On hearing my news Dr. Novy was disappointed. For ten years he had tried to beat honesty and accuracy into my head in the tradition of Robert Koch and Emile Roux. Now what would happen to me in the streamlined elegance of the Rockefeller, where sensational scientific events were often portended but seldom came off? What would become of my discipline absorbed from the dedicated, austere Frederick Novy when it was exposed to the atmosphere of a scientific emporium where it didn't very much matter if one made mistakes, what with Rockefeller prestige backed by the big money? What would happen to the scientific conscience of Novy's boy, Paul, when he consorted with the Rockefeller star, Dr. Hideyo Noguchi? Noguchi, a gay little Japanese, had earned fame resting partly on his discovery of a spurious spirochete that turned out, alas, to be definitely not the cause of yellow fever. You forgave Noguchi because he was a nice little guy, but Novy, the master of spirochetes, took Noguchi apart without mercy.

In the midst of this triumph of landing a job in the microbe-hunting big time, life was bad for me that spring of 1920. In the lab far into the night with Tom Le Blanc I tried to prove the hunch that those strains of streptococcus pouring out high yields of blood-dissolving streptolysin were the ones that were most virulent, the most savage killers of mice . . . and maybe of men. But the mice said no. Hundreds of experiments yielded contradictory results. Big doses of streptococcus might leave mice in a given experiment alive while smaller doses killed their fellow mice in the same experiment. I hadn't the wits to see that my mice, not being litter-mates, might individually vary vastly in resistance. My head was in a whirl. I lost confidence. There seemed to be gremlins clobber-ing the most carefully set up tests of streptococcus virulence. I was distraught in the night in the lab, and then on top of this came bad news from Rhea.

With reluctance she had consented to see me for a short eve-ning in Detroit, and at dinner at the Hotel Ft. Shelby she broke the news to me that after this we must never see each other any more at all. In a taxi after dinner—we had no other place to be alone—I was on my knees, sobbing, begging her, "Wait for me. You'll see. In a couple of years in New York I'll make the grade for you." The girl with the compassionate eyes couldn't stand the tears and said, "Yes, I'll be waiting."

Then an instinct came to my rescue. Many times, when life got scrambled as a result of my turbulence, violent activity in the out-doors calmed me down, dragged my ashes, let me start over with a clean cortex and hypothalamus. How to get away from it all, to clean my mental and emotional house before starting work in the autumn? My wife, Mary, forlorn, neglected, and justifiably bit-ter, took our two little boys to Maine for the summer. Then Tom Le Blanc and I, on a dark, starlit June evening, shoved off from Cheboygan, Michigan, in an old fifteen-foot canoe: nearly swamp-ing in the Straits of Mackinac in the icy water in a very rough following sea when we came out from under the lee of Round Island; landing with the canoe low in the water at St. Ignace with our gear all soaked; then paddling past Les Chêneaux islands and up the St. Mary's River; then going by train over the height of land north of Lake Superior; then paddling down the Pagatchewan, the Kenogami, and the swift Albany River all the way to Ft. Albany at the foot of Hudson Bay, three hundred miles north of nowhere. And back again, paddling and poling and tracking more than a thousand miles, in all, that 1920 summer.

On that cruise we were often short of food. We saw not a liv-ing soul for many days. Tracking with a tumpline back up the Albany River, I slipped and cracked my head on a rock and conked out, and that could have been curtains for us. We lived on sow-belly, corn pone, wild blueberries, and strong tea. We paddled back to Michigan down the St. Mary's River, tanned and tough and with bellies corrugated like Jack Dempsey's in his prime.

"By God," said Tom Le Blanc, "we must look like the old *voyageurs!*"

I saw Rhea in Detroit for a few bittersweet hours and we held each other tight. "It's done you good, dear," she said. "You look tough enough to lick anything now."

"I've got to lick them. For you—no, for *us,* darling," I corrected. "You'll wait for me?"

"Yes, I'll be waiting," she said, and in her eyes there were little tears. "You'll write me?" I begged. She looked troubled. She had promised her father and mother to have no contact with me till I'd kicked free.

"How do they know about us?" I asked. "Mary—your wife wrote them all about us and they're upset. You can't blame them," she said. "You may write me as much as you want. I'll try to let you know how things are going. . . . "

And she did just that, sparingly, for the next year. We held each other tight at parting and I was mad about her and so proud of her. Her work was going well at Parke Davis and she'd been put in charge of the laboratory's anaerobic microbes, of their vaccine and serum production. She told me how she was bleeding horses from the neck vein; horses she'd immunized with Welch bacillus toxin. She was getting to be a microbe-hunting pro. "You must have to stand on tiptoe to get the needles into those neck veins," I said, laughing, and proud of her. She was a little girl only five foot two and it was for me a lovely picture, this little lady calmly bleeding big horses. "You're wonderful, baby," I said. Though she was thin owing to a series of bad sore throats and looked peaked, though her face had no color, to me she was beautiful and I wanted her but could not have her.

"Be a good boy. I love you, Paul," she said, for the first time, that August afternoon in Detroit. Walking toward the train for New York, down Woodward Avenue, it was for me once more as if walking on air; it was an energy, an ecstasy, transfiguring life; it was superturbulence, the kind of illumination Fëdor Dostoevski says comes before an epileptic seizure. And this will never die in my memory.

"What are your plans for research?" asked Dr. Simon Flexner, at the Rockefeller the first day of September. He had listened with urbane astonishment to my account of that crazy cruise to Hudson Bay and back. Dr. Flexner must have wondered how such a bushwhacker could fit into the polite world in that ivoryest of all ivory towers of medical science. And well he might wonder. How could I behave respectably?

"No plans, Dr. Flexner," I said, and went on to explain that this past summer had wiped my head clean of bacteriology. "My brain's a blank blackboard," I said.

Now Dr. Flexner revealed the directorial steel under his urbanity. How different he was from Frederick Novy, who was the apotheosis of free inquiry, who never gave me a directive, who looked every inch a lab man, a searcher. Dr. Flexner looked as if he might be high in the College of Cardinals in Rome. Now he revealed his own plans for my research. His cold face beamed at me with benign power—high kilowatts for all its benignity. Dr. Flexner informed me his department was about to launch a project of study—laboratory epidemiology—of upper respiratory and pulmonary infections as they afflicted rabbits, along lines begun by Professor Topley in England. That would be an excellent project for me to start on.

Of ideas for investigating the sniffles of rabbits I was innocent as a newborn babe. But if I could only turn myself into a microbe-hunting trained seal, that wouldn't matter. My new chief would be the idea man.

What a temple of science the Rockefeller Institute was! It gleamed, materially, in comparison to the department of bacteriology in the old Medical Building at Ann Arbor. That grubby den of research reeked of guinea pigs, white rats, and rabbits. At the Rockefeller you did not smell the animals. They were brought to you from a beautiful animal house in the bowels of the Institute by a servant, a diener. In the primitive days of one's work with Novy one raced three flights down to the basement and back up with wire baskets teeming with guinea pigs and battery jars alive with white rats, and one cleaned the cages and fed the animals when our major domo, George Lutz, was not available. At Ann Arbor one burned one's hands, blowing one's own glassware for complex apparatus, and one washed one's own test tubes and cooked the culture medium to feed one's microbes. At Ann Arbor science was do-it-yourself.

At Ann Arbor I did these chores mornings and taught medical students afternoons and then jogged a mile down to the Huron River mill race to swim hard for half an hour and then, far into the night, together with Frederick Novy, we worked alone, brewing the most powerful poisonous anaphylatoxin so far discovered. By incubating relatively harmless normal rat serum for fifteen minutes at body temperature with a few drops of semisolid agar-agar we turned that serum so toxic that a quarter of a cubic centimeter into the jugular vein would kill a 250-gram guinea pig in three minutes. "It's as if we're pulling a sword out of its scabbard," growled Novy poetically. In those nights in 1914 as we walked home—for me it was a high comradeship—far past midnight, the Professor and I thought we'd surprised the secret of anaphylactic death and maybe of all forms of allergy. Those were the days.

Here at the Rockefeller all was different. Lab servants washed the glassware and cooked the culture medium and if you had a well-enough trained technician, he could even do your experiments for you. But there is this to be said in praise of the Rockefeller Institute: it was a shrine where the world's medical great came to pay homage. Here I was awed by the chance to know the world-renowned Belgian, Jules Bordet, who just this year, 1920, had been awarded the Nobel Prize in medicine. Here I stood in respectful silence while Dr. Simon Flexner explained the method of Rockefeller's streamlined science to Dr. Bordet. "Here we have technicians trained to do the experiments," said Dr. Flexner. "This relieves the investigator, who can go for a stroll in Central Park to think out the next step in his problem."

Bordet, a wispy little Belgian genius—all brain, no front—looked at Dr. Flexner with an apologetic smile. "It is an admirable idea," said Bordet. Then he raised his shoulders and shrugged in seeming self-depreciation of his own old-fashioned methods. "Such discoveries as I've made," he said dryly, "have all been stumbled on by accident, making my own experiments with my own hands." Jules Bordet had earned his own Nobel Prize.

One day Jules Bordet played his part in starting me on my hoped-for second life, writing. That afternoon he managed to slip away from his routine of visits to the Institute's distinguished characters. He came to my lab for a jam session, the two of us alone. The frail, famous small man with his drooping, pathetic mustache sat chain-smoking cigarettes that he rolled in brown paper. He answered my eager questions as to how he had developed his complement-fixation reaction that had resulted in the Wassermann test. He was a progenitor of the science of serology.

He recounted how he had isolated the bacillus of *coqueluche*—the whooping cough—from his own little son's dirty handkerchief that had lain neglected on a lab bench for days. He told how he had been the first to spy the spirochete of syphilis, before Schaudinn, how he didn't dare publish such a tremendous discovery without confirmation by his master, Metchnikoff, at the Pasteur Institute. "I sent my stained preparations—Giemsa method—to Metchnikoff," Bordet explained. "But Metchnikoff was getting old," he said smiling, "and couldn't see too well through the microscope. He wrote me he wasn't sure about my new spirochetes. He warned me against publishing. So I lost that one," said Bordet with a shrug and a sad smile.

What an afternoon it was, and what fun it was to write to Rhea to tell her how Bordet had praised my Ph.D. thesis on the toxicity of normal serum, and how intrigued he was by the terrific toxin Dr. Novy and I had produced by treating rat serum with agar-agar. At the end of that afternoon Professor Bordet said something that shook me. Mind you, I hadn't confided to him my ambition to become a writer. He looked at me with a gleam in his watery blue-gray eyes. "Your style of scientific writing is pure," he said. "What you should think to do is a *roman des microbes.* I can see you feel they are as much *roman* as science." There should be *une histoire de science des microbes* as it actually happened. That night, with only the desk lamp burning in the lab, I told all that great day in a letter to my far-off Rhea. How excited, how pitiful were my hopes. And, given a publisher, how would I find time to write it, busy as I was with research on the *Bacillus lepisepticus,* of the genus of Pasteurella, the cause of pneumonia in rabbits? How could little good Jules Bordet know of the difficulties of this not-yet developed or not-yet discovered style of writing?

The shrine of science, the Rockefeller, was an education to me; it was a new and strange kind of college. Back to it early in the morning a few hours after a night late in the lab sniffing for scientific leads among the snuffy noses of my rabbits sick with pleuropneumonia, I'd climb the front steps of the Institute. Inside the door, a bust faced me. Of Hippocrates? Or Leeuwenhoek? Or Pasteur? No indeed. As was meet and proper, here was a sculpture of John D. Rockefeller, Sr., the greatest of all searchers for God's gold. "We're paying you well, we're giving you every advantage, now come through with a discovery," old John D. seemed to exhort me through thin lips. Every morning I paused to bow a bit before the bust of this most pious of all men of money.

At noon, after a drab morning with my rabbits that had so far told me nothing new, giving me nothing to report to my chief, Dr. Flexner, at the lunch break there was balm for my discouragement. Here I could listen to the scintillating talk of my betters, a scientific elite, a bevy of bacteriological, biological big names. It was thrilling to sit at Jacques Loeb's table listening to that parent of fatherless sea urchins, a veritable eighteenth-century encyclopedist come back to life, making offhand wisecracks about Voltaire and Diderot and pouring sarcasm on contemporary scientists. "As a physicist he is a good husband and father," said Loeb of one eminento, his Mephistophelic eyebrows arched, his black eyes flashing. "Medical science?" said Jacques Loeb, chuckling. "Dat iss a contradiction in terms. Dere iss no such thing." "You should begin with the physical chemistry of proteins, as I do," he admonished his tablemates, who were hard put to it to swap mental punches with the famous founder of the philosophy of a mechanistic conception of life.

What a *Kopf* he was, Jacques Loeb. He gave the Institute a high scientific tone. In addition to his advanced researches, he served as the Institute's front man. I can see him now, piloting Albert Einstein—who looked every inch a concert violinist—about our spotless halls. I adored Jacques Loeb and tried to ape his tart dialectic and I was a thousand miles behind him and would never catch up. In those days I thanked him for encouraging my atheism; he was the peerless leader of the militant godless. But best of all he was the exponent of scientific method as against the prevailing twaddle—*that* was his word—of medical science and I tried secretly to copy him. He was kind to me and backed me up in a semantic hassle over terminology with my chief, Dr. Flexner, reviewing my first manuscript published from the Rockefeller.

Those luncheon sessions were a kindergarten in my stumbling study of character. I never tired of listening to the philosophy of Alexis Carrel, who had won the Nobel Prize in medicine for his ingenious end-to-end anastomosis of arteries, so that he could transplant a kidney, from cat to cat, with its blood supply intact. This worked, too, in men. Carrel, who had been in America a long time, had carefully preserved his French accent, which made him sound to me even more learned than he was. In his lab, in his black surgical gown and cap, Carrel was a magician keeping a bit of chicken heart muscle beating, in a bottle, transplanting it from bottle to bottle ad infinitum over the years, hinting the awesome possibility that physical life is (potentially) immortal. From time to time the birthdays of those bits of chicken in their bottles, tended with devotion by Dr. Ebeling, made newspaper front pages. Dr. Carrel's publicity genius astounded me and I secretly practiced his French accent, hoping it would fortify my own taxicab driver's French if I ever got back to France.

Then at the luncheon table there might be Dr. Peyton Rous, refined, gentle, exquisitely cultured. He had uncovered the virus of a cancer, a sarcoma of chickens; it hinted that all cancers might turn out to be viral, as it now, forty years later, becomes possible that they are. Dr. Rous was so amazed at his own discovery that it was rumored he couldn't stand the mental strain of going on with it and you couldn't blame him.

In this refectory there was an air of solemnity to be expected and appropriate to the unveiling of mysteries. Yet, the old Pasteurians of the Rue Dutot in Paris—Roux and Chamberland and the martyred Thuillier—might have felt out of place in this Rockefeller Institute lunchroom. For all its seriousness, its culture and learning, those old Frenchmen might have felt a lack of that all-out desperation characteristic of their master, Pasteur; a lack of his divine fire.

Among the eaters in this scientific beanery the most picturesque was the enigmatic Japanese, Hideyo Noguchi, a scientific Trilby, the creation and at the same time the slave of his Svengali, Dr. Simon Flexner. In the winter of 1920 I was asked to hitch my wagon to Noguchi's star. Three months had passed and I was excited at what seemed a new fact that gave interest to the sniffles of the pneumonia that decimated the rabbits in the laboratory. Suddenly—it was a bolt out of the blue—Dr. Flexner asked me if I'd drop that research and go to Vera Cruz, Mexico, where a yellow fever epidemic was said to be raging. Purpose of mission: to isolate and bring back strains of *Leptospira icteroides,* claimed by Noguchi to be the cause of the dread Yellow Jack.

Would I like to? I wouldn't like to. Dr. Novy was pretty sure that what the misguided Japanese searcher had discovered was only *Leptospira icterohemorrhagiae* of infectious jaundice. I still believed Novy's view of Noguchi. Then too, I didn't want to go that far away from Rhea. I pleaded with him to let me keep probing into the miseries of my snuffy rabbits, to find the cause of the curious behavior of the lepisepticus microbes that murdered them. It seemed as if we were on the trail of something hot. Dr. Flexner relented.

And so it came about that my rugged assistant, Tom Le Blanc —who loved to globe-trot—packed up and was off for dangerous Vera Cruz. "Go to the best hotel and rent a portion of it," Noguchi directed Tom, grandly. "Buy a dozen silk pajamas and do not worry about expenses. But bring back the Leptospira."

Now I was alone without any assistant except my diener, Frank Foucek, with whom I boxed, afternoons. Writing Rhea that I wanted to stay close by her in the United States, this brought a quick answer that she was glad. Rhea worried me. Repeated streptococcus sore throat was getting her down. "But it doesn't keep me from work. I'm enjoying the work with the anaerobes. I love you more and more."

It was a lonely, blue winter in 1920. I'd made no contacts with magazine editors or publishers to help me start the dreamed-of second life of writing; and there was no writing to show them, anyway. Bordet's proposed romance of microbes gathered dust on the shelf of my imagination. There was only a funny quirk of behavior of the rabbit sniffle microbes to excite me. Certain colonies of germs, when they were streaked on serum agar, changed their appearance and at the same time turned out to be harmless, gentle—instead of virulent. So what? Well it was something to chew on.

For all its lavish facilities, its endless apparatus, its technical know-how, the Rockefeller Institute in 1920, at the end of some twenty years of existence, seemed to have fallen somewhat short of its glorious promise. As a shrine of research, the Institute had had a curious origin. It had not blossomed out of a great discovery like that of Pasteur and his living vaccines, or like that of Robert Koch and his invention of a solid culture medium that had enabled the isolation and trapping of most of the deadly anthrax and TB microbes.

The idea of the Institute had been born in the brain of a remarkable man of God, the Reverend Frederick T. Gates. He was known as Mr. John D. Rockefeller's chief almoner. In the service of the greatest money-man the world had ever known the Reverend Mr. Gates was faced with a difficulty. When your master has made that much money it is probable that some of it has come from people who feel that by rights they should have been allowed to keep it. Mr. Gates, a pious man, was aware of the saying of Our Lord, "It is easier for a camel to go through the eye of a needle, than for a rich man to enter into the Kingdom of God." Here was the ethical difficulty: how *does* a very very rich man get right with God? The Reverend Mr. Gates turned out to be just the man to write the prescription. Mr. Rockefeller, in his autobiographical fragment, *Random Reminiscences of Men and Events,* pays a compliment to the philanthropico-commercial genius of the good dominie. "Right here," writes Mr. Rockefeller, "I may stop to give credit to Mr. Gates for possessing a combination of rare business ability, very highly developed and exercised, overshadowed by a passion to accomplish some great and far-reaching benefit to mankind."

The Reverend Mr. Gates was just the man to help Mr. Rockefeller squeeze through the needle's eye on the way to bliss among the Baptist cherubim and seraphim. To lubricate this maneuver Mr. Gates melded a compound of commerce with holiness. He began by a close study of a then standard textbook, Dr. Osler's *Medicine.* Horrid facts appalled him. Despite the world's highly developed medical science, despite Pasteur, despite Robert Koch, despite Claude Bernard, despite Dr. Osler himself, the Osler textbook told a terrible story. Against almost every major disease, doctors remained helpless at the start of the twentieth century. The Osler book was a masterpiece of medical teaching in lofty prose. It told doctors the signs and symptoms proving that TB, or cancer, or syphilis, or pernicious anemia, or lobar pneumonia, or malignant hypertension have snuck up on patients and are maybe about to do the poor devils in. The book was a marvelous textbook of differential diagnosis to teach the physician to tell this disease from that. Alas, at the same time, the book showed only too clearly that against a host of maladies—including those here mentioned—the doctors couldn't do a damned thing.

Now our Reverend Mr. Gates saw how to fix it. He was inspired, shaken to his shoes by what he saw as a chance for Mr. Rockefeller's salvation. He would mitigate the miseries of millions by the use of the gold that God had left in the stewardship of Mr. Rockefeller. Out of the Osler book Mr. Gates compiled a list of maladies, all the way from mild to deadly, all the way out to the sad sicknesses that the great English Dr. Sydenham had dubbed "continuate and inexorable," such as one-hundred-per-cent-fatal pernicious anemia. This list Mr. Gates placed before medical dignitaries, authorities at the Johns Hopkins, among them Dr. Osler and jolly Professor William H. (Popsy) Welch, who, in addition to his learning in pathology, was a connoisseur of terrapin à la Maryland, and had a memory that rolled delicious dinners around his tongue years after.

Mr. Gates posed these savants a question; given ample funds furnished by God's steward, Mr. John D. Rockefeller, Sr., might it not be feasible to launch a grand attack on sundry sicknesses such as carcinoma, cerebrospinal meningitis, and the lobar pneumonia that was then plugging up the air sacs of lungs, killing a hundred thousand and more Americans yearly? The Reverend Mr. Gates put a challenge to his advisers. What was it that their medical science lacked? Not brains. Not curiosity. Not Pasteur's wild boldness. No, not these. It was money it lacked. Such at least was Mr. Gates's insight. Given enough of the yellow metal, the moolah, you could buy the bricks and mortar, the microscopes, yes, even the men; you'd find plenty of men if you paid them decently. Then you could organize all the facilities for grand researches to discover the cures of those deaths lamented in his textbook by Dr. Osler. It was a vision. It was a natural.

Mr. Gates drove his point home. Might not the cure of all these incurable diseases become possible if Mr. Rockefeller could be enlisted as the research angel? Might it? They'd say it might! And Mr. Gates was sure he could get them their angel. Mr. Rockefeller, reputed to be an avaricious icicle by some who did not really know him, had hidden deep within him a boundless benevolence. That Mr. Gates knew. And so it came to pass that the philanthropist took fire from his almoner's "passion to accomplish some great and far-reaching benefit to mankind." Now Mr. Rockefeller waved his golden wand and so an Institute, temporarily housed in a small building, was prudently started at Sixty-sixth Street on the banks of New York's East River, across from the bleak poorhouse on Blackwell's Island. And the director and guiding spirit of the new Institute was Dr. Simon Flexner.

Soon after the take-off there was what seemed a stunning success, a new serum, evolved by Dr. Simon Flexner and his minion, Dr. Jobling, to cure epidemic cerebrospinal meningitis. This remedy was reported to lower its mortality by many per cent—statistically significant. Without controls. You did not need them. This vindicated the Gatesean hypothesis, so it seemed. It hinted that the medical unknown was like a slot machine: feed it enough gold pieces and you're bound to hit the jackpot of a cure. The sad thing was that Drs. Flexner and Jobling had not so much initiated as repeated the discovery. Two German searchers, Drs. Jochma and Kruse, had seen ahead of them.

Such was the beginning of the Rockefeller Institute for Medical Research in the first decade of the brilliant new twentieth century. But yet, and alas, as the years wore on the hoped-for parade of cures did not come off. Could it be that the slot machine had turned out to be a one-armed bandit, stealing God's gold from Mr. Rockefeller? It is true that the hospital of the Rockefeller Institute in the century's second decade did bring forth serums against Types I and II and later many other types of lobar pneumonia, not downing their death rates sensationally, but for all that, seemingly statistically significant. But still in the opening years of the 1920's citizens went on dying like flies from the great majority of the maladies which, said Dr. Osler, lacked a curative medicine.

To Dr. Flexner, to the Reverend Mr. Gates, to Professor Welch this must have seemed baffling. All the factors for success seemed there: the bricks, the glass, the hands, the well-trained heads, the master directorial mind. Yet the hoped-for scientific offensive against multiple deaths can hardly have been said to have achieved a break-through; on wide fronts it can indeed have been said to have fizzled out. (Though, curiously, the public did not think so. To the man in the street, and to many a humble physician the Institute was and still remains the temple in medical research.)

The study of this phenomenon of money—lavish amounts of it—failing to bring forth cures became my private hobby in these years at the Institute. It is a major mystery. I do not, down to this day, understand why huge grants for research are not necessarily followed by a cure for cancer. There seems to be a reluctance on the part of mortal ills to fall before an organized onslaught on the part of men, materials, and money. One can only retreat into mysticism, into theology for an explanation; it may be in the realm of the eschatological. It may be, alas, that God does not always smile too quickly upon His servants who are eager to thank Him, materially, for His having blessed them, materially, by letting them gather in great gobs of God's gold. Could it be that certain monies are tainted, as was hinted by our muckrakers in the opening years of the century? Ridiculous! Money is money. *Pecunia non olet.*

In the winter of 1920–1921 there came an opportunity to see my forbidden Rhea. Into my lab one day walked a kindly old public health man, Colonel F. F. Russell, who acted in an advisory capacity for the Rockefeller Foundation (not the Institute). In a fatherly way he told me there was the chance of a job for me to run the clinical laboratory in a hospital in Buffalo—not a research position but routine clinical pathology. And would I go take a look at it if the Buffalo people paid my expenses? To me this should have been a blow, and below the belt. In the first place I didn't know enough pathology to run a clinical laboratory. In the second place Colonel Russell must have known that it was not going to be my destiny to sit on my seat peering through microscopes at stained sections of kidney or liver or brain, routinely. I was a bacteriologist, a researcher, right this moment hot on the trail of a peculiar type of microbic behavior, a possible explanation of the mechanism of attenuation of virulent germs. Colonel Russell must have been told this by Dr. Flexner, who apparently had given small importance to my observations. Dr. Flexner must have sent Colonel Russell to me as an undercover emissary to aid in getting me out of the Rockefeller Institute.

"When offered a job, one ought to take a look. Thank you, Colonel Russell," I said. And why didn't I save the Buffalo hospital my expense money by telling Colonel Russell of my unsuitability? Why didn't I ask him why Dr. Flexner wanted to get rid of me? Well, the wild-goose chase to Buffalo would pay my expenses halfway to Detroit. To see Rhea.

At Buffalo it took the hospital people only a few hours to find out that Paul de Kruif was hardly the man for them; and, next morning, shaving in the Pullman coming into Detroit, a fellow shaver asked me: "Why you whistling? You seem happy." "I'm going to see my girl," I said.

My heart hammered when I rang the doorbell of the apartment where Rhea lived with two college girl friends. And there she was. And there was the maddening scent of her. And there we were tight in each other's arms and away from the world for a long moment.

"What's wrong, darling?" She was thin. She was sallow. There were circles under her eyes. She was sick. She was beautiful. She was my own true love. She tore my heart.

Our few poor hours seemed minutes. I couldn't take my eyes off her high-cheekboned face with its clean jawline. I wanted never to leave her and to hell with the Rockefeller and to hell with my research she was so wonderful.

Rhea told me her troubles and her triumphs with her anaerobic microbes at Parke Davis and how embarrassing it was to tell her boss that the blackleg spores they'd shipped out in a supposedly living vaccine were dead. All dead. Useless to guard Argentine cattle from blackleg. They'd have to call all the vaccine back. She'd make them. She was brave.

Then we snuggled close as I showed her my research notebooks, telling her the new phenomenon I'd found—"microbic dissociation." A rabbit septicemia culture isn't simple. It's constantly

21

splitting, dissociating into two distinct types of microbe. One type virulent. The other type harmless.

How did I spot the harmless ones? asked Rhea. "Stumbled on to it," I said. "Streaked out a drop of exudate from the pleura of a dead rabbit on a serum-agar plate. Incubated it. And here were two absolutely different types of colonies mixed up together."

"How d'you prove one of 'em wasn't simply a contamination?" she asked.

"The microbes from the two different colonies look exactly the same under the microscope; both lepiseptics, for sure." One colony was fluorescent, smooth. Another colony right beside it was dull gray, granular, rough-edged. But the smooth fluorescent colony, subcultured into serum broth, was virulent. And how! Dilutions, out to one-hundred millionth of a cubic centimeter of a subculture from a gray rough colony—undiluted—are harmless. Attenuated!

"Will the attenuated ones immunize rabbits against the virulent ones?" she asked. She knew that was just the point, an *experimentum crucis*. What fun we'd have working together! But when?

CHAPTER TWO

W~HY~ did Dr. Flexner want to get rid of me? He had seen the dissociation experiments and was beginning to understand their possible significance. But it turned out that he was disturbed by other, far from scientific events in my laboratory. It had been reported to him that I was fooling around with not one but two young women in the Institute. It was, to say the least, improper here. Dr. Flexner had me up on the carpet and scolded me. "Your conduct indicates that you are either a knave or a fool," he said. Miserably I admitted to being a bit of both. My conscience, monogamous, was at war with Turkish instincts for the exercise of which I was in the wrong country. Dr. Flexner smiled almost understandingly. I didn't tell him that what tortured my conscience was the possibility of not being true to Rhea—of whom he knew nothing.

What had driven me to this moral confusion? Atheism, partly. Long ago before the war I'd read a book, *Sanine,* by Artzybasheff. Sanine was free-thinking, ruthless with dames, with the negative ethics of Dostoevski's Ivan Karamazov, who'd argued: "If there is no God, then all things are permitted." I was sure there was no God. God was accident merely, mathematics of permutations and combinations. This was an excuse to coddle my inner enemy, sensuality, steamed up by my turbulent energy.

All this except my love for Rhea was disclosed to Dr. Flexner. I begged him for another chance. He said he liked my work. He was intrigued by the harmless rough-type microbes arising from the smooth type, virulent. Excited, I pointed out that this might explain how all microbic attenuation might come about, how harmless, attenuated cultures arise by a process of natural selection. It might throw light on the mystery of the gentling of chicken cholera and anthrax microbes that had enabled Pasteur to use them to guard chickens and sheep. This might be that not too common thing, a generalization. It might be and it might not. Wasn't Dr. Flexner pleased with this dissociation work? He certainly was. Would he let me go on with it? He said kindly that he would, and would I please get busy and write up the results, so far, for publication in his *Journal of Experimental Medicine?*

I went back to the lab, elated and ashamed of myself, with only the honesty of my experimental observations to comfort me. Only that and a tender worship for Rhea so far away. In the lab I woolgathered at two rows of test tubes; serum broth cultures of virulent smooth type in the front row, of attenuated rough type,

23

back row. How elegant. How lovely. The virulent lepisepticus grew in silky smooth turbidity; the harmless ones settled out in great granules, in contrast.

I took a grip on myself and in the beginning of 1921 in the winter in New York, life opened up for me after this crisis. I found myself among the *literateurs* of the Big City, thanks alone to the prestige of being on the staff of the Rockefeller Institute for Medical Research. That was the open sesame for me. I got to know that gentle, humorous martyr to rheumatoid arthritis, Clarence Day, as the result of a fan letter written to him in admiration of his book *This Simian World*. Clarence wasn't bitter about his affliction, against which medicine was helpless, and he laughed at my comments on the impotence of medical research, even at the Rockefeller. Himself crippled, he was delighted at my turbulent energy. Only five hours sleep? Wow! He had a bald head, round surprised eyes, and looked like a man from Mars. He was an audience for my egotism, and yet my teacher. Late afternoons in his hermitage high over the North River he told me his still unwritten stories, taking his father apart, yet loving him.

Clarence introduced me by a casual note scrawled painfully with his arthritic hand to Francis Hackett, critic on the *New Republic* and as witty a man as I've ever known. Hackett was then meditating his funny book about the sad wives of that unfunny king, Henry the Eighth. Hackett, with his gentle, blond Danish wife, Signe Toksvig, a writer too, lived in that literary oasis, Turtle Bay, and here I was their pupil. "Are all Danes blond and beautiful and brainy like you, Signe? And you're beautiful too, Francis, in a rococo Irish style." Francis laughed. Did this moujik from Michigan know what rococo meant? He didn't exactly. But Francis and Signe would teach him and they did.

They appointed themselves my unpaid literary agents and introduced me to Norman Hapgood, editor of Hearst's *International Magazine* and father of the five-foot shelf of books selected by the august President Eliot of Harvard. Norman was querulously learned, a keen scout of writing talent, and he might be a market for my writings, yet unwritten.

And then through the kindness of Clarence Day and Francis and Signe and Henry Mencken came the chance to get a toe hold in the world of the writing big time. A book seriously laughing at so-called civilization in our country was being put together. Its authors were a galaxy: Henry L. Mencken, George Jean Nathan, Van Wyck Brooks, Lewis Mumford, and many others all aiming to take America's cultural pretensions to the cleaners. The contract for the proposed book had been signed with the spectacularly successful new publishing house of Harcourt, Brace and Company. The book's editor—a mysterious, sloppy bohemian but keen intellectual, Harold Stearns—asked me would I write the chapter on American medicine.

My suitability for this job could hardly have been other than that I worked at the Rockefeller Institute and the University of Michigan Medical School. I was no M.D. What did I know about the art and science of medicine? All I knew was that America had many eminent doctors using many medicines and that with the medicines the doctors did not cure many people. Doctors were priests, medicine men, layers on of hands, exponents of the bedside manner—that was my brash estimate of their noble profession. This tickled Harold Stearns.

Yes, I'd try to write the chapter if he'd let me remain anonymous. "Why anonymous?" asked Stearns, who wanted to exploit the reputation of the Rockefeller. "If you print my name with that connection I'd get kicked to hell out of the Institute," I said. I sat down to write about what I knew: not much, my only source book being Garrison's *History of Medicine*. Writing far into the night in the lab after the day's dissociation experiments were done.

Then presently there was good news to write to Rhea. Joel Spingarn—who'd been a Columbia professor and was a scholarly man—declared my essay to be maybe more effective, *journalistically,* than any other in the symposium. It got around New York that here was an amusing new journalist in medical science.

My fee for the work was fifty dollars, the first writing money I'd earned.

. . .

In the lab the work was booming. How did I know that the rough, harmless type of the lepisepticus microbe really arose from the smooth, virulent? Mightn't they exist together side-by-side in sick and dead rabbits and then appear together on my serum-agar plates? How to prove that the virulent ones actually changed into harmless? How to prove that the rough types weren't mere contaminants, as Rhea had suggested? Only one way to prove it, fishing one lone single microbe out of a culture swarming in billions under the microscope—it was a most delicate and difficult technique—by means of a Barber pipette. Trying it again and again I failed miserably. Then a young microbe hunter at Cornell Medical School, Dr. Kahn—I don't remember his first name, alas —showed me how and did it for me. And presto, here were cultures originating from a single microbe. Pure line strains. I do not know which of these pure line cultures were Kahn's and which mine, or were all of them Kahn's? In my publication I didn't even thank Kahn in a footnote, and of this discourtesy I'm ashamed to this day.

Now we were in business. That single virulent smooth-type germ multiplied into fluorescent smooth types in subcultures. Then, when subcultured again, a few flat, gray rough-type colonies began to show up on the serum-agar plates among the fluorescent virulent. I hurried to Dr. Flexner. I had it. Here was microbic *mutation*. My chief objected to this word mutation applied to microbes. These rough types might only be variants, Dr. Flexner exclaimed. I begged him to let Dr. Jacques Loeb referee our semantic hassle. Loeb beamed through his black eyes at me and turned to Flexner. "De Kruif iss correct," said the great biologist. "His attenuated rough types do not revert to smooth, virulent. They breed true. They are sports, mutants. It iss a true mutation in the sense of Hugo De Vries."

Dr. Flexner, bowing before Jacques Loeb's verdict, let it stand as "mutation" in the scientific report. The mysterious splitting, the dissociation of a culture into two dramatically distinct types is a business of a deadly microbe mutating into harmless. How? Nobody knew. Ambitious dreams swam in my head and I wrote them in long daily letters to Rhea. We'd start a new branch of bacteriology; we'd isolate harmless mutants from other microbic species and maybe turn them into living vaccines against sundry killers of men.

The man who cooled my cockiness was Loeb's associate, John Howard Northrop. This tall, nonchalant physical chemist—later to win the Nobel Prize for crystallizing the enzymes pepsin and trypsin—warned me to take it easy. Northrop's china-blue eyes looked at me as he tugged at the tips of his splendid long Nordic blond mustache. He was like a Viking come back to life. Northrop outwardly didn't give a hoot about science; he was a noted hunter and fisherman and these pursuits he regarded as far above muddling with microbes in the lab. Yet his head held what seemed inborn chemical knowledge and his skill with his hands at the lab bench made me hold him in awe. He was not only a performer of chemical prestidigitations but gave chemical advice offhand to the great Jacques Loeb while Northrop himself seemed to be away in the world of the grouse and the speckled trout. He was nonassertive—a scientific Lao-tse.

Jack Northrop shamed me, he was so definitely not on the make. "Why are you knocking yourself out, working like three men and not sleeping?" he asked me. "For Rhea," I said. "You'll never get her the way you're going, you're knocking yourself out, you're shooting yourself to hell," he answered. He thought me crazy trying to do science and learn writing at the same time. What did these indoor pursuits amount to compared to wing-shooting? Telling me his outdoor exploits he played down his own part in them and of his science he spoke apologetically. If only I could learn Jack's *sang-froid*. Yes, if only. He kept getting me to tell him about Tom Le Blanc's and my wild cruise to Hudson Bay. "Come along to Newfoundland this summer," he urged. "Let's see how good you are at poling a canoe up fast white water. Newfoundland—that's where you get the big fighting salmon." But where would I get the money to go?

Soon after that, the late Glenn Frank took me to lunch. He was the brilliant editor of *The Century* magazine, which spread culture to aspiring intellectuals. He was handsome and affable and later became the boy president of the University of Wisconsin. He'd seen my piece in the new book spoofing American culture. Could I expand that into a book, first running it in *The Century*? Would an advance of say, five hundred, be okay? Would it!

"You can write it on the shore of the Sandy River," said Jack Northrop. "Only you'll have to first help get us up there with that setting pole—there's some fast white water."

What would have happened to me if I hadn't gone to Newfoundland with Jack but had stayed in the lab and my hole-in-the-wall bedroom that hot 1921 summer in New York? I was alone and unstable. In June I went to pay a last call on my two little boys and Mary my wife, who was leaving to teach at Wellesley. The boys seemed to sense they wouldn't see me again and they waved at me out the window, calling me to come back to them as I walked away from their drab apartment building. "Come back, Daddy," they shouted, and for twenty-four years I didn't see them.

What would have happened to me if strong, steady Jack Northrop hadn't dragged me out of the stinking city that summer? How lucky I was. Who was watching over me? For many years now, when deep in doldrums, uprooted, somebody or something was there to help me. In the war in the Argonne it was Sergeant Savage, a laundryman from Fitchburg, Massachusetts, tall and imperturbable in his hip boots, who made me ashamed to be yellow under fire. Then Rhea had calmed the wild, shell-shocked sensuality that all but ruined me after the war. Then Dr. Donald van Slyke had got me into the safety and scientific luxury of the Rockefeller—when I'd really wanted to come to New York only to be close to Henry Mencken and to get to know editors and writing men. But still I had no roots. I was restless. And though in my work I was a lone wolf, I did not want to be alone. I wanted Rhea fiercely but she was away, and what would happen to me in New York with women a dime a dozen and *faute de mieux*?

Clarence Day, Francis, and Signe tried to teach me to write

and always seemed happy to see me and they were a haven from the danger of the maddening attraction for a dame, any dame. But I couldn't impose on my friends' kindness and didn't, and many nights walked the streets trying to burn off this damnable turbulence, this energy boiling in me. Furious at this weakness I'd drag myself, dead-beat, up to the hall bedroom, falling on the narrow iron bed in the narrow room, trying to read myself to sleep with the essays of Schopenhauer, the German philosopher whose pessimism, Jacques Loeb said, was due to an incurable gonorrhea. How I dramatized myself those dreadful days! How I pitied myself, at last falling asleep not much caring whether I lived or died.

Now, in late June of 1921, Jack Northrop and I were sweating, bending over our setting poles in fast water, paddling up quiet stretches of the Humber River in Newfoundland many miles till Jack, opening our packs at the first night's camp, stretched, chuckled, and said: "It appears that the salt has left us." Next morning we laughed and paddled back to the base camp and got the salt and started all over and nothing mattered. Nothing much mattered to Northrop, the Nordic Lao-tse. At last we made camp in a wood on the bank by the Sandy Lake Rapids where Jack said there must be salmon. Early morning and in the evenings the hermit thrush sang for us. At our meals of brook trout the camp-robbing Canada jays snatched morsels of fish out of our fingers on the way to our mouths. For weeks we saw no one.

During the day Jack, hip deep in the rapids, fished the pools for salmon. All day I sat, propped against a tree, with a pencil covering pages of one notebook after another with the first draft of a book that was sure as hell going to get me kicked out of Rockefeller. Turbulence had faded. Noons I thrashed a crawl stroke in the cold water of Sandy Lake. In Newfoundland's northern air there was an elixir to stir one to write, not giving a damn for anything.

What was getting down furiously in those notebooks was a montage of what I'd seen, heard, read, felt, and experienced in the past eleven years close to medicine—in medical school and teaching medical students; in the lab in the night with my austere master Frederick Novy; in the library reading Pasteur and Koch in the original; in the war in France drinking *clos de bouche* with Hans Zinsser, William Elser, Stanhope Bayne-Jones and many other men of all medical disciplines, the elite of American medicine; at the Pasteur Institute sitting at the feet of Emile Roux and Maurice Nicolle—and at the Rockefeller where we worked with docility under the guidance of Dr. Simon Flexner. It was the tale of the past eleven years as lived under the influence of too many medical and scientific celebrities and too few family doctors. What was getting written—flip, snooty, occasionally hilarious—was a farrago of youthful foolishness with a seasoning of insight.

What was trying to get written was *Arrowsmith* but without Red Lewis's skill as a writer. In this callow creation I was alone on my own. Good Jack Northrop was of small literary or scientific or philosophic help to me. He tugged at his magnificent mustachios and smiled while I despaired of medical progress. For Jack there was no such thing as progress, except backward toward the American Indians. According to Jack the great days of the American continent were done when the Pilgrims landed and began to bother those poor Indians; everything after that was a downhill road to doom. "Turn round, quiet, look," whispered Northrop, eyes shining as he pointed to a mother duck leading her ducklings off the nest for their first trip into water.

I turned back to my notebook. What, in these early 1920 days, was the condition of the science and the art of medicine? Relief of pain by anesthetics and a few analgesics. Saving of life from malaria by quinine and from syphilis by mercury, but these were ancient remedies found long before our so-called medical science. Look at the disappointment in Paul Ehrlich's spectacular 606. It had turned out far from the one-shot *therapia-sterilisans-magna* he'd hoped and the long treatment needed to cure was dangerous and sometimes killed. This brave beginning of chemotherapy might be its end as well. Chemicals synthesized by thousands were bad not only for microbes but for men. My mathematical god seemed to play it impartially between men and microbes.

And what had happened to hope for cures by serums? Big start with the serum cure of diphtheria and then the old bog-down again. Pneumonia? Two of my Rockefeller colleagues had actually evolved a serum that saved a proportion of the victims of Types I and II pneumonia—if you got them early. But it turned out there were distinct types of pneumonia microbes almost ad infinitum; and while doctors were waiting round for labs to tell them what type was infecting their patients death might not wait. Over-all, pneumonia death rate was not going down.

What had become of the brave prophecy of Pasteur—that it was now in the power of men to make microbic maladies vanish from the face of the globe? Where were the hoped-for preventive vaccines? It seemed the mathematical god was good only to chickens and sheep. Even of the preventive power of a vaccine for human typhoid fever there was serious question. Again, the bog-down.

And to add to my bitterness, manufacturers of phony alleged curative vaccines were exploiting medical credulity. You shot it in if you thought a patient had a disease—almost any disease— and if the patient got well, it was the vaccine that cured him. No need for checking on it by control cases, untreated. It was a swindle made in the name of Pasteur.

But wasn't scientific surgery wonderful? Life-saving? Under aseptic technique they could cut, they could sew, they could tat, they could mend, they could patch; but this was glorified plumbing, mechanics, surgical hemstitching, trying to take death out of people, not keeping it from getting into them. And how many wretches were being operated upon not for appendicitis—but for one hundred and fifty dollars?

I couldn't praise the conquests of public health without pointing out that certain of its other activities were ridiculous. Of course, many lives were being saved by the sanitation of milk, water, and sewage. Healthmen were bravely squirting oil on the breeding places of mosquitoes to cut down deaths from malaria and yellow fever; they were boldly battling bubonic plague by fighting the flea. Side-by-side with these heroes a distinguished professor of pathology, Dr. Aldred Scott Warthin, of Michigan, was suggesting to his students that masturbation might be an economical preventive of the microbic consequences of venery. Side-by-side with him was a Belgian professor, demonstrating the dangers of alcohol to an audience of workingmen. The earnest savant poured alcohol down the throat of a guinea pig till it went into a coma and died. "And that proves—" he cried. "And that goes to show that alcohol is bad for such little animals," interrupted a workman.

So under the inspiration of Henry Mencken I tried to make monkeys of well-meaning professors who, though lacking scientific weapons, conducted a futile moral fight against alcohol, syphilis, and gonorrhea. What poured on to the pages of my notebooks on the bank of Sandy Lake Rapids was fixing to finish me in medical science. Mencken might kid politicians that way, okay, but I was kidding medicine, and didn't I realize you'd better not kid the doctors?

Jack tried to cool me down. "Let's go down the river," he said, "and out to the railroad to get the mail." Jack's wife, the lovely Louise, was expecting a baby this coming autumn. Jack, outwardly calm, had been building up an inner inferno of anxiety. "What was that, a gunshot? Did you hear that?" asked Jack as we paddled down the river. Impossible. We were thirty miles away from nowhere. "Maybe they're trying to find us. Maybe there's bad news." He fired his rifle in reply and only an echo answered. But up out of his imperturbability surged terrible energy and he dug his paddle savagely into the dark water and I did too, infected with his worry, wondering if there might not be bad news from Rhea.

That day we broke some kind of private record for distance covered by land and by water. We shot rapids we should have portaged. We slogged across feather-bed swamps. Jack with his long legs walking like an Indian crossed them easily, while I— breathing hard—bogged down in them. Jack waited for me. He roared with laughter. "You look like a great big goddamn frog," he said, as I pulled myself up out of a sinkhole. We got to the little railroad station, some forty miles from our camp. Thank God, Louise was all right, said her letter, and from Rhea far off in Detroit there was a little note saying she hoped the book was going well and maybe I could come to see her in August. "I love you more and more," she finished.

Our good news was a needle to our anterior pituitaries and in turn our adrenals and, still full of beans, despite the forty miles of paddling and mushing we started right back, mushing, paddling, and poling up the dark V of the chute of a rapids, our canoe hanging motionless on the crest for a dangerous moment against the force of the cold dark water. . . . But one more big shove and we'd make it. We got back within not too many miles of Sandy Lake Rapids and Jack figured we'd covered more than sixty miles that day. Feeling the physical fatigue that's the salt of life for bushwhackers, we made camp in the shelter of the canoe. We built a big fire of birchwood and drank big cups of strong cocoa, bitter for lack of Klim and sugar. The cocoa's theobromine woke us up and by the firelight I read to Jack about the Dempsey-Carpentier fight from the New York *Times* that had come with the mail.

That cruise didn't calm me down; far from it. Back at Sandy Lake camp—after the longest sleep in my life—all afternoon and all the next night, I woke up next morning feeling empty but wonderful. Now my exuberance drove me into an ultimate heresy, a spoofing of the high priests of medical science. I laid about me, not neglecting the eminentoes who had the say over my bread and butter.

One of my colleagues at the Rockefeller Institute—Dr. Rufus Cole, a gentle man who had been kind to me—had published an essay proposing the thesis that medicine had now developed so far that it could be looked at as an independent science, on a par with physics and chemistry. What a mental *gaffe!* While disease must be studied in a modern hospital, at the same time nothing should be left undone to cure the patient, wrote the eminent author. What a howler, what hooey, what a contradiction in terms! To study a disease, to get to know it, shouldn't the student abstain from interfering with the cause of the disease he was looking for? How otherwise would you establish your base line? What had Pasteur done in his immortal experiment with the fifty-two sheep at Pouilly le Fort? He'd vaccinated only half of them and left the other half as controls and had left everything undone to save them; and they had died—*les témoins,* controls, Pasteur had called them—sad witnesses to the power of the vaccine to save the others. That was science. And had my eminent author of the essay done likewise? He had not. He'd ordered his pneumonia serum given to all patients so that not a single one would die per adventure the experimental serum might save. Yes, *might* save. But without the serum that single one might have lived anyway. Who knew?

To study a disease but at the same time not hurt the patient by withholding what might help him—what kind of nonsense was this? Myself, I preferred the cold honesty of that old therapeutic nihilist, Josef Skoda of Vienna, who believed God meant His children to suffer and to die but not to be cured. Good old Skoda. There was a scientist for you. He lost all interest in patients after he'd found what was wrong with them. Take them away. Wheel them out. We know there's no cure. It isn't in the cards.

Then why had I written a chapter glorifying our family doctors? They were sentimentalists too, but they did not pretend, the good ones, to be scientific. In their humble way they were therapeutic nihilists, though not in the stern style of old Josef Skoda. They knew that, now and again, though lacking serums, they did pull a patient through by the mysterious medicine of words, of tender loving care. By faith. Why had I stopped the study of medicine and switched to bacteriology? Partly because there was not the love in me that's the driving force in good doctors. My years of cool butchery of thousands of rabbits and guinea pigs—to find a few facts that didn't even promise to save a human life—what did that show but a lack of reverence for life?

I was destructive. I wasn't only a therapeutic nihilist but a nihilist, period. For me, the world was too full of people and animals. Having no spark of reverence for all life, I had no ethics. I was for myself—and Rhea. I wrote furiously under the tree by the Sandy Lake Rapids to one end, for one goal. Anything that would bring the great day closer, that day when Rhea and I could hold hands and look the world in the face as man and wife. Any activity that would bring this to pass was good.

What was the use of knocking myself out at microbe hunting these days of the beginning 1920's when the universal life-saving advances predicted by the immortal Pasteur seemed to have come to a dead end? The blooming golden days of the old microbe hunters were done. But right now this 1921 summer, far west from Newfoundland, a scientifically self-taught man, Dr. Frederick Banting, who laughingly called himself an unemployed surgeon, was sweating over a few doomed dogs in a hot attic with a med-ical-student assistant, Charles Best, in the University of Toronto. They had not the money for enough dogs and in the twilight they sallied out, bringing in stray dogs, using a necktie for a leash. They worked without benefit of big money and on next to no money at all. They were breaking open a whole new science of life-saving hormones. They were discovering insulin.

Back in New York in the early autumn of 1921 over the scientific grapevine I heard gossip of this Banting business, bandied about in our Institute beanery. I shared the pervading skepticism about Banting, though only partly. Ignorant though I was, a tempera-mental optimism fought my doubts. The brave days of microbe hunting were done. Where were the swashbuckling heroes—like old Professor Pettenkofer—who swallowed a culture of virulent cholera vibrios to prove that these microbes found by Robert Koch did not cause this disease? These heroes were dead. Their brave days were over.

But had Banting spotted a new and totally different type of villain, not, like microbes, attacking us from without, but arising within us? Was diabetes the result of a mysterious messing up of our own body chemistry? Our metabolism? Metabolism—that was the Greek word summing up what we did not know about the complicated chemistry that goes by the name of life. Were Banting's brews of pancreas gland the first crude weapons of a war against messed-up metabolism? Were the seemingly inexorable diseases—juvenile diabetes, pernicious anemia, rheumatoid arthritis, even cancer—were they not microbic, but instead, metabolic?

In New York that autumn at the beginning of the Roaring Twenties life for me became exciting and almost happy. My sister Lois was joining me, having got a job in the New York Bureau of Laboratories with Dr. William Hallock Park, and together we had fun finding a little hole-in-the-wall apartment where we planned to live with our witty, sharp-tongued, and loving mother. And before Mother's arrival Rhea—it was a looming, incredible happiness, it was too good to be true—was coming to visit us; she was coming to meet my sister, she was coming into our family; we were going to show her New York for the first time.

The microbic dissociation experiments were going great guns; the harmless, rough-type microbes, when shot into rabbits, protected them against the smooth type, virulent. We had a living vaccine. Nights, after the next day's experiments had been got ready, I began typing the final draft of my foolish book about doctors, written longhand by the Sandy Lake Rapids. Clarence Day, Francis Hackett and his wife, Signe, were proud that the book they'd sponsored was actually getting itself written, and over all this seventeen-hour-a-day, fiery activity there was a strange glow. Rhea would soon be here. Not for a few furtive hours as always up till now, but for a whole week we'd be together. Openly. There was a gay electric feeling of life this 1921 autumn.

We clung together, laughing, saying we'd never forget our long kiss, alone, in Grant's Tomb; we tired our eyes and our feet in the Metropolitan Museum of Art. Mornings we stayed late after Lois had gone to work, holding each other tight, away from all the world and wanting each other with a madness that might only be calmed by marriage. She had a mysterious quality of almost but not quite letting herself go, as if this was not yet the appointed time; and it was strange how her patience calmed my turbulence.

Then we would set out in the tangy New York October weather to do the town.

We kissed atop the Woolworth Building and then on the Statue of Liberty and then, surreptitiously, in the Aquarium. We embarked on the little sight-seeing boat that took boobs around the big city, and going up the Harlem River Rhea spotted a sign, BARE-ASS BEACH, above boys playing naked in the water, and I blushed and felt shy but Rhea looked up at me, laughing. Francis Hackett and Signe gave us dinner in their apartment in Turtle Bay and were charmed by my girl. She said not much. When Francis asked her had she read John Dos Passos's *Three Soldiers* she said she'd never heard of it. She never commented brilliantly on any book she had never read. Signe felt she was fierce for me for all her calm, cool *comme il faut;* and at parting gave Rhea a little book about two lovers very long ago—Aucassin and Nicolette.

One evening Clarence Day's big car and chauffeur picked us up and Clarence took us out to a splendid dinner and then to a revival of *The Merry Widow*. I carried Clarence—as helpless as he was distinguished—into and out of the theater. The days flew by in a happy blur. Night after night we went to the theater to shows and plays picked out by Rhea. Sitting huddled close to her, holding her hand too tight, I watched Joseph Schildkraut in *Liliom* make rough love to Eva le Gallienne, who in her part seemed to me gentle and resigned like Rhea.

Now followed a burst of lab work with results that drew the praise, "Dat iss very pretty," from satirical old Jacques Loeb. By making careful counts of the number of lepisepticus microbes per cubic centimeter of serum broth culture, and then diluting the culture serially way out to one-to-one-billion, one cubic centimeter of one to one-billionth of the original culture, injected into the pleural cavity of rabbits, brought eight out of ten of them down with fatal pleuro-pneumonia. It worked out arithmetically that one single wee microbe from a smooth-type virulent culture could do a healthy rabbit to death.

And marvelous—one cubic centimeter, undiluted, containing

close to a billion rough-type attenuated bugs—shot into a normal rabbit's chest, caused it to bat not an eye. It was elegantly quantitative, the kind of science Jacques Loeb called science. Now one could quantitate, could measure the precise degree of resistance to virulent lepisepticus of rabbits immunized with the harmless, attenuated ones. I was proud. This was more than pretty; in its precision it was beautiful.

That autumn and winter it was wonderful to have my mother back taking care of me after so many years. She kept house for Lois and me in our little apartment, getting me breakfast at six-thirty and sending me off to walk all the way from West 114th Street across Central Park to the Institute at East 66th Street and the river. She listened sharply to the dissociation work as I told it to her and to Lois over the dinner table and was proud of the approval of Jacques Loeb. But she was especially excited about the coming funny book about the doctors, which Clarence Day had now christened *Our Medicine Men;* a title that in a swoop put the ancient priests of a witchcraft of healing on a par with the superdocs of today. She never showed worry over the fierceness of my drive, going back to the Institute by bus after dinner to work at the dissociation, to type more and more of the final draft of the book, to write a letter to Rhea, to get back home in the small hours of the morning.

"Paul, Paul, how do you keep it up?" she said, but she goaded me on to the writing. From my earliest boyhood I remembered her as a tremendous reader. She had read Dickens's *Tale of Two Cities* aloud to me and his *Child's History of England* over and over. She was, in her obscure western Michigan way, an authority on George Eliot and Mark Twain, and I remember her reading deep in *Anna Karenina*—which she considered a bit too rough for me—reading, preoccupied by the star-crossed lives of Anna and Vronsky. Her reading of illicit love would have got her severe censure by the Calvinistic elders of our village of Zeeland, Michigan, had they known. But she was safe with the passion of Anna Karenina; not only in our village but in the surrounding region that book was not known. Evenings, while she sat absorbed in it, my farm-implement-selling father—who had never read a book in all his life—snoozed over the pages of the *Literary Digest* and the *Review of Reviews*. And now her turbulent son was giving hints of becoming a writer.

I was going to have to leave the Institute even if they didn't fire me. About this necessity I kept my own counsel, saying nothing about my still vague writing plans for the future to mother or Lois or Jack Northrop—only writing about them in nightly letters to Rhea. We must marry, and soon. I was mad for her. To set up our household we were going to need more money than we could ever get microbe hunting—what with Mary's two little boys to take care of. About that responsibility Rhea made a stern demand. No matter how many years we would have to meet this fixed charge, we'd take care of the boys before we ate.

At the Institute in my work all was serene. Dr. Flexner, who edited my dissociation papers for his *Journal of Experimental Medicine,* told me he was amazed to have to make so few changes in their text and none at all in their form. He confided to me he had to tear many a manuscript to pieces and demand drastic rewriting. "Where did you get this economy with words, this *style?*" he asked. Didn't he know Dr. Frederick G. Novy? Hadn't he served on a bubonic plague commission in San Francisco with Dr. Novy? Wasn't Dr. Novy a great and severe stylist in scientific writing in his own way? Certainly, admitted Dr. Flexner. Well, Dr. Novy had been more than my master, teaching me experimental method. "Did he rip my first scientific reports to bits!" I exclaimed. "He looked at the six conclusions of my first report. In his precise, minute handwriting he wrote 'bosh' and 'twaddle' and 'rot' on the margin. He growled that every one of my conclusions was unjustified, exaggerated, untenable. Then he sat down by me and said, let's start over."

"Thomas Henry Huxley—I've studied him too—and H. G. Wells—I know his work backward and forward—they've helped me too." One thing was certain, I added cockily, I hadn't learned anything about writing at the University of Michigan. Except about how not to write stuffily. They flunked me in Rhetoric One, my first year.

"But your papers read like a story," said Dr. Flexner. I didn't tell him that this was what I really wanted to do, not make science, but write stories. Yet it was a lift that Dr. Flexner no longer tried to direct my work but gave me my experimenting head. Proudly I showed him rows of little serological tubes, with washed microbes suspended in buffered solutions from pH 8 on the alkaline side all the way down to pH 2.5 on the acid. "Look," I said. "The smooth, virulent bugs stay perfectly suspended, stay turbid, all the way down to pH 3. But the rough, attenuated begin flocking out just below neutral at pH 6!"

Here was new stuff, a deep physical difference in the two strains of microbes, and tied up to their deadliness or lack of it. Here a twinge of conscience bothered me. My old Michigan associate, Arnold Eggerth, had come over for an afternoon from Long Island College and suggested this trick of titrating the stability of the bugs in serial buffered solutions. On publication I didn't give him credit, as I should have, in a footnote.

I confessed to Dr. Flexner that Jack Northrop wanted to collaborate with me on the mechanism of what makes microbes clump together—on the physical chemistry of bacterial agglutination. "Fine," said Dr. Flexner, "go ahead." It was Arnold Eggerth's trick that got Jack Northrop started on our experiments on the mechanism of bacterial agglutination. In these studies Jack took off into a rarefied region of physical chemistry of which I knew nothing. What I contributed to the publications by Northrop and De Kruif—which later became obscurely famous in immunology—was mainly to furnish Jack with the washed microbe suspensions and buffer solutions. It was Jack's brain that did the thinking and devised the experiments. My name should have been on the papers only in a footnote of acknowledgement by Northrop.

In these matters my conduct smacked just a wee bit of the unethical. In fact there's no such thing as a wee bit unethical any more than there's any such thing as a lady being a wee bit pregnant. You are honest or you are crooked. There is no such thing as a man being "intellectually honest." A man is honest in his guts and his brain and his heart and all of him or he is not honest. What had led me into these little crookednesses? Ambition, that was it. On the make. My trouble was I didn't yet have Rhea to be by me day and night, not only to calm my turbulence but to guide my conduct.

Now the drive to break away from bacteriology into writing and to win Rhea as a wife opened in the early months of 1922. Henry Mencken planned the strategy. I'd got to go away from my job and the Institute for six months to Reno for a divorce, but where was the money?

At last I got up nerve to confess to Dr. Flexner the need to kick free from my old life, to build a new one, to make a new life with Rhea. He generously offered me leave of absence with pay to which I said no, thank you, I'd find the money. Mencken suggested I tackle Norman Hapgood, editor of Hearst's *International Magazine* that was trying to bring intellectual exclusiveness to the masses. Long before, in *Collier's Weekly,* Mr. Hapgood had rocked the country with a series "The Great American Fraud," by Samuel Hopkins Adams, on the horrors of patent medicines. Now, at our luncheon conference, Mr. Hapgood, lean-faced, drawling, and a terrific valetudinarian, sprinkled bran upon his strawberries, ate a dish of prunes, and put me a question.

Might there now be new and different but similarly sensational news in a series to prevent citizens from dosing themselves to their doom with new nostrums? Norman Hapgood had a strong nose for reader interest. It was Norman who had made the world happy by needling Conan Doyle into bringing his great sleuth back to life in a series, "The Return of Sherlock Holmes."

I told Hapgood that there was a different kind of nostrum racket, fooling not merely the public, but some of the doctors. The drug manufacturers—not yet called pharmaceutical houses —were advertising ethical remedies to physicians. Some of these concoctions were as spurious as S.S.S.—Swift's Sure Specific— for syphilis, curing only those people who did not have this sickness. "Are there doctors who are that gullible?" asked Norman.

Thus was born a project, "Doctors and Drugmongers," that would finance the coming months at Reno, that would bring me toward the goal of facing the world holding hands with Rhea, and that got us years of headache and feeble fame. But how to document the facts I'd told so airily to Norman? How begin the legwork for my first tough job of reporting and where? All I knew, firsthand, were facts about a bacterial vaccine manufacturer who sold physicians, ethically, among other preparations, vaccine cures for pneumonia and consumption; and the curious science of a famous drug house that sold doctors toxic microbic filtrates to be shot—at some risk to life—into already very sick people's veins. But where to get the documents of the danger, the damage, maybe the resulting deaths? Mencken to the rescue. "I'll give you a letter to Dr. Morris Fishbein, at the American Medical Association in Chicago."

Walking into 535 North Dearborn Street in Chicago, I was cordially greeted by Dr. Morris Fishbein. Brilliant is the most frequent description of Dr. Fishbein today and brilliant was how he impressed me in 1922. Though not yet in his middle thirties and only an associate editor, his hand was firm at the controls of the *Journal of the American Medical Association.* He was precocity personified. He in no way impressed me as a man on the make; he was made. He held me in awe of him because he gave the impression of having arrived, at birth, not in the sense of arriving in this world, but in the sense of being, at birth, a success, congenitally—than which there can be no more startling precocity. He was not yet, when I met him, Mr. A.M.A., but he gave the impression it wouldn't be long before he would be.

To my delight, as we discussed doctors and their bedevilment by drugmongers, Dr. Fishbein never fumbled for an answer. He had rapid-fire conversation of fantastic precision, making you believe that what he said was so; and it was not necessary to ask any questions; uncannily his monolog anticipated them. His narrative of the fooling of physicians by drugmongers was convincing, amusingly anecdotal, and, in its learning, encyclopedic. I felt as if caught in a didactic avalanche and then run over by a steamroller upon reaching the bottom. And yet, strangely, when this brilliant briefing was over, I remembered little of what Dr. Fishbein had said.

Divesting me of such modest scientific distinction as I thought I had, Dr. Fishbein introduced me to all and sundry as a "feature writer," to my embarrassment because I had written no features. Technically I did not even know what features were. Then Dr. Fishbein turned me over, as a feature writer for the Hearst magazines, to Dr. Arthur J. Cramp. Bearded, professorial, and in his modest reserve the antithesis of Dr. Fishbein, Dr. Cramp now took me figuratively by the hand and led me into a weird world of pseudoscientific shadows, a strange realm where men of business became rich by selling doctors medicines that could kill people and sometimes cure them. It stirred me to fancy myself a knight on a crusade for truth in medicine. Dr. Cramp brought out massive evidence. What wonderful poop, as the reporters say, was mine for the digging. The drugmongers' serums, vaccines, chemicals, and dubious hormones—displayed in ethical advertisements in medical journals laid before me by Dr. Cramp—were an indictment of sinister misinformation of the doctors. This scandal was unknown to the public, who up till now had trusted the science advertised to the doctors to be sound and true.

"Why does the medical association pound patent medicines and soft-pedal this ethical proprietary business that's just as quackish?" I asked Dr. Cramp. "Why haven't people been informed of this long ago?" Dr. Cramp had no answer, not a direct one. "Breaking this stuff to the public may get you into a peck of trouble," said Dr. Cramp sympathetically. "Just let me at it," I answered happily. "Dr. Fishbein will back us up when we say in public what he says to his doctors inside your organization."

Regarding the taboos of Big Medicine I was an innocent lamb. It didn't occur to me that the doctors might think their being hornswoggled was none of the public's damn business. Who was I, a featureless feature writer, to dare to expose it? The doctors hadn't appointed me as their spokesman. Dr. Fishbein seemed

to be their spokesman. Spokesmanship? A curious art. A spokesman is "one who speaks for or on behalf of another or others;
especially one deputed to voice the opinions of a body, etc.—
a mouthpiece" so says the dictionary. I thought of Dr. Fishbein's
job of medical spokesman with awe. You need not only to
have profound knowledge, but also to be mentally agile to be a
mouthpiece for a hundred thousand doctors. You must have insight. You may start out, talking straight out of the middle of
your mouth. Suddenly, protests from county medical societies.
Then you may have to switch from talking straight out of the
middle of your mouth to talking out of the middle and both sides
of it at the same time. Dr. Fishbein needn't worry, though. He
talked so fast it took a quick thinker to know out of which part
of his mouth he was talking. And he was on the side of the
doctors and against the quacks who were not doctors, the
doctors knew that. But if you could look inside Dr. Fishbein's brain
you'd find it a kaleidoscope of immensely varied, and even con-
flicting, knowledge. To be the medical mouthpiece on all subjects from the cause of cancer to the high cost of medical care
and to snap out the answers at the drop of a hat—that must require possession of a final, supreme characteristic: self-assurance.

I wrote my first blast at the drugmongers and took it hopefully
to Mr. Hapgood. Alas, it seemed my writing life was over before it
got fairly started. Mr. Hapgood took me for dinner to a German
restaurant on Third Avenue. Sprinkling his bran liberally over I
forget what course in the dinner, he beamed at me kindly through
his spectacles and broke the news to me that I could not write.
Not for the man in the street. Not for the readers of Hearst's
International. My facts were well documented but the writing
was pedestrian. It was scientific, lacking reader interest. It was
dull. And here he'd already paid me for the first article. What to
do? Then Norman Hapgood revealed himself as every inch the
marvelous mass magazine editor that he was.

"You've been living in a remote scientific world of your own,
Paul," said Norman. "You're off for the West on the trains. Talk
to everybody. To people in the washroom and the observation car.

To the conductors and trainmen. Lead them into the subject you're working on. Tell it to them like a funny story. When you see they're interested, when you've hooked them, then write like that. Write it the way you tell it to me. *Write as you talk*—you know you can hold me spellbound."

On the observation platform of the rear car of the Overland Limited the floodlighted white tower of the Wrigley building in Chicago grew smaller in the east and vanished as I told the conductor the story of an ogre in California who was fooling doctors, selling them gland extracts supposed to be full of hormones to bring bouncing health to patients tired at the end of a hard day. "Would you believe it, the gland extracts are phonies," I ended, past midnight along with my fascinated audience of one.

CHAPTER THREE

Now I was alone on my own, a free lance, but there was still the comfort, the security, the scientific prestige of the Rockefeller Institute. Surely I'd be back there in November, married to Rhea. But would I? There was my funny book, *Our Medicine Men,* up-coming serially in *The Century* magazine this 1922 summer. True, it was to be published anonymously. But if certain members of the Institute should find out that their colleague, De Kruif, was the author? I'd hinted about it—my mouth, alas, was like a torn coat pocket—to a couple of Institute acquaintances. Mightn't they tattle on me to the big men who were victims of my satire? It even seemed as if, in a moment of bravado,

I'd planted this news deliberately to reach the big men's ears. It was my streak of mischief, no, my turbulence.

That 1922 spring and summer and autumn live in my memory as a montage of crazy adventure. In the first place, I established residence in Reno to sue my wife, Mary, on the grounds of desertion and this was a fiction: she hadn't deserted me. I had deserted her. In the second place, Mary had given me no assurance that the divorce would be uncontested. And what if she fought it? How could I win? Mary was furious with me and rightly so. It was a marital crackup in which all the blame was on one side, my own. The suit to kick free was the wildest kind of Brodie. "Why do you love me?" I'd asked Rhea. "Because you don't give a damn," she had answered. This was her criterion for manhood and surely a shaky basis for the establishment of a safe, steady, happy life. But then, if Rhea was one thing besides brave and honest, she was a gambler—with her life.

To her I wrote long letters daily from Reno and could hardly wait for their short, devoted, daily answers. Her little letters—ending "I love you more and more" were the only stabilizing influence—these, plus fierce, concentrated work, learning to write about doctors and their exploiters, the drugmongers, in language plain people would understand.

Day after day I marched two miles to a pool below a dam on the Truckee River carrying a heavy briefcase packed with drugmonger deviltries—documented—given me by Dr. Cramp of the American Medical Association. Under a cottonwood tree I labored mightily to turn these doings into the kind of vernacular that had fetched the conductor on the Overland Limited. Good news from Norman Hapgood. "You've got it, Paul," and quickly three articles were accepted and paid for. Toward the end of each afternoon I jumped into the cold water of the pool in the Truckee, swimming free style back and forth across it, and then marched back to Reno to eat dinner alone and then to my rooming house to make sketches for the next day's writing and to write to Rhea.

Then more good news from Norman. It seemed that, with this

new vernacular writing style, my efforts needn't be limited to a sad saga of doctors embattled against false vaccines and serums. I was going to have to go to Los Angeles to beard a glandmonger in his den; why not meet movie celebrities and upon them write character sketches? It seemed to Norman that my forte was going to be to write about people. Why not try to tell what made movie stars tick? I might convince the public of my versatility. Enclosed check for expense money.

Only two movie characters interested me—Chaplin and Fairbanks; how to get to know them? Norman arranged with Mr. William Gibbs McAdoo to make contact with these heroes of the cinema. Mr. McAdoo—who was then busy fixing to run as Democratic candidate for President—admitted me to his presence. He was obviously not impressed with my importance either as a visiting fireman or as a writer, yet he gave me introductions to Charlie Chaplin and Doug Fairbanks. From Mr. Chaplin, silence. From Mr. Fairbanks an invitation to luncheon and to spend the day with him on the set of *Robin Hood*. Surely Mr. Fairbanks, who was Chaplin's friend, would help me meet the tragicomic genius. It was stimulating to see Mr. Fairbanks as Robin Hood bounding through the air with the greatest of ease with the boodle he'd robbed from the rich to give to the poor. At luncheon I tried to find out what made the great acrobat tick. He was a most serious man, with a grievance. When he learned of my acquaintance with Henry Mencken and George Jean Nathan, Doug took up our time probing me for why those two critical nabobs hooted at his pretensions to high cinematic artistry. "They consider me a guy who just jumps around," said Mr. Fairbanks forlornly. Could I correct their impression in my proposed story, and to them, personally? Doug kindly phoned Chaplin, who turned out to be not available.

At parting Doug mentioned casually he was off to hunt lions in Africa with the Duke and Duchess of Sutherland. Doug was impressed by dukes and nobby persons.

I tried to do a sketch of Mr. Fairbanks as more than a bozo who bounced about, bringing out his self-appraisal as a creative artist whose portrayal of human emotion was not appreciated in the world of the critics. To bring this out, I compared him favorably to a movie queen famous for her cosmetic baths in pasteurized milk. The sketch was hurried off with high hopes to Mr. Hapgood. Never was there a flop more resounding—it turned out that this movie star was a friend of Mr. Hearst's.

In San Francisco, on the way back to Reno, Dr. Karl F. Meyer picked up my spirits. Karl was a formidable Swiss microbe hunter; a mountain climber, famous pathologist, epidemiologist, and philosopher—a man of culture of the type bred only in Europe. He had the harsh, handsome look of a young Prussian field marshal, lean-jawed with a toothbrush mustache, and this appearance hid one of the kindest hearts I've ever known. He was a blend of the high medical academic and the economically practical. He was right then deep in saving the California packing industry—beset by contamination of its cans of olives by the deadly botulinus bacillus, the toxin of which was killing people in various parts of the land. Karl was fearless; and his weapon was scientific truth; with his laboratory facts he genially knocked the heads of the captains of the California canning industry together. In his thick German-Swiss accent he showed them how they'd have to apply bacteriological science to their slipshod canning methods in order to kill every last resistant spore of the awful Bacillus botulinus. Dismayed but no fools, the captains made Karl the czar of their industry with full powers to hire and to fire, with the result that all the millions of cans of California olives became safe as so many churches.

Karl was a man of versatility. On an unforgettable Sunday we crossed San Francisco Bay on the ferry to Sausalito and walked through the grove of the big trees in Muir woods and then—*au pas* and *langsam aber deutlich,* "dat's how we climb in Switzerland"—up the rugged path to the top of Mount Tamalpais. Here, alone, we held a jam session on the condition of American medical science. Karl's hard, kind gray eyes regarded me from between mountaineer's wrinkles as I told him of my book, *Our Medicine Men,* about to appear serially. "You'll never go back to the

Rockefeller," he said, roaring with laughter. "Now you haf *got* to be a writer. Anyway, you aren't interested in our damn bugs so much as in people. Why don't you plan a novel? Tell dem where de scientific bodies are buried." That afternoon on Mount Tamalpais, where the clean breeze off the Pacific made everything—even writing a novel—seem possible, Karl Meyer planted the seed for a book, not my own, later to take form as *Arrowsmith*.

Toward the end of the summer came the catastrophe Karl had predicted, exploding in the form of a letter from my boss, Dr. Simon Flexner, at the Rockefeller Institute. It was icy. It outlined a scandal. Anonymous articles were appearing in *The Century* magazine. They were signed "K—, M.D." It had been reported to him that these were by De Kruif. I was no M.D., only a Ph.D. Dr. Flexner found it hard to believe me guilty of such imposture. (In fact the by-line was an editorial mistake with which I'd had nothing to do, of which I knew nothing till the magazine hit the newsstands. *Mea culpa*—I hadn't read my page proofs.) It was nice of Dr. Flexner to find it hard to believe I was such a fraud. He also wrote he found it impossible to believe me guilty of such tirades as the articles were. The writer of the articles had seen fit to lay about him, not sparing certain important people at the Institute. Surely I would not be guilty of such treachery. That was generous of Dr. Flexner. Would I please reply immediately, assuring him he'd been misinformed of the authorship of these indiscretions?

The pledge of anonymity by the editors of the magazine had been broken. I was in for it. I'd had it. My microbe-hunting days were done. Immediately an answer, to this effect: Dear Doctor Flexner: your information, alas, is exact. I am not guilty of signing the articles "K—, M.D." However I *am* guilty of writing them anonymously. What date would it be convenient for you to see me? I'll be there.

On September 1, 1922, around ten in the morning, I was admitted to Dr. Flexner's presence and he did not rise to shake my hand but was polite enough to ask me to sit down. Then, with a mixture of relish and regret, the good doctor launched upon a discourse. I interrupted him, quickly and politely. "Please, Dr. Flexner, may I have stationery and a pen? To write you my resignation from the Rockefeller Institute, to take effect today, September 1, 1922? And please don't scold me, even though I deserve it. What's done is done, and I'm sorry to have upset you." He gave me pen and paper and the resignation—our American euphemism for firing—was accomplished in a single sentence and I rose to go. "Please sit down, De Kruif, I'd like to talk to you," said Dr. Flexner. His ascetic, power-scarred face was a mixture of warring emotions: of relief, of indignation, of exasperation, of pity, even of solicitude. Before Dr. Flexner launched upon his sermon—it wasn't a scolding as I'd feared—I understood the elements causing his suffering, for which I pitied him in my turn. He was relieved, of course, that I wasn't going to fight his firing me by raising the issue of academic freedom, that I wasn't going to ask what was American science coming to if a searcher couldn't say out loud what he—and many others—believed to be true.

"This resignation is between you and me; it will not be aired in the press," I said. Dr. Flexner was gratified. Then I listened in astonishment as he explained his indignation. Of course he was proud of the accomplishments of his Institute—including my own, he interpolated with an almost friendly smile—but the Rockefeller's distinguished scientific achievements were not what had made him most happy throughout his years as its director. No, it wasn't the Institute's scientific output, its undoubted saving of human lives, its contributions to basic knowledge, it was not any of these that had meant the most to him. No, it was the harmony, the serenity, the brotherhood with which the staff had always worked together. Like a big happy family. My amazement was due to our deep difference in point of view as to what it took to make real science. My belief demanded that in science every man, all out honest, must call them as he sees them. Science was men—individuals—each one sure he was right and making no bones about it. It meant Louis Pasteur hating Robert Koch's guts and vice versa. It meant Fred Banting bitter about J. J. R. MacLeod's trying to appropriate Banting's discovery of insulin and Banting's saying that out loud, so that the University of Toronto's Chancellor, Sir William Mulock, had MacLeod removed from Canada, sent back to Scotland.

I felt deep in my bones that a spirit of competition is what makes truly hot science and what is science if it is not hot? To cross over to other creative disciplines—who'd ever heard of artists or composers or writers who amounted to a tinker's damn working together under one roof in an atmosphere of brotherhood and loving kindness and live and let live? All creation, including science, is a war against precedent. Science to be vital must grow out of competition between individual brains, foils one to the other, each man mad for his own idea and where do we get if a man can't shoot off his face? This was my vernacular for academic freedom. If science must be made by a collection of contented human cows or a happy herd of trained seals, then to hell with it, I was through with it. Though I didn't say it out loud, such was the deep difference between Dr. Flexner and the turbulent man he was firing, this day, September 1, 1922, for the writing of obnoxious features.

Doctor Flexner now became concerned about my personal fate. He would like to change the date of my resignation from September 1, 1922, to March 1, 1923—that would give me six months' pay while I looked round for a position. On Dr. Flexner's part this was pure kindness. But like a Michigan moujik I'd never heard of separation pay. Suspicious as a peasant, I thought this offer lagniappe, to tip me, to keep my mouth shut. I stood up. "No, thank you, Dr. Flexner, let's make it a clean break. The resignation stands, as of today."

That noon of September 1, 1922, my feeling was one of freedom. Free, free, free—that was the word for it. Free for what? It was clear as clear that no other institute, no university department of bacteriology, not even a commercial pharmaceutical laboratory—of which in those days hardly any could be called scientific—would give a job to a man who had been kicked out of the Rockefeller Institute. What I had done was kick my scientific career in the teeth.

I did not ask, as I might have, where would I find enough features to write? Except for Banting's insulin there was then no hint of the explosion of medical science that today gives swarms of "science writers" comfortable livings. Before shoving off back for Reno I went to see Norman Hapgood and told him I was free to write full time for him, but he seemed a bit worried at this rupture from Rockefellerian prestige. I went to Glenn Frank, editor of *The Century* magazine, and told him The Century Company was now released from its pledge to anonymity and could publish the forthcoming *Our Medicine Men* boldly under the name of Paul de Kruif. "It's too bad the forms are locked on Foxe's *Book of Martyrs,*" he said, laughing. "Appearing as a martyr might make you a hero and get your book a lot of attention." Glenn was bothered. For *Our Medicine Men,* Clarence Day had designed the dust jacket, black with white skull-and-bones dripping red blood; lurid, sensational, and not conveying the style to be found between the book's covers. It showed that Clarence did not take the book seriously. Yet, adoring Clarence, I thought his contribution sensational. Glenn Frank knew it would keep customers away in droves. Advance orders for the book were not encouraging.

Then came the first quarrel with Rhea. Till now toward each other we had been nothing but tender. Now on the way back to Reno, I stopped off in Detroit to tell her the exciting details of my being fired, and the news from my lawyer, Mr. Lunsford, that the divorce would be uncontested if a sum of money in cash would be forthcoming together with a stiff alimony to take care of the boys. And the further good news, from my mother, that she'd like to see me to discuss a loan—with interest—to meet the cash-settlement demand. Mother would be glad to meet me in Chicago.

Now our romance was really rolling and we held each other close and were happy and Rhea said she was resigning her job at Parke Davis to go home to Freeland, Michigan, to rest and get ready for our marriage. Then, the second happy day of this reunion, the telephone rang in the apartment shared with her girl friends. I listened to her side of a conversation that seemed to embarrass her. No, she was all right now. Yes, she was feeling much better, thank you. She'd be back to work tomorrow. Please don't worry. It had only been a cold. It's awfully kind of you to be solicitous. . . . Long pauses on Rhea's part listening to what, in my imagination, was someone's impassioned impatience to see her. Though she didn't mention the name of the worried person at the other end of the line, it was obvious to me that he was some sort of suitor, and serious.

At the end of her talk I was in a jealous fury. She explained. It was Mr. So-and-So, Parke Davis executive. Bothered at hearing of her illness. That had been her excuse for taking these days away from work. I kept asking questions. Was Mr. So-and-So married? No. Was he interesting? "No, stupid, but shouldn't I have been polite to him?" Her face was open-custard-pie honest and serene as always. Her lovely openness, her obvious innocence should have made me feel the heel I was. But the inner turbulent bad man in me had command. False self-pity swept over me. Nobody is true. Not even Rhea. I'd adored her as the one perfect woman, spotless. I'd kicked my science out the window for her. I'd turned myself into that most pathetic human being, a male divorce-seeker at Reno. What was I doing? Only defending myself against the guilt of my own sensuality. Didn't I know that the root of causeless jealousy is the jealous one's inner badness? As I talked, with self-righteous self-pity, her face showed perplexity, then deeper, deeper trouble.

Suddenly Rhea broke under this barrage of cruel, crazy self-pity. She rushed out of the room, I following her, scared now, into her bedroom, where I'd never been. She lay face down on the bed, shaking in a fit of weeping, sobbing completely out of control, convulsive, utterly abandoned. The depth of her desolation frightened me. What had I done to our dear dream? What kind of suspicious so-and-so had I been? I knelt by her, clinging to her, incoherently begging her to forgive me. What kind of a mean man was I? Forgive me, darling. You know I love you. I *know* you love me. Desperate at losing her; if I'd lost her I knew I'd lost everything.

She wrenched free of me. With the ultimate desolation of the unjustly accused she looked at me out of eyes swollen and bloodshot and forlorn. My own gabble of forgive me forgive me was silenced. She looked at me with a little sad smile. At last she found words. And these will be with me till the day I die. "To think I've waited for you these three years. . . . " That was all. It was a self-accusation, deep in sincerity; her devastating self-criticism of her own folly to have wasted her time on such a man.

"Darling, forgive me. Please don't send me away. I'm so scared, honey. Please wait for me more. I love you so. You're all I have. Please go on loving me."

Rhea put her arms round me. "I'll wait for you. I do love you, I do," she said, with a little shudder of ebbing sorrow.

In Chicago, on the way back to Reno, there was the best of good news. Here was Mother not a bit worried about this obvious debacle of a career. She was glad to say the money for the divorce settlement was ready.

"There's a divinity that shapes our ends, rough-hew them how we will." Up to the first week of September, 1922, I hadn't rough-hewn my ends; in my turbulent don't-give-a-damn I was chopping my ends to pieces as if with mighty swipes of a double-bitted Michigan ax. The day after seeing my mother there appeared an agent of the divinity, in the form of the then most famous author in the wide world. This was Mr. Sinclair Lewis.

I was in the office of Dr. Arthur Cramp at the American Medical Association, gathering dope for the series on doctors and drugmongers for Norman Hapgood. Here now in the door of Dr. Cramp's office there loomed, in tow of Dr. Fishbein, a young red-headed man, very tall and slightly stooped, nervous, his face spotty red as if about to explode into a dermatosis. His light-blue eyes fixed sharply on me for a moment, then peered, dartingly, round the office. An unearthly character, not to be forgotten once seen; a man in the stylish accouterments of an English country gentleman or retired guards officer—without a mustache—but totally lacking in the phlegm and equanimity associated with one. Here was a creature who was wild, freewheeling, intense, outlandish.

Dr. Fishbein was proud to introduce me to the greatest living best-selling American novelist. *Main Street* rocked the country. *Babbitt*—rumored to be a far greater book—was about to hit the bookstores. If we hadn't read *Babbitt,* said Dr. Fishbein, mysterious in his foreknowledge, we hadn't read anything. Meanwhile, Mr. Lewis's blue gimlet eyes ranged over a shelf of bottles of nostrums, sinister exhibits in Dr. Cramp's sanctum. Off the shelf came a bottle, twitching in Mr. Lewis's nervous hands. It was a big vial of bitters made in Baltimore. Sinclair Lewis peered at the bottle's label. "My God, it's high in alcohol," he exclaimed. "Do you mean they let people buy that over the counter in drugstores?" Then he whirled round and fixed me with his fierce blue eyes.

"You're an investigator, you're a scientist, do you dare to taste this bottle's contents?" asked Lewis, and the severe tone of his voice hinted my possible cowardice or, to say the least, my lack of scientific curiosity. When he put this question, Mr. Lewis was sober.

"Do I dare to *taste* it?" I answered. "I'll drink all of it!" No, no, he wasn't asking me to be that foolish; but as Dr. Fishbein moved to intercept it the bottle was at my mouth and, head thrown back, with gusto and bravado I gulped all the bitter-tasting stuff with one mighty swig, choking and coughing at the end of it. There was a look of real concern on the faces of Drs. Cramp and Fishbein and a look of alarm—tinged with admiration —on the spotty visage of the great author of *Main Street.* "My God," said Lewis, "have you ever had any of that stuff before?" Then he turned to Dr. Cramp: "Has any one ever been known to have downed a whole damn bottle of it?" I tried to explain: "It is my rule to try anything—once." With mounting alarm, Mr. Lewis, who under his outward violence was a careful man, asked

Fishbein and Cramp, "What'll happen to Paul—shouldn't you pump his stomach?"

What did happen to me was really something. The first tingle of warmth in my middle gave way to a bitter burning and then to the beginning of nausea. As the many ounces of the violent remedy—recommended dose, one tablespoonful—attacked my brain cells there began a chaos in my consciousness. I remember being hurried into a taxi by Dr. Fishbein and Sinclair Lewis. I recall having vomited violently though with propriety in a bathroom in Dr. Fishbein's home. Then oblivion. At last awakening lying on the bathroom floor and in my ears a sweet sound of the birdies singing. And Dr. Fishbein was bending over me ministering to me medically, holding my head and feeding me tablespoonsful of paragoric.

I awoke clearheaded and feeling myself, instead of a plain drunk, a seeming martyr to science under Sinclair Lewis's anxious gaze. "Forgive my misconduct, Mr. Lewis," I said. "They call me Red," he said. For Red I had become the man who would try anything once.

Then the three of us fared forth on the town. At Red's command Dr. Fishbein phoned for a limousine. We must go to Elmhurst to pay our respects to the great Carl Sandburg. On the way to Elmhurst we stopped for refreshment and dinner at a roadhouse—a Capone joint. Lewis and I quaffed several glasses of what was said to be fine old whisky. Dr. Fishbein, knowing his Chicago, took it easy. Near the front door close to our table hovered a formidable character in black tie, a bouncer. "Could you lick that guy, Paul?" asked Lewis, apparently hoping I'd try anything once. "Please come over here," Red begged the bouncer. "We've got a big boy here who thinks he can lick you." "My redheaded friend is a little plastered," I said to the bouncer, shaking his hand hard and giving him a wink. "I know damn well you could kick the hell out of all of us." The bouncer and I stood face-to-face as he sized me up and then, liking my compliment, broke out laughing and patted me on the shoulder and told us all to enjoy our dinner.

"By God," murmured Red, "I believe that guy was scared to tackle you."

At Elmhurst there was no Sandburg. His lovely gray-haired wife, Paula, explained he was off strumming his guitar. Carl would be sorry to have missed us. But did we know that Gene Debs, the eminent socialist, was sick at the Lindlahr Sanitarium, close by? It would be an errand of mercy for us to pay a call on the old hero of labor.

Red Lewis was ecstatic. Gene Debs! The greatest socialist since Karl Marx. The man he hoped might be the protagonist of the labor novel he was hoping to write. Dr. Fishbein said it was reported that old Gene Debs was close to the end of his rope. "Poor Gene, let's hurry, maybe you can do something for him, Morris," said Red. Dr. Fishbein asked how scientific medicine could do anything for a patient in a chiropractic sanitarium like the Lindlahr? But here we were, propelled by Red, who was volcanic.

Red was tender to poor old Debs, who sat in the back seat of the limousine with Red's arm solicitously round his shoulder, Red showing obeisance to him as one of the great men of our time. To Red's eulogy Gene returned a pathetic smile. "No, I'm finished," said Gene. "But I know a little philosophy to comfort me. You'd like to hear it?"

"Sure, Gene, go on tell it. It might be just what I need for the labor novel," said Red tempestuously.

Gene smiled. "Here it is. You might call it the ninth beatitude. I don't mean it irreverently. *Blessed are they who expect nothing, for they shall not be disappointed.*"

That was all. These were maybe the deepest words of the many deep ones I had heard from this old fighter for human rights. I'll not forget his gentle, tired, discouraged voice—terrible in its resignation—as he intoned his ultimate philosophy. What a contrast old Debs, a failure, was to Lewis, the new great man of letters, and to Fishbein, medicine's coming Prolocutor—both of them comets in the American sky. It gave me the creeps.

Beginning that evening Gene Debs's words became the ninth

beatitude for me, and then later for Rhea and me together they became a rallying cry in fair days and a comfort in foul. To put beside it later we had only one other watchword, tougher, grimmer. "Let's not kid ourselves," Rhea would say when the going got rough.

From worshiping at the feet of Gene Debs, we took Dr. Fishbein back to his home. At last we could get words in edgewise. So Red and I went to his apartment at the Hotel Morrison to make a night of it. Red Lewis, sober now, became every inch a writing pro. For him I became a specimen under his intense, searching, baleful eyes. I was astounded by his knowledge of family doctors till he told me his old father had been one. He astonished me by his insight of what was now about to happen medically, at what he felt was a new age, the real birth of a new medical science.

He cross-examined me about why I'd left medicine for research on viruses, spirochetes, trypanosomes, and anaphylaxis under austere Frederick Novy. His questioning stirred me to make Professor Novy come alive, a figure of medical romance— our lab window the only one lighted far into the night in the medical building at Ann Arbor. Red cackled with glee at my stories of life among the trained medical seals at the Rockefeller. He was made reverent by my eulogy of Jacques Loeb, who'd taught me that quantitative science was the one discipline dependable in a vague, fuzzy world. He drew me out to tell him how I'd been fired deftly by Dr. Flexner for irreverently daring to write—à la Henry Mencken, Red's own hero—spoofing Rockefeller science, for disrespect to medicine's holy of holies. He tested my erudition, making me recite inside fables of the foibles of microbe hunters— from the first one, Leeuwenhoek the improbable dry-goods storekeeper in Delft, to the last great one, gay Paul Ehrlich, who deprecated his discovery of 606 for syphilis by telling how he had had one moment of good fortune after seven years of bad luck.

Red Lewis could be a terrific listener. He asked a hundred canny questions and they were never silly. He roared with laughter at my desecration of sacred scientific cows. Medicine and medical science? It seemed it was like *Main Street,* and many of its greatest names turned out to be oafs like *Babbitt.* He drew me outside myself, stirring me to talk like a real writing pro, though what I'd written up till now amounted to next to nothing. My narrative seemed to him to be an epic of medical debunkology, skeptical, yes, cynically satirical; and debunking—that was what Red Lewis truly loved, and of muck-raking in other fields Red Lewis was the master.

In the gray of the morning Red asked me a question: why shouldn't we collaborate on a book? About doctors? About what was alleged to be medical science? What would be funnier? What would be more sensational? What could be more timely? I did not hesitate. Why shouldn't we, indeed? When do we start?

"There's a detail we've got to settle, first," said Red. "I've been talking to Morris Fishbein, asking him wouldn't he like to work with me on a book about doctors. But the trouble about that is he's their spokesman. He's *official.* He's brilliant and learned. But *you*—" His interrupted sentence meant that I was the final opposite of official, a man who gave not a hoot, who'd try anything once, who was reckless, who could floor himself with a bottle of bitters and come back for more, who knew where scientific bodies were buried, who hauled medical skeletons out of closets and could tell about esoteric medical matters with buffoonery.

I left the little ethical detail of settling matters with Morris Fishbein to Red. I do not know if he ever talked about it to Morris. Indeed, Dr. Fishbein is said to maintain that he suggested me to Lewis as a collaborator. We parted, sentimentally, as conspiratorial brothers. We must get together right after I came back east with my divorce from Reno. We drank one for the road to the man who was for us as if a pope. "To his Holiness, Father Mencken," said Red Lewis, lifting his glass with reverence. I left his apartment in a haze, floating as if on air, safe on the other side of the turbulent river. A writer, or a collaborator on a novel. A writer at last, or so it seemed.

The next day came danger. Exhilarated, I wrote more details of the thrilling news of the coming work with Lewis to Rhea, again asking her forgiveness and telling her I loved her more and more. But I was wild with happiness at having—so it seemed—the world by the tail. I must celebrate. You can't celebrate alone. I was, in my accursed sensuality, precisely like a lush, long on the wagon, who must calm his inner tension—unbearable—by reaching for a drink. What I now reached for was a dame to admire me. Any dame.

Beside myself with the need to share my success with somebody, I reached for the telephone book and then for the phone. In Chicago at this time I knew there was a wonderful woman, remembered from World War I, alluring, mysterious, unattainable, making me frantic with wanting her, famous for her being wanted by many other men, a true *femme fatale*. Now she was living alone in Chicago. In World War I she had been mildly amused at me as an energetic young bumpkin bouncing back and forth between Dijon, the front, and the Institut Pasteur—full of inside scientific war dope, seasoned by an unbacteriological zest for Voltaire, Rabelais, and Anatole France. And busting with untamable ardor.

Now when we met this 1922 afternoon in Chicago it was a *coup de foudre* for me, not of love but of passion. The lady was languorously acquiescent. Gone were my true, constant, loving thoughts of my Rhea. It was as if she did not exist. My long-bottled-up sensuality exploded into a fierce flame and I was proud to be this lady's temporary hero. This lasted for two days. But I must get back to Reno. At the end of the second wild day came a pitiful little note from Rhea. I'd missed a disaster. The letter told me how—distraught—she had almost taken the train to Chicago, planning to come right to my hotel to feel my arms around her, to see me off on this final trip to Reno, to make sure as sure that all was love between us. But now that my letter had come telling the generosity of my mother and the great news of the chance to write a novel with Sinclair Lewis, her trip wasn't necessary.

"Be a good boy, darling," her letter ended. "I love you more and more."

That night, feeling like a dog of dogs, brooding alone on the observation platform of the Overland Limited west out of Chicago, I watched the white tower of the Wrigley Building grow smaller down the long straight stretch of track. Memories of the days with Sinclair Lewis and the Prolocutor and then the *femme fatale* were swept out by remorse for what I had done to my Rhea.

The old conductor—now my fan—came for a chat.

"Do you know the hot story I've got?" I asked him. "No, tell me," he said. "Well, there were seriously sick people whose doctors had shot a microbe soup into their veins and it had killed them dead as doornails."

CHAPTER FOUR

THOSE last months in Reno turned out to be by far the worst—up till then—in my life. I came apart at the seams. With me it was now as with an alcoholic, sober, then falling off the wagon for a spree and getting back on and telling himself never again—now we take the veil for keeps!—and then finding that the fall had sensitized him to a need for more debauchery. It turned out, alas, that there is a parallelism between the disease of innate need for alcohol and of innate need for a woman, any woman. Thus now those last months in Reno swept me into a sensual whirlpool and sucked me under.

Thinking back now to that time, it must then have been that in my life a main current began to appear, though so far not discernible among the anecdotal eddies and swirls of this narrative. The story wasn't the big jump from science to writing. It was the beginning of an agony of self-knowledge. It was lonely, a search for a part of a conscience that in me was almost nonexistent. It was a feeble fight toward honesty, not only in writing but a personal fight against inner lies, great and small, against mere peccadilloes and mortal sins.

Rhea wrote from her home in Freeland. Might she pick out her wedding ring, a circlet of small diamonds, not expensive? The letter ended as always: "Be a good boy, darling. I love you more and more."

Good boy. That was what I was now not being. The writing was going smoothly and with a new component of originality inspired by the marvelous session with Sinclair Lewis. I now gained an audience. It was a tall, dark, lovely lady, seeming slender but actually what French connoisseurs of women call "*fausse maigre*." She was a ringer for Rosamonde Pinchot, who played the nun in *The Cathedral,* produced by Max Reinhardt. This dark lovely lady's face was sad, like Pinchot's. The dark lady's past was tragic. She had been married briefly and her marriage had crashed; she had not been awakened. She was an expert secretary and after working hours typed fair copy of my manuscript, and our relation was proper except that its propinquity was always perilous. I told her about Rhea and this history of the big battle to win her and she said—sadly—that such a romance must be wonderful. Wasn't I lucky and I couldn't know how drab a life—like her own—was without it.

Evenings in her home where she lived with her mother we sat proofing the manuscript, gradually closer, insidiously more propinquitous, till at last—unconsciously—knee touched knee, we not aware of it except for a slight flush on her face and my deeper breathing. The dark lady was lithe and athletic with a stride like Diana and we began to go for long walks in the clear autumn Nevada twilight out toward the sun setting behind the western hills. "It's so good to be with you, Paul," she said. "You're like windswept hills." Alas, in her innocence she judged me wrong; and I pitied her for her unfulfillment and she was sorry for my having to restrain my boiling energy in these last days of the long wait for Rhea.

I remember us, one evening so long ago, but sharp as if only yesterday. The sun was setting behind the western hills. We were all alone and miles from her home and in the sun's last glow she was forlorn and her profile, framed in her dark wind-blown hair, was ravishing. Now we were close and then the lovely dark lady turned to me and her mouth found my mouth in a long, deep, wild kiss. She was lost. I was lost. We were lost together. And where was Rhea? She was twenty-five hundred miles away and did not know.

It was more than a flirtation. It wasn't that I loved this dark lady and she said, no, she did not love me, as night after night she swept me away to satisfy the insatiable hunger overwhelming both of us. We must not see each other one night more. "You must stop wanting me," I pleaded. "I mayn't fall in love with you, you're Rhea's, I know," she answered.

To the last day, cravenly, I wrote those letters to my Rhea, long letters desperately telling her my love and my wanting her. I was going to hurry back to my Rhea by the first available train on the day of my divorce. Back to Rhea who would love me and guard me and cure my black lust.

On the day of the departure from Reno, right after the perfunctory rigmarole of the uncontested divorce, Judge George Bartlett took me by the arm and led me to the west windows of his chambers. The western sky was a riotous sunset, a conflagration reaching from the rim of the hills. Judge Bartlett was one of the saddest and gentlest of men; sad because of all the sin and sorrow he had seen, gentle in his tolerance and forgiveness of the kind of sexual skulduggery he knew was mine. Judge George put one arm around my shoulder and swept the other toward that sky—wild, turbulent, mad with the colors of the palette of the year at Arles of Vincent van Gogh.

"Look at it, Paul," said the Judge with kindly solemnity. "Don't forget it, Paul."

Rhea met me in Detroit and she was more lovely than ever and radiant. I showed the bit of paper, the proof of the divorce she had waited for and that I'd fought for over more than three years. Her father, mother, and sister, her family—pronounced with a drawl stressing the first syllable—were coming down from Freeland to Detroit the day after tomorrow and at my expression of being nervous about meeting them she smiled. "Don't worry, honey," she said. "They're just plain people—but I know you'll like them."

They turned out not to be just ordinary; their extraordinary ordinariness made them remarkable. Her father, George Frederick Barbarin, had brought with him a bottle of prewar Scotch to celebrate our meeting. He was the leading pharmacist of the Saginaw valley and a staunch Democrat in a region that was then black Republican. He had the ruddy, weather-beaten face of a riverman. He had Rhea's candid gray eyes that knew no fear, brave as his father who had been brave and badly wounded when a captain in the famous Iron Brigade at the Battle of Gettysburg. There was depth to this clan that had sprung from the Frenchman, Noël Barbarin, a colonel on the staff of General Washington. "Barb"—that's what his customers called him—hated suffering of man and beast. He was more than a dispenser of drugs, herbs, and simples. He was a comforter and a salty counselor. For misbehavior and sins his understanding and tolerance knew no bounds. Though agnostic, he attended all funerals, including those of village and country scalawags. He seemed limitless in his sympathy for all sorrow. Rhea said he gave sinners and sufferers a feeling that he'd been through all of it himself.

We had our first family meal together at the Hotel Statler in Detroit, and what a serene family they were. I fell to musing, later, about my own family.

In my boyhood in our family my father would be stony silent for days, gloomy, preoccupied, only opening his mouth to read the inevitable chapter of the Bible after every meal. He was a tough, totally self-made man whose formal schooling had ended at the second grade. He was a natural mathematician who would offhand give me the answer to a stated problem in college algebra without so much as having heard of a quadratic equation. He solved the fiscal angles of profit and loss in his hard-driving farm-implement business at a glance. He had contempt for the economic calfishness of his farmer customers and foreclosed them without too much mercy.

My father made what was big country money in those early nineteenth-century days but then often tossed a part of these profits away in bold investments, such as an as yet unsuccessful paper milk bottle, and in portland cement companies. These disasters made him furious, not at himself but at my mother, who was then reduced to tears. Outside our home he was considered a jolly man; his round face smiled and his round belly shook with hearty laughter.

He was true to my mother, who feared him and loved him. "Your father was a hard man," my mother summed him up to me just before she died. On his black days, for minor peccadilloes, he bared my back and had at me with a horsewhip with the abandon of a Captain Bligh. Afterward he seemed to feel better and might take us out for an auto ride—for a spin as he called it—and then would like as not treat us to an ice-cream soda.

He was determined to get me away from our small town, wanting me to become an engineer or a doctor or a "rattling attorney" though he never made it clear to me why an attorney should rattle. Yet he had no great hopes for me, considering me a coward because I couldn't keep what he called "a stiff upper lip"—I whimpered when he beat the hell out of me. The streak of cowardice in me must have stemmed partly from fear of my father. I do not blame him because I now know that for many years—beneath his being outwardly robust—he was, subclinically, a sick man; and his irritability was that of an undiagnosed diabetic. In his last years, slowly starving to death under diabetic treatment on scant calories, he became gentler to me. He was proud of my going great guns at the university, microbe hunting under Professor Novy. Happily my father told me Dr. Novy said I might turn out to be one man in a million.

A few years before that, I had been glad to announce to my

father that he was relieved of all financial responsibility for my education. Though well-off, these outlays had always irked him sore. But now he would be happy to know—this was in 1912— that I'd quit medicine for a Rockefeller research fellowship in bacteriology under Professor Novy to work for a Ph.D. and my schooling wasn't going to cost him anything more at all. From then on out he began to respect me somewhat. Of him—in his last five years as he slowly starved toward diabetic death—this is my best memory.

But what a contrast to my father, the hard man, and to my mother who feared him, what an opposite was Rhea's family, these easy-going Barbarins with whom I made first acquaintance at the dinner at the Hotel Statler in Detroit in November, 1922. It was plain to see that Rhea's mother, a gentle lady, had no fear of her husband. It was obvious she adored him, yet in a low key she kept kidding him for his mild eccentricities. They were a kidding family, all of them, including June, Rhea's younger sister; not jeering at each other but making fun of one another with down-to-earth north Michigan salty humor.

That first evening began the narration of what turned out to be Tittabawassee Township folklore told to me over the next thirty years. "There was this fellow, Ed Smith," said Barb. "He was quite a drinker. One morning our village pastor met him on the street and asked him: 'Why is your nose so red, Mr. Smith?' 'It's blushing with pride at the way it keeps out of other people's business,' Ed said, quick as a flash."

Barb smiled. "But that wasn't the best one," he continued. "One night Ed came home stewed to the gills and snuck into bed, balancing on the edge of it with his back to his Missus. 'You might as well turn over, Ed,' said his wife, 'you're drunk clean through.'"

Now I was off for New York for the coming meeting with Sinclair Lewis to plan the work on the novel that he enthusiastically seemed certain we must do together. Again that night as on the last trip home from Reno I had qualms not only about my own turbulence but about an instability apparent in Red Lewis that first mad day with Prolocutor Morris Fishbein in Chicago.

Would Lewis really go through with our plan for the novel? He seemed unpredictable; he was the self-confident captain of his soul that rationalized its ethics. Look what Lewis had done to the poor Prolocutor, Fishbein, making him happy they'd write the book about doctors together, then throwing it over when he'd met me. What if he'd since met up with another learned doctor or a really brilliant bacteriologist? Would he throw me over as he had the Prolocutor?

But I was then wrong in my doubts about Red Lewis; he would not let me down either. He had promised to see me in New York and he did, the day of my arrival—by accident. I hadn't the least notion where to find him. To get information on his whereabouts I went to the offices of Harcourt, Brace and Company, his publishers. Would they bother the great Lewis on the town on the celebration of his *Babbitt?* Had he left word about me? Providentially, as I reached the top of the steps the front door flew open and there was Red. He greeted me with a whoop, hugging me.

"By God, here is the boy who'll try anything once," he cackled. "Let's go to the Gotham for a drink. You've got to meet Gracie."

This was the first of the Mrs. Sinclair Lewises, and together Mr. and Mrs. Lewis were terrific in this heyday of the best-selling novel, *Babbitt*. In my life I'd never seen such a determined, dashing lady. She greeted me with a somewhat British "Hah d'y'do." She scrutinized me. So this was the young man that Hal—her name for Red—said would try anything once. She was stunning. She was like an American duchess. She was a mixture of haughty and democratic cast in a bohemian manner. I had never seen the likes of her. She was *sui generis*. It was plain that Red worshiped her as a stylish, sophisticated luminary of the emerging international world of café society.

I'd hardly recovered from my awe of her spectacularity before Mrs. Lewis—"call her Gracie," said Red—asked my medical advice. "I'm putting on too much weight, with all this *pawtying* around over Hal's new book. What can I do?" I gallantly assured her she was not an ounce too heavy and then she mowed me down. "Nonsense. You can see my rump's too big," and with a pirouette she displayed her rump in profile. "How do I take it off?" she asked, and her question was an imperious demand. "Your rump's just right as it is," I said. It seemed as if my retort was a bit forward. Gracie looked at Hal narrowly. She seemed to know little of Hal's intention to work with me.

"Paul is going to help me with a book," explained Red, in a tone of voice that suggested that he was a bit scared to admit it. Then Red in his turn bowled me over. Our novel, projected in Chicago, seemed to have evaporated from his memory. To Gracie —this was what he insisted I call her—and to me he rapidly outlined a scheme of which I hadn't heard. We were going to do a series of short stories, not a novel; stories with a new type of hero, a character—bacteriologist, doctor, public health detective —all in one. A kind of scientific Clarence Budington Kelland production. My god!

"It'll make a great magazine serial; we'll take the idea to Ray Long and Norman Hapgood at Hearst's," said Red. "It'll be sensational. They ought to pay us a hundred thousand," he said confidently. "What a genius," I thought, "even in regard to money." The scheme smacked of slick magazine fiction, not of a work of art, but of fiction slicker than slick, having nothing to do with the book we'd planned that September night in Chicago. What would Henry Mencken think if he knew? Reviewing *Main Street,* Henry had given an accolade to Lewis, "who had come up," he wrote, "his face blanched from years in the hulks." Henry meant the years of Lewis's hack writing before he had become a literary artist.

I was stunned. Red seemed about to drag me with him on a relapse into the George Horace Lorimer school of literature. What could I do? I'd hitched my wagon to this glowing red comet and could but cling to its fiery tail. To hang on, to make the money to marry Rhea—that was all that mattered. Gracie, too, seemed apprehensive of this threat to Red's new high literary respect-ability.

Ray Long and Norman Hapgood were, as Red predicted, vigorously interested in his idea for a magazine serial, introducing a new fiction character that Red was sure might rival Sherlock Holmes. At this time Ray Long, a shrewd, genial, thin-lipped Hoosier, was himself on the way to his zenith as a buyer of big writing names for big money. For Ray Long, it wasn't great writing that boomed circulation so much as the big name that wrote. Here Ray really had it. What was then a more glittering name than that of Sinclair Lewis? He was hotter than a brace of of pistols. Ray realized that; Red realized it too; and so did Norman Hapgood, though Norman thought that writing came first. But Norman had confidence in my scientific solidity as Red's collaborator. The deal seemed to all three of them to be a natural. I contributed my share of enthusiasm because it might speed my marriage to Rhea.

Did we have some stories ready, or at least some plots? In grinding out slick fiction the plot's the thing, "John Henry Plot," in the words of Rex Beach, the great forgotten slick-fiction master. We did not have finished stories. We did not have a single plot. "Don't worry, we'll get you the stories," said Red. "Have you spoken to your publishers about this?" asked Ray Long. "Not yet," Red admitted. But he was sure they would be as thrilled as we were.

Red's publishers, Alfred Harcourt and Donald Brace, were thrilled, but in reverse. They were thrilled with a quiet horror and told Red so, carefully. Publishers must go easy with great authors who believe their own publicity. At the beginning of our conference, Red had introduced me to Messrs. Harcourt and Brace as a distinguished bacteriologist who had been fired from the Rockefeller Institute for Medical Research and notable as a tough boy who would try anything once.

Red was quick to sense his publishers' disturbance at their star's proposed short-story hookup with Hearst. Gradually Red switched the negotiation around—and I helped it a little—both of us steering the discussion to our original plan for a new type of iconoclastic man of medical science, back to our novel projected in September in the night in Chicago. Now Alfred Harcourt and Donald Brace caught fire. Red poured on the coal, boosting my technical—and even artistic—qualifications, the latter then unborn.

Donald Brace and Alfred Harcourt were the publishing sensations of the early 1920's, even as Red was the sensational author. In rapid succession *The Economic Consequences of the Peace,* by John Maynard Keynes, *Queen Victoria,* by Lytton Strachey, *Main Street* and *Babbitt* by Sinclair Lewis, had appeared on their list and had rocked the country. All of these titles were popular yet distinguished; all were top best sellers though in the category of beautiful letters. Now Mr. Harcourt and Mr. Brace agreed it would be really something if we'd write a serious novel in the realm of medical science. Who'd ever done that? Nobody.

Now our four hearts beat as one. We were excited. But Red? He was unforgettable. He was off to the races. He held us spellbound. His clever cortex did a superswitch. Its ten million neurons performed simultaneous somersaults. What happened in that creative brain was awesome. Proposing slick stories! What had he and Paul been thinking? The Hearst name would be poison to any true work of art. Alf and Don—as Red called Messrs. Harcourt and Brace with affection—needn't worry. They shouldn't have had to warn him that slick paper would lower the Lewis prestige in the world of lovely letters. How could we have been so stupid? Red's avidity for the big Hearst money evaporated. In broad strokes he painted a picture of our narrow escape from literary whoredom.

"Let's get going on our plan for the novel seen by both of us as in an illumination, as in a vision, in Chicago. Let's block it out. Let's go. Now listen—"

Then Don and Alf and I assisted, as the French say, at a revelation, a veritable eruption of literary creation. *In situ,* as it were, Sinclair Lewis fashioned an epic, or at least a saga, instinct and informed with the spirit of medical discovery, with a handsome, stubborn-minded young medical scientist the embattled hero. The action opened in the frowsty office of an old Midwestern doctor; it leapt to a modern medical school; it swept to the tropics to a death fight sad and sinister under the Caribbean moon. Out of Red there belched plans, plots, and characters not dreamed of in our first Chicago session—a flamboyant Swedish epidemiologist, a money-mad professor of otolaryngology, a buffoonish missionary of public health—all of them foils to our stark microbe-hunter hero. Sinclair Lewis that morning showed himself as if a seeming master of medical narrative. He exploded a drama out of his imagination. Not a word of it had yet got down on paper. All of it was in the air and a great deal of it—on sober second thought —might be described as hot air as well. But such was his mastery with words that we bowed before him as a veritable *Ganzemacher*.

"You've got something here," said Alf Harcourt, sagely rolling another brown-paper Bull Durham cigarette, and Don Brace said yes, he was sure we had it, and they both of them—Alf cordially, Don kindly—welcomed me into the house of Harcourt, Brace. Next day at the Columbia Club, Red, Alf, and Melville Cane, who was the firm's lawyer as well as a good poet, met with me to draw up the contract for a medical novel, yet unnamed. That day Red could not have been more generous. He could not have made me more happy. Terms: full collaboration by Sinclair Lewis and Paul de Kruif, with me sharing top billing, my name on the title page and cover. All royalties—book, serial, and movie—to be split fifty-fifty.

This was too generous. "That isn't fair," I said. "It's Red's name that's going to bring in the dough. Okay to make it full collaboration but let's split the royalties 75 for Red and 25 for me." It was so agreed. Alf Harcourt out of his shrewd, sharp eyes gave me a long look. It was not unkindly.

What a day. To finance my end of the expenses for Red's and my proposed travels in search of tropic color, an advance on royalties of twelve thousand dollars was stipulated in the contract.

Then my heart was heavy. What about Rhea? We'd forgotten the poor child in the mad shuffle. "Can't go before we marry," I said. "But we can't take her along to the tough places we'll have to go," Red protested. "All right, but we're going to be married before I go or the deal is off," I said. "How about our shoving off the first week in January?" Red mollified me.

"Okay," I said. It was then the first week in December.

Alas, Rhea had planned that we were to be married on January 17—her father and mother's anniversary. What to do? Together Red and I hurried from the Yale Club to the Hotel Astor and dispatched a wild wire to Rhea in Freeland, Michigan. The telegram was excited. It was peremptory. It was frantic. It was seasoned with buffooneries inserted by Red Lewis with his by-line. It was a first example of my stupid hurry-hurry-hurry, of my go-go-go under which Rhea was to suffer almost throughout her life. It was my turbulence. It was my wanting her, *now*.

That evening a wire came back saying all right she'd meet me at the Michigan Central train in Saginaw the morning of December 11 and we'd take the train to Detroit immediately after the wedding. Her wire was submissive. It was sad but I didn't see that then. There'd be not even the semblance of a celebration of her father's giving her in marriage, not even a bottle of Mumm's *Cordon Rouge* that he'd put aside for the occasion.

Now in New York under Red's direction there was feverish planning: passports; steamship tickets; a portable typewriter; a library of fat, formidable medical textbooks in which to look up plagues that were to endanger our heroes; pith helmets to make us look like the English explorers that we weren't; reams of paper on which to report the results of our literary safari.

There was no time to be sorry for my rude change of Rhea's plans. My letters and telegrams shouted my hot impatience to marry her after all these years of waiting; they impressed her with the necessity of fitting our feeble fortunes into the great author's plans. He was mercurial. He was unstable. He was a genius to whose caprices we had best kowtow, or he might blow the deal and roar off to write a labor novel, maybe.

We must, I assured her, take the bull by the forehead, as Roy Fritsche's old lumberjack was wont to say. There was every reason why we must marry December 11, 1922, instead of waiting till January 17, 1923.

Rhea, her father and mother and little sister June and I stood in a huddle in the parsonage of the Congregational minister who was liberal enough to marry a divorced man of no religion to a girl who did not wear her deep spirituality on her sleeve. During the short ceremony Rhea and I stood close and when we said "I do" we held hands fiercely. Her grip said: "Never leave me." Mine, responding, said: "I'll be true."

"You look so beautiful and tired, darling," I whispered. "I didn't sleep at all last night," she said. "What was bothering you, honey?" "Worry," she said.

If her father and mother were worried they didn't show it and they seemed proud and quietly happy—despite their gamble of giving their daughter into the care of a turbulent man. It was a lowering North Michigan winter gray day, raw, cold, Siberian. In the diner on the train to Detroit we faced each other and laughed, triumphant.

"You little louse," I said happily. "Big louse yourself," said Rhea. And the sun broke through and shone upon my bride.

CHAPTER FIVE

How to recapture the twenty-four days of the whirl of the honeymoon before shoving off with Red Lewis for the Caribbean—the wonder of Rhea's abandoned yet low-keyed love, loving deep with shattering intensity, all gone, yet never clamorous; afterward our returning to the realm of sanity, both of us only able to say it's worth all the years of waiting. Rhea made it for me as if there had never been any other woman, *ever,* and this made me hate it that there had been any other at all. There is this that is remembered as most strange: a little communion in the middle of the first night as we woke from a coma of sleep, loose in each other's arms. This transcended our ecstasy. I whispered that this awakening with her by me was so strange because it was the first time—after love—I hadn't wanted to be away by myself.

We went to Chicago and here there were days and nights of getting to know each other in the Hotel LaSalle. The weather all these days was foggy and snowy and lowering and up to our room drifted the weird wail of the high-pitched whistles of the traffic cops—to this day, hearing them, they remind me of our being in each other's arms.

That first week of our honeymoon we began to combine work with our happiness. Dear old Norman Hapgood had asked me to do a close-up sketch of the great Dr. Frank Billings for Hearst's *International,* before leaving with Red. And Dr. Morris Fishbein —the coming Prolocutor who already knew almost all the medical angles—clicked me with eminent internist Dr. Billings, who specialized in eminence. He looked eminent; he was eminent; he had eminence thrust upon him. It turned out that Dr. Billings took a dim view of being splashed across the sensational pages of this mass-circulation magazine by a Hearstling feature writer. Not quite respectable. A bit off the orthodox medical beam.

"Don't pull the rug out from under me again, Morris," I said to the Prolocutor, looking him hard in the eye over the lunch table.

But other meetings went better. We were both thrilled when Carl Sandburg, bringing his wife, the beautiful Paula, and their little daughters, paid us a call in our room in the Hotel LaSalle. "You know what I said to your man when we first met at Morris Fishbein's?" Carl asked Rhea. "I said to Paul, sizing him up— *you* don't look like a bacteri-*ol*-ogist—you look like a *Mich*igan Dutchman driving into town on a load of *tur*nips." Carl said it in his wonderful baritone drawl in a rhythm stressing certain syllables and as if intoning one of his poems.

This mysterious Swede with his lean face and lank hair and china-blue eyes became our hero—above Mencken and Red Lewis and on a pedestal alongside my master, Frederick Novy; and for years I tried my damnedest to write with Carl's rhythm in his little words that were grass-roots music in the American grain. I never came within a thousand miles of him. I stayed the Michigan Dutchman on my load of turnips. To work like Carl Sandburg with words you have to be born with it, and this I was not.

Then, as its pitiful too few days went by too swiftly, our honeymoon went into high gear. We were off from Detroit in the fast overnight train to New York City, to show my modest bride to Alf Harcourt and Don Brace and Gracie and Red Lewis and to Red Lewis's friend, Hal Smith, the distinguished editor; and to Norman and Elizabeth Hapgood and to Clarence Day and Henry Mencken and Jack Northrop. "Shoot straight with that little girl," Jack had warned me in 1921, when he first met her. "Don't you lose her; if you do, you're sunk." Red, though not having met her, already knew Rhea from my bemused babbling about her and my furious impatience to make her my wife. Red would be thrilled to see us, proud lovers, legitimate, and strong in our oneness against the world of the big literary Bohemia. And Gracie, Red's duchess, surely Gracie would feel toward Rhea as a kindred spirit, what with Rhea's *comme il faut,* her high style not of dress but of manner and heart.

It was with this anticipation that we boarded the train to Hartford, Connecticut, where Mr. and Mrs. Sinclair Lewis were in residence. Mark Twain long ago had set the precedent for celebrated authors to mitigate the dullness of staid old Hartford; and I'd heard that this was why Red had gone to live in that conservative city.

Red had no sooner let us in the front door of his elegant rented mansion—there wasn't even time for us to take off our wraps—before he wheeled on me, giving me bad news in a tone of sincere regret. "I'm so sorry to have to tell you this," he said, "but Alf Harcourt says there's liable to be a seventy per cent drop in the advance sales of our novel if your name's on the cover along with mine." "Why's that?" I asked, puzzled and lacking privity to the theory behind such predictions in publishing. Red's red face became redder than ever. "Well, you see," he explained, "Alf dopes it out this way. If the critics and the book buyers see Lewis and De Kruif on the cover, they'll say Lewis is finished. He's hiring an unknown to help write his book for him."

This sounded like what's on the floors of stables to me, but I know little about the book trade. Paranoid thoughts raced through my head—is this celebrated author trying to provoke me? Does he want me to blow my top? Does he bank on my wounded pride making me call off the deal? Doesn't he remember our joint top billing is written in the contract? What will this do to the kudos I'd expected from my name appearing on the cover of the first truly scientific medical novel ever written?

This was the first time the ninth beatitude was to sustain me: "Blessed are they who expect nothing for they shall not be disappointed." It worked.

"Does this change our royalty arrangement—75 to you, 25 to me?" I asked Red coolly.

"Of course not, Paul, that stands firm as ever." Now Red summoned up his real talent as a rationalizer. Didn't Rhea and I see how disastrous it would be for all of us financially to have the book get off to a bad start in the advance sale? The critics and the trade would be sure Sinclair Lewis was slipping, et cetera, et cetera, and et cetera. When Red came to an end of his admirably syllogistic oration, "It's okay with us, Red," I said. "Isn't it darling?" I asked, turning to Rhea. "Of course," she said with equanimity and a faintly dangerous smile.

"That's mighty generous of both of you. Now we'll do a great book. Maybe it'll make us all rich. Let's get going. What'll be the title?" There Red had me. How the hell do you title a book that still lacks substance, of which not a word has been written? "Let's scan the telephone book," said Red enthusiastically. "That's where you can get some of your most effective name titles."

But what's the damn book really going to be about, I kept thinking. Looking for the title before you'd got it clear about the story seemed working backward to me. Had Red fallen under the influence of the movie magnate, one of the Messrs. Warner of Warner brothers? In December Red and I had waited upon that marvelous man, Red negotiating with him in the sale of the movie rights of *Babbitt*. As Red gave this Mr. Warner the hard sell, extolling the terrific literary and popular success of *Babbitt,* Mr. Warner's eyes looked far away as if into an enchanted distance. "*Babbitt* might make a great movie, but it's a bad title," said the sage of the cinema. "Now we've got a great title, ready made, in *De Beautiful and de Damned*—you know, Scott Fitzgerald's."

Now I came back from my reverie over that revealing meeting of two great minds. "Would be wonderful if we could find a title as catchy as *The Beautiful and the Damned,*" I said. "This is no laughing matter," said Red, testily. "A name title is best," he continued. "I never'll get another as good as *Main Street*. That's actually become part of American common speech."

"But what's our book going to be?" I persisted. Red seemed deep in a trance in his creative, best-selling, business imagination. In all these fields he was a triple threat. At last he said: "Well, they're already calling businessmen *Babbitts*. We've got to find a name that'll fit all iconoclastic great medical researchers."

We've got to find a name to intrigue Christians and Jews, I thought. Christians mightn't go much for a Jewish hero, but Jewish ladies are terrific book buyers. Mischievously I remembered one of Henry Mencken's combinations, recommended for Jews on the make, yet wanting to make their monikers palatable to anti-Semitic Christians. We might call our main character, I thought, "Darwin Shapiro."

While the heads of the three of us were close together over the telephone book, Gracie made her entrance, not so much walking as sailing down the stairs. She was smart in a tweed suit and apologized for not having been on hand to welcome Rhea and complained of a splitting headache and said it was divine of

Rhea to have come along with me and what were the three of us doing? Oh, just like Hal to put us to work right away looking for a title. She had one for us. It's going to be a medical book. Wouldn't *White Tile* be just the thing? They have so much white tile in hospitals. When you think of hospitals, don't you think of white tile? Not bad, I thought. Better than Darwin Shapiro. But wait, they have white tile in men's rooms, too.

"Wouldn't you like to freshen up and dress for dinner?" Gracie asked Rhea. "I don't have a dinner dress, Mrs. Lewis," said Rhea. "I've an afternoon dress—" Gracie looked at poor Rhea with pity. "I'd no more think of dining without dressing for dinner, than I'd think of going to bed without my pajamas," said Gracie. Rhea looked at me with her rare puzzled frown as if to ask how we'd got into this strange society, and since she had no dinner dress hadn't we better leave on the next train?

"The Hepburns—you know the famous surgeon, Dr. Hepburn? —are joining us for dinner," Gracie explained, *avec impressement*. Hepburn in those 1922 days was not yet a name to drop; the Hepburns' daughter Katharine was still far too young to make the name illustrious. Our predinner drinks failed to lift a pall that descended over the scene. The gloom seemed to center in Rhea, who was grimly furious.

Gracie's second, precocktail entrance was a sight memorable in our annals. Her swoop down the stairs was spectacular. It was no less than regal. I retain only an impression of a kind of tiara trailing off into gauzy streamers; of a face as animated and haughty as it was handsome; of a neckline plunging ahead of its time; of an astounding ensemble that even down to this day would have excited the envy of all of the ten best-dressed ladies in the land. Jewelry gleamed. Bracelets tinkled. There seemed—this may be a wrongly remembered impression—to emanate from her a mysterious perfume. What a gorgeous Gracie, what a stunning lady.

The dinner that followed was unmemorable except that Red, toward the end of it, now tight, gave his famous imitation of an

Anglican bishop, a prince of the church. The Hepburns were pleasant people, in no way throwing themselves about. Gracie, pleading a splitting headache, broke up the party early and went up to bed and Red and Rhea and I were left alone and went into a huddle in a corner of the drawing room and got back on the plan of the book. Red was a taskmaster.

Then it came to pass that Red was not only a taskmaster but a real companion and friend. It promised to be a wonderful end, for Rhea and me, of a day that had been rather rugged. I was happy. Rhea was tired. Red was magisterial in his bold creative bursts of imagination. Then there appeared a little fly in the creative ointment. It thrilled me that the three of us were kindred spirits but now it disturbed me that Red was getting a bit too kindred with my Rhea. He edged over closer to her. He snuggled up to her. He began at first surreptitiously and then openly to try what could only be called necking with her. His idea seemed to be that the three of us might now be as one. Rhea remained oblivious. She seemed not indignant. She sat still as a mouse in danger. Her eyes did not appeal to me for help. It was for poor Red as if making love to a statue of a female wooden Indian, as if all his love's labor would be in vain. For me it was bad, turbulence rising toward boiling, left fist clenched, left arm cocked ready to throw a hook with all of me behind it. But why clobber him when Rhea was handling it so well? Red's heat cooled under Rhea's imperturbability. During all this time he'd gone on with his creative monolog. Now the frustrated great man looked at Rhea. Her *sang froid* had saved the project. From that night on out and during all our work Red's conduct toward Rhea was correct, platonically affectionate, admiringly avuncular.

We were to return to New York on the afternoon train next day, which seemed not too soon for Gracie and she was fertile with devices to speed her parting guests. Hal had promised to take her to an afternoon movie and together they whirled us to the station in an open Cadillac in the cold and through the snow. Hal bid us an apologetic farewell. Gracie's headache was gone and she was relieved and gay. "You won't mind waiting a while for the train, my dears?" she asked. "It won't be long." She wanted to go to a movie. We waited long for the train in the station, stuffy and teeming with a holiday crowd.

Red and Gracie joined us two days later at the Chatham in New York and their deportment toward us was as if it was a reunion of old friends. It seemed as if Red had emerged the victor in what must have been a serious battle in the war between men and women. I say it seemed, advisedly, since Gracie could not have been more gracious. We must hurry to complete our outfitting for the coming literary safari. Red took me—an amused Rhea tagging along—to Rogers Peet to buy raiment, not only for the tropics but to make me presentable for the smart literary world and for a possible high scientific *conversazione* at the Royal Society in London. Black tie. White tie—full soup and fish with what Red called "come-to-Jesus" collar. Red was serious in his selection of my wardrobe. It must be not expensive but adequate for all British occasions. It must be inexpensive Rogers Peet; it didn't have to be Brooks Brothers or Gray and Lampel. Yet in good old Red's defense it must be said that he knew his sartorial stuff. He was the arbiter of my second-rate *elegantiarum*.

Now, two days before the date of sailing, Red and Rhea and I —minus Gracie—went on an expedition. Our principal luggage was Red's notebook, Rhea's handbag, and a New York City telephone directory. We were on the way to Washington to keep an appointment with the highest U. S. Army Medical Corps brass. It was encouraging how on the train a vague yet definite design for the novel began to emerge. The characters seemed to take on reality simply by our giving them names to fit them: Fatty Pfaff, Clif Clawson, Angus Duer, Roscoe Geake—there was a real bastard—Almus Pickerbaugh, the great political public health mafoofsky. . . . Their names made you see them. The telephone directory also gave us Martin Arrowsmith for the leading man and I was happy when Red coined Leora for the name of the leading lady. Rhea contributed little as Red expatiated on the imbecilities or virtues of emerging characters. Except once she offered: "He wouldn't do that, Red." "Shut up, Rhea," said Red mock seriously, "you're talking too much."

At the office of the surgeon general of the U. S. Army, Major General Merritte W. Ireland was most helpful. His son Paul had been my assistant at the University of Michigan. And here too Colonel Joseph Siler was most gracious. He remembered me as an obstreperous captain in the A.E.F. in France in the First World War. Red heard Colonel Siler as remembering me to have been turbulent yet hard-working in those war days.

That evening in Baltimore it was my fair lady—not Red—who turned out to be the guest of honor at a brilliant if alcoholic dinner, thrown in a private dining room in the Marconi restaurant by Henry Mencken, then at the peak of his gastronomic, his bibulous, and his writing prime. Rhea was not only the only lady present but the only woman. Then there was Red—scintillant as always —and along with Mencken came good old Tom Le Blanc, now a graduate student at the Johns Hopkins School of Public Health, rougher and tougher than ever, surer than ever that I was merely lucky and would never be a writer, just as in the days at Ann Arbor. "*You*—a writer," Tom then had said. "It's just as if you announced you were going to be a capitalist. What would you use for money, kiddo?" Now his look said he hadn't changed his mind.

Mencken was wonderful to Rhea. Meeting her and looking at me, Menck said to her in a courtly manner: "Condolences, Mrs. de Kruif." Turning to me, beaming, he pronounced: "Congratulations, Paul." Mencken explained to her the merits of the waiters at Marconi's. "When they come into a room in this joint, when you're entertaining a gal alone, they knock on the door, wait, and then come in backwards."

It was boisterous, comradely, gay; an epically alcoholic evening. Mencken and Red—both masters of monolog—dominated the conversation, both of them pronouncing their satires simultaneously in a counterpoint that made their wisdom incomprehensible. Their wit was lubricated by Martinis, dry sherry with the soup, *Liebfraumilch* with the fish, *Nuits Saint Georges* with the beef, *Moet et Chandon* before the dessert, and brandies brandies brandies—fine old brandies—out of big snifters with the cheese and coffee.

Now our honeymoon drew to its close. Now Rhea must go back to her family in Freeland to wait till March when she would sail to join us in England. The night before our parting we excused ourselves early from a party Red and Gracie threw. The night was ecstasy and sadness. That night we did not sleep till just before dawn. Wild happiness gave way to foreboding. We loved and wept and loved in far-gone desperation—as if this might be the last time, forever.

CHAPTER SIX

O N the S.S. *Guiana* Red and I both wore steamer caps and carried walking sticks. We were trying to seem like world travelers. Red was almost one, though he had not been in Africa, Asia, or the lands of the South Pacific. Red gave the impression of an eminent British author lately escaped from Sauk Centre, Minnesota. He look distinguished—a lurid, brilliant personality. He looked anything but dull and dreary. Except for my stylish steamer cap and trench stick I could have passed for a Michigan Dutchman coming into town on a wagon load of turnips. On the S.S. *Guiana* we did not have to be impressive. There was nobody on the grimy little cargo boat one could awe. Red was rehearsing for greater things to come.

The first morning out Red unlimbered his Corona in our cabin and we settled down to build the skeleton of a novel—still tentatively called *Barbarian*—but gradually becoming *Arrowsmith*. It was for me as if to be in a new wonderful world to be working with Sinclair Lewis. It was astounding how rapidly he developed the scientific and spiritual agonies of Martin Arrowsmith, a tough young man hell bent to become a microbe hunter. Red gave me exercises writing a fictional biography of Arrowsmith's master, Max Gottlieb. I tried to make him a blend of gaily wisecracking Jacques Loeb and the dedicated truth hunter, my old master, Frederick G. Novy. Loeb was brilliantly surface; Novy was deep and difficult to do. Also I wrote a treatment—as the movie Shakespeares call it—of the career of Martin Arrowsmith. As his apprentice, Red toiled to transform me into a writer in his, Lewis's own image. Beware of clichés, he insisted. Clichés were anathema.

Where Red was, there was work and fun and fury. Where Red reigned, there was the reward and the solace of alcohol after the day's work was over. No drinking while writing, that was then Red's virtuous watchword; but, oh boy, when the day's work was done. He began to teach me to forget the stuffy, stilted prose of scientific reports from the Rockefeller Institute and to write all out—free style.

On the night before the day of our landfall at Saint Thomas in the Virgin Islands there was the first of Red's turbulent parties. Our company consisted of a Welshman who was the ship's chief engineer, and a pleasant, pie-faced man; and the ship's doctor, handsome, dark-haired Hamilton Frobisher, who, believe it or not, was the descendant of Martin Frobisher the explorer. Then there was Red (to stir up trouble) and then there was me (not saying much in order to avoid it).

That night we drank late and deep. Irked by Red's advertisement of Dr. de Kruif, the man who would try anything once, Dr. Frobisher became nasty. "You think you're tough," he snarled.

"Why don't you try standing a watch in the fireroom? The stokers are poor little consumptive Peruvians half your size." "The fireroom ventilating system isn't working," said Frobisher. "Temperature around 165 in front of the furnaces. Why, you big Dutch bastard, you couldn't take it for half an hour." The chief engineer put in his oar. "You'd like to try?" he asked. "You got a jumper big enough for me?" I asked. "Sure," said the Chief. "Wear nothing but the jumper and your shoes. Report to the engine room just before eight in the morning. No breakfast. Just a lot of strong coffee. On a full stomach you'd puke your guts out." "Okay Chief," I said as we weaved off to bed. Red was horrified at what he had wrought. "Don't worry, kiddo," I said.

The first job was to clean the fires in number two boiler. Right away the hellish heat combined with my hangover to make me queasy. I remembered good old Roy Fritsche who'd taught me to clean fires in the Zeeland, Michigan, municipal light plant long ago. I knew how to drag out the clinkers and roll the coal buggy to feed the fires. So I began helping the poor consumptive little Peruvians keep up a head of steam. I had to vindicate Red's boasting about me. Gradually my nausea and hangover dissolved in a flood of sweat.

After an hour the Chief came to see how I was doing. "By God, boy, you're pouring on the coal," he shouted above the roar of the fires. I laughed. "Hell oughtn't to be bad if you can stand this," I said. Half way through the four-hour watch the Chief brought Red and Dr. Frobisher to the door of the fireroom. Red, tall, distinguished, and British in his pith helmet and Palm Beach suit, bizarre in this environment, peered in at me and cackled his pride to Dr. Frobisher, who seemed discomfited. "See, Doctor," said Red. "I told you this boy is tough."

All went well through the four hours of the watch and at the end I was going strong and there was a singing in my heart as I reported to the Chief. He deflated me. "You did all right Doc," he said. "But the skipper says our speed's down a couple knots. Steam pressure low. Could it have been you?" He smiled.

That night the Chief, Red, Dr. Frobisher, and I resumed

our libations. Dr. Frobisher apologized for his calling me bad names. I said forget it. Then the Chief gave warning to Dr. Frobisher. "Don't provoke this cove again. He's a slow burner. Watch out. Good-natured guys like the Doctor will stand a lot. But if he ever did let go it might be bad for you."

This pleased me. I'd never murdered anybody and never had wanted to, but it was romantic to be regarded as a potential killer. The Chief's psychological estimate disturbed our author, Red, about me, his apprentice. He looked at me with a new respect mingled with worry. Had he taken a latent killer to his bosom? He looked at me as if he thought he'd better stop trying to get me into drunken combat. That day Red and I turned a corner together. He never tried to get me into a fight again— with anybody, himself excepted.

In our cabin in the S.S. *Guiana* the framework of what Red called our fable grew by jumps. Once facts had pinned him down, Red never tried to make do with phony movie science. . . . He kept teaching me to let myself go to dramatize real science. He kept prying out of me Frederick Novy's deep, simple spirit of the science Novy had got from Pasteur and Robert Koch and Emile Roux—an esoteric philosophy different from that of the scientific church of John D. Rockefeller, Sr. There couldn't be the littlest lie in Dr. Novy's work. This contrast filled Red with glee.

What a blissful experience this was for me, to try to learn to write all out, wildly, yet sticking to facts. If you could keep your stuff true, if you could make it a *Tatsacheroman,* you might write something new and out of this world. But it was tough to try to write like Red Lewis. There must be hard, cold, accurate men—in a chiaroscuro against characters that were caricatures. Of the invention of these, Red was a master. You didn't have to be kind about them. For Red, they epitomized his own contempt for much of humanity. Red brought out my latent puckishness trying to write memos on such characters for him. I didn't in my heart believe they were that bad, but okay, if that was what he wanted.

At every Caribbean island stop of our dirty steamboat, Red dragged me off to sight-see. Red was a tremendous tourist with a keen eye and the accuracy of a Baedeker. I was bothered by these trips ashore—the hammer of the tropic sun pounded me through my pith helmet. On a Sunday in Martinique I learned that Red was a seemingly deep though phonily religious man. At the mass in the dim cathedral, Red gazed up with reverence at the Bishop shepherding the procession down the aisle and to impress him Red acted like the devout Catholic that he wasn't, on his knees praying to the God he didn't believe in at all.

From the mass we went to a cockfight and here Red wept over its cruelty and over the gallantry of the battling birds. He exclaimed, if only we human beings could be that brave. He admired all bravery of man or beast if he didn't have to take the risks. We both were stirred by the grace of the high-yellow ladies weaving their seats as they walked, balancing heavy loads atop their heads, their arms swinging free at their sides. We were told that if the burden of these beauties was only a postage stamp, they'd put it on their heads with a brick atop it to keep it from blowing away. I looked at them, yet thoughts of my absent Rhea kept the sensualist from rising in me.

While Red kept peering from island to island for backgrounds against which to stage horrible epidemics, my hobby was to look for outlandish characters, and in Bridgetown in Barbados I found one that even Red with all his genius couldn't caricature as a phony. This was a wonderful old man, a superbly healthy old man, past seventy, Mr. Aldous, from Winnipeg, who did not care if he lived a day longer or died right now. Mr. Aldous was well-heeled and in his pleasant life had had all of it. He was a strong swimmer with his old-fashioned breast stroke that never tired him and he took me for swims in Bridgetown harbor. I swam rings around him, free style, and, looking down through the clear, buoyant water, saw long dark shapes cruising beneath us. "What're those big fish?" I asked Mr. Aldous. "Sharks," he said. "Mightn't they take us?" I asked. "Might—but not likely. They get plenty of food from stuff off the boats."

"What if one of them would prefer live human meat?" I asked, a bit uneasy. "Young man, it would be an easy death," said Mr. Aldous, bobbing along placidly with his breast stroke. Then he told me his philosophy. "You see, I've had my life. It's been good. If a shark took my leg off clean, I'd bleed to death quickly. It would be preferable to a lingering senility."

This Chinese calm of good old Mr. Aldous impressed me as the quintessence of don't-give-a-damn. Day after day this serene patriarch and I swam farther and farther out in the bay. I reported these exploits to Sinclair Lewis. He looked at me and said: "You have a will to destruction, Paul." "You've got me wrong," I said. "It is only the determination of a coward to conquer *fear* of destruction." Mr. Aldous was a character and I tried to sneak him into the book in some capacity, but Red was unimpressed.

In the club at Bridgetown we made an alcoholic discovery, the rum swizzle, introduced to us by a Britisher named Menzies—pronounced, to Red's delight, "Mengies." We retired each night well swizzled. Our letters of introduction and Red's international fame got us a conducted trip around Barbados with the island's health officer, little Doctor Hutson. He showed us that horrible epidemics were improbable on his salubrious island. This irked Red, who was on a hunt for tropic epidemic backgrounds, yet he was bothered more by Dr. Hutson's tiny pocket flask from which at the end of a thirsty morning he poured us out what he called a "modicum" of Scotch totally inadequate to raise our alcohol blood level. We thanked Dr. Hutson and on our return to Bridgetown made a beeline to the club. There the swizzles dampened our drought and soothed our failure to find the tragic background for the coming death fight by hero Arrowsmith.

In Port of Spain in Trinidad we found a spot sufficiently sinister. It was the Ice House, a bar, famous for its planter's punches in cold tall glasses beaded with moisture, and when we'd sipped enough of them they took us into strange worlds of our imaginations. They made us see a tropic island where death stank—the black death of the bubonic plague. This imaginary island became the battleground not only for Martin Arrowsmith's death fight but for his war with his conscience. "Am I justified in leaving part of the plague-threatened population unprotected, as controls, as witnesses to the hoped-for power of my antiplague remedy?" Red wrote about this with emotion.

In this Ice House I wept at Red's decree that Martin's wife, the devoted Leora, must perish of the plague, dying pitifully alone while her Martin was off fighting the black pestilence. I cried because Red's portrait of Leora—lovely in her abnegation—was growing more and more to be the image of my Rhea. I wept because of this and because of the planter's punches and the swizzles. Oh well—it's all in the never-never land of a novel and then I must remember Rhea is very much alive; and the emotion is mainly sentimentality, stirred by the swizzles and the planter's punches.

The punches and swizzles must bear a certain responsibility for the bizarre narrative that boiled out of Red's brain onto the sheets of yellow foolscap in his typewriter. Leora's death kept making me see Rhea dying. What artistry it was to make readers cry over events that only grew in Red's brain in the evenings in the sinister gloom of the Ice House in Port of Spain!

At Barbados we had joined another ship, a tidy little Dutch vessel, the S.S. *Crynssen,* that first took us to Trinidad and then along the north coast of South America and then to Panama and then doubled back along South America and across the Sargasso Sea, gay with the bubbles of Portuguese men-of-war bobbing on the quiet water, and past the Azores and at last to Merrie England, Red's beloved England, the isle of his aristocratic dreams.

"Always sample the wine of the country," said Red, and in a spotless town—Willemstad—we sipped too much Curaçao, and Curaçao, alas, gave us no atmosphere for a black-plague epidemic since the Dutch authorities would not permit rats on their clean little island. But Red was enchanted, listening in the night to the darkies singing sad Caribbean songs. We crossed to La Guaira, the port of Caracas.

A deadpan Venezulan drove us up a twisty mountain road with no guard rails at fifty miles per hour in a Buick with a governor on its engine. It could go fifty, no matter how steep the grades. Our demon driver cut across to the left-hand side of the road on the curves. He hung dizzily on the right-hand edge of straightways and this got Red's wind up. We knew no word of Spanish to restrain our Jehu. Red's red face blanched and his gestures failed to slow our wild ride down—any moment we might be in for it. Then at last the driver pulled up at a little tavern overhanging the edge of the mountain, and Red implored the bartender to tell our driver for Chrissake to take it easy.

"Why are you so scared, Red?" I asked him. He looked at me earnestly. "It isn't that I'm afraid," he said. "I just want to live to finish Martin Arrowsmith." Red did not fight fear, he rationalized it. There was always a good reason for prudence. Driving prudently had survival value and physical prudence was one of the secrets of Red's success. "It isn't fear," Red explained. "It's my overactive imagination."

Shakespeare, as always, had a gag for this. "Cowards die many times before their deaths; the valiant never taste of death but once." It was too bad for Red that he hadn't served along with me in the Argonne under fatalistic Sergeant Savage, who told me, when he saw me scared of the incoming heavy stuff, that nothing would get me till my number was up. But then again, Red's prudence had its creative uses. It was his timidity that, by contrast, helped him to imagine the bravery of Arrowsmith and his Leora. It heightened his admiration for the boldness of the reckless. Physical caution in the artist makes him worship the brave, stirring him to write about them with high emotion. It is, perhaps, an example of a secret of art, the secret of contrast, of chiaroscuro, as the old painters called it. It is rare to find brave men who can write deeply of bravery.

It was great luck for Red our being on the Dutch boat *Crynssen,* because among our fellow passengers there were rich Britishers and about Britons—especially if they were rich and nobby—Sinclair Lewis was enthusiastic. There was a Mr. Mappin, a handsome and reserved man, a partner in the famed firm of bauble and gewgaw merchants, Mappin and Webb. There was generous Mr. Walter Martin, the proprietor of Martin's the tobacconists in Piccadilly, and his dear wife, Mirksy. There was a man of noble blood, the Honorable Mr. Gideon Murray, Master of Elibank, who later became Lord Gideon Murray—he was a rosy-cheeked, gentle man and every inch a noble lowland Scotsman. Then lastly, dominating this coterie, there was the vast Mr. Prévité, absentee owner of fabulous asphalt deposits in Trinidad. He was a dignified and elephantine personality. He had never had to dig the asphalt personally but he owned it. I dubbed him "Mr. Privy" and though it disturbed Red—always awed by fiscal eminence— he cackled and congratulated me on the pat name for this majestic personage. "For Godsake don't call him that to his face," said Red. Mr. Privy wore shoes with heavy crepe soles— the first I'd ever seen. These enabled him to float his vast bulk on the soles of his tender feet. His gait was a bit ataxic.

Red's celebrity quickly made him intimate in this distinguished company, and on its fringes I tagged along. Arriving at Colon in Panama, Red invited the British contingent to a dinner ashore in the Hotel Washington. Red put on his acts, brilliantly mimicking Babbittesque American businessmen and stuffy American Anglican bishops. He had even the pompous Mr. Privy in stitches. At last came the moment for the settling of the bill. Red was our host. He scanned the reckoning. "Let's make it Dutch," he said. The faces of our British guests showed amazement. Was this an example of American hospitality? I signaled the waiter, took him aside, and settled the check.

If Red could be stingy, I could be roguish in return. In those days I hadn't got past the Biblical admonition "an eye for an eye, a tooth for a tooth." Our good ship *Crynssen* bound east from Panama was pitching in a head sea kicked up by strong winds against the current of the Gulf Stream. At each plunge of the nose of the little vessel into the trough of every wave, its propeller was out of the water, racing madly.

"Could this be dangerous?" Red asked me. "It couldn't be,

it is," I said solemnly. "What might happen?" asked Red. "The goddam screw might spin itself right off," I explained. "Where'd we be then?" asked Red. "We'd be at the mercy of the waves. No steerageway. We'd be like up you know what creek without a paddle. We'd drift on a rocky shore."

Red disappeared. I went to bed, and awoke next morning to find his berth undisturbed. On deck First Officer Vander Heuvel greeted me. "What did you do to Mr. Sinclair Lewis, Doctor?" he asked. "Has he been lost overboard?" I asked. "No, but he stayed up on de bridge with me all night. He seemed to want to stay close by me. He kept worrying me about our losing the propeller."

At the breakfast table there was Red. He greeted me severely: "Do you know, Paul, you have a streak of real cruelty in you?" "Who've I been cruel to?" "You know damn well who to," Red snarled. "To me!" "Oh—about our maybe losing the propeller?" I asked. "The first officer said there wasn't a chance of it," said Red. "You made a fool of me." "Then my saying that must have scared you?" "No, but it got my imagination going." "You mean you could see us piling up on the rocks? All night you could see it? Gosh I'm sorry." "You should learn not to be cruel—people would like you better," admonished Red. "These English seem to like me. But the English don't have what you call imagination," I said. "Their minds are matter-of-fact. They wouldn't begin fretting about the propeller till it had flown off."

This being before the days of airmail, letters from Rhea were few; and getting a packet of them on our final stop at Barbados en route to England, I read them, lovingly. She had got her passport and had her passage on the S.S. *France* to arrive at Plymouth March 18. Would I meet her? Would I meet her? Would I? My God, we'd never part again, ever.

In our work on *Arrowsmith* Red and I were true collaborators; sheets of yellow foolscap kept pouring out of Red's typewriter and we made the landfall at Plymouth with more than sixty thousand words of a complete scenario of the life and times of Martin Arrowsmith; we had down on paper the scientific philosophy of

Max Gottlieb (who was a blended Jacques Loeb and Frederick Novy) but who should have been much more Novy if Gottlieb was meant to portray the soul of a true searcher; we had sketched the life and death of brave small Leora who was worth the whole kit and caboodle of all the characters. Despite ruinous rum swizzles, despite the perils of planter's punches, despite dangerous Holland gin and bitters—despite this voyage in a vapor of ethyl alcohol in all these forms—Red had brought off a miracle and knew it and I knew it and there once more was a singing in my heart. To have kept my promise to Alf Harcourt and Don Brace and to Gracie and Rhea—to keep our genius, Red, this side of delirium tremens. He had been kept this side of going off a deep end— though there were times, mornings, when his shaky hand poured some of his Scotch onto the table and some into the glass. Yet he'd got the nub of his novel down onto paper; and now the task of dialoging it, for so great a writer as Red, ought to be coasting.

Red and I were never so close, before or after, as now when we leaned on the ship's rail, shoulder to shoulder in the dark, and peered toward the lights of Plymouth. "England," said Red with choky emotion, as if coming back at last to a long-lost home.

Red was at his best when met at railroad stations by reporters or friends or hangers-on or all three together. Getting off the train in London at Paddington Station I saw Red living up to his distinction as a lord of language. Debouching from our first-class carriage he created a sensation that stopped the passengers hurrying from the train. Red threw his arms round a great big genial giant of a man—Frazier Hunt—who'd come to meet us. Attending Hunt, a world-famous reporter, there stood a little bearded bundle of anonymity, Mr. C. E. Bechhofer Roberts, a nice, modest man whose fame as an author was known to few. Red and Spike hugged each other like brothers who had not met since childhood. Mr. Bechhofer's duties were those of cupbearer. He gently agitated a huge silver cocktail shaker. He looked at me solemnly. "Neat gin and ice, Doctor, no vermouth," he explained.

It was a sinister potion. We were on the way to tight before we left the platform. We grew more gay by the minute. In an hour we were plastered. Such was my introduction to London.

For such tosspots as Red and Spike, being plastered only meant exhilaration; for me it meant disaster. It came to a climax by my turning pea-green in the Café Royal. I saw a dozen Reds and Spikes and Bechhofers; they floated in the air in the whirling dining room of that historic café. I was sick and ashamed. Hunt, veteran of a hundred booze battles worse than this one, kindly ministered to me in the men's room. "Remember to eat plenty of hors d'oeuvres when you begin drinking, kid. Then you can go on forever."

As his technical adviser—as Gracie called me—Red assigned me to select the scientific eminentoes with whom it would be educational for him to hobnob. This job was exciting and soothed the *cafard* of my exile from research and helped to pass the crawling days of two weeks of waiting for my Rhea. We had the honor of dining with jolly little gray-bearded Sir William Bayliss and his brilliant physiologist collaborator, Sir Ernest Starling, in Starling's modest house. They'd been knighted for their work, which included dreaming up the word "hormone"—today on every tongue. These noble men of science had no opportunity to instruct Sinclair Lewis, who led the conversation in his scintillatingly magisterial manner.

At the laboratories of the Medical Research Council at Hampstead I was excited to meet Dr. H. H. Dale, who was to become Sir Henry Dale for his discovery of the anaphylactic effect of histamine. There was a rumor he was already on the way to knighthood. At the Hampstead laboratory we met poker-faced P. P. Laidlaw, about to make his name as a fighter against dog distemper.

Best of all—and for me this was momentous—Red and I swapped scientific gossip with Mr. Clifford Dobell, an obscurely famous protistologist, a tremendous authority on intestinal amoebae, who far into the night as a hobby engaged in researches into the life and work of Antonie van Leeuwenhoek. This was the old Dutch dry-goods storekeeper and janitor who had been the first of all men to see microbes. The meeting with Dobell was, for me, an embarrassing conference. Dobell was an acid-tongued detester of all things American, especially noisy Americans. He held himself haughtily while Red asked questions that revealed his knowledge of bacteriology. "Wasn't Sir Ronald Ross's discovery of the mosquito transmission of malaria remarkable?" Red showed his reverence for British science. "Ross did not discover that," said Dobell icily. "The Italian, Grassi, did."

When Red was away for a necessary moment, Dobell said: "This Mr. Lewis is a dreadful man. May I give you dinner some day this week? You'd be interested to see my Leeuwenhoek."

"What do you find different about these British searchers?" I asked Red next morning. "Different from, let's say, the Rockefeller Institute scientists." "I've only met Loeb and Northrop—what's wrong with them?" Red asked. "They're exceptions," I said. "Well, go on, shoot," said Red, expecting a trap. "How are these Britishers we've met different?"

"They know a real experiment when they meet it on the street," I said. "They have respect—for truth." This roused Red's latent Americanism. It worried him. Though he yearned to be a nobleman—"I just might buy a baronetcy and settle down here," he liked to say—yet he was proud to be a son of Sauk Centre, Minnesota, especially when sober.

"You mean these Britishers are more honest?" he asked. "They don't tend to get their science mixed up so much with dollars as we do." "Can ours be bribed?" asked Red. "In a way, some of them. They might lift another guy's work without giving him credit," I said, "if their boss thought it would help his institute or whatever." "But how are these British researchers really different?" Red kept at me. "If our boys have to choose between true and phony," I said, "then more of them know on what side their bread is buttered." "Would you say many of our scientific boys can be trained like seals?" Red asked. "You almost said it," I answered.

The spirit of this dialog got into *Arrowsmith,* though invidious comparisons of Americans to British were not mentioned. Red fascinated our British scientific friends with the exception of Dobell. "His insight into the scientific method is remarkable," said one admiring savant. Clifford Dobell—Mr. Dobell—he scorned a doctorate—was a mixture of objectivity and prejudice. He was objective about his amoebae; about Leeuwenhoek he was as objective and loving a biographer as ever lived. For Clifford there were few authentic creative great men: chief among them he placed Leeuwenhoek the microscopist, Vermeer the painter, Chopin the composer, and the biologist, D'Arcy Thompson. "But Darwin?" I asked. "Darwin? His *Origin of Species* is about as true as the first chapter of Genesis. Maybe Genesis comes nearer to the truth," said Dobell.

At the end of the first dinner tête à tête with me, Dobell said: "You're going to try to do the story of microbes—you'll have to start with my old Leeuwenhoek. I'll put everything about him at your disposal, if you wish." This got me off on the right foot in my coming test as a writer.

March 16, 1923—two whole days before the S.S. *France* was due at Plymouth, I was there, waiting for my Rhea. I wasn't impatient but spent those days in a happy daze, walking in a great park, gazing at the formidable rear elevation of Sir Francis Drake, where he had stood imperturbable for centuries looking out to sea, waiting for the Spanish Armada.

Now at last Rhea and I were huddled snug in the dark in a carriage behind a team of splendid horses making cloppety-clop over the cobbled street on the way to our hotel.

In an expensive, small, but elegant Georgian House in Bury Street, St. James's, Red received us with affection as if we were his children. This was on the eve of a battle, not, as before, the battle for credit for the book, but a contest to see if Rhea and I could call our souls our own.

Red and I had finished work in his apartment in the late afternoon. "Spike and Emmy Hunt and you and Rhea and I are going to Bath—Red pronounced it 'Ba-a-a-th'—for Easter," Red announced happily. "But Red, we can't," I said. "We've invited my sister Lois over from Brussels."

Lewis exploded into indignation. His red face went redder and its blemishes became glowing points of fire. He choked with fury. He recovered enough at last to give tongue. First he looked at me with cold disdain. Now he saw what I was. An ingrate. No respecter of his greatness. Not his obedient servant, but chained to Rhea and to Lois. Now he delivered his opinion. "Paul," he said, "you are not a fit man to work with me on Martin Arrowsmith." "Red," I replied, "you can take the book and shove it." "All right," said Red, "I can get a Berlitz bacteriologist to help me finish it." "Good-by, Red," I said, and walked out the door, not slamming it, and went upstairs to Rhea.

"What's wrong, honey?" asked Rhea. "Nothing," I said. "Only we've just been fired from working on Arrowhead."

Then came a bewildering series of events. The steward of Georgian House, the imcomparable Dunger, an admirable Crichton right out of the pages of James Barrie, was at the door. Apologetically he came bearing my medical and bacteriological textbooks and monographs, the source material of *Arrowsmith*. He returned again and again, at intervals, with various possessions I'd left in Red's apartment. Pencils. An eraser. A lovely photograph of Rhea—1920—it had been my ikon at the Rockefeller, at Reno, and on our long voyage while we made Arrowsmith come alive in the Caribbean.

Then there was the sound of the buzzer at our living-room door, a long buzzing and insistent. There stood Red, in tears, and trembling. He threw his arms around me. "Brother Paul," he said, "forgive me." He was abject. "Okay—forget it, Red," I said.

"Sorry I got tough." It was an emotional if somewhat opportunistic reconciliation on both sides. But the net of it was we did not go to Bath.

What about the credit for who wrote *Arrowsmith?* Over the years it has become plain that the majority of people who have talked to me about *Arrowsmith* had no idea I'd had anything to do with it at all. Then there is a small school of friends who erroneously believe it was not really Sinclair Lewis but De Kruif who wrote it. Nothing could be farther from the truth. Sinclair Lewis wrote it. Yet there is evidence that, during the early phases of the book's composition, Red thought I'd been of some help to him.

Just after our knock-down-and-dragout, in the glow of our reconciliation, Red showed me what was to be a letter to our publisher. *"And in all this there's a question as to whether he (de Kruif) won't have contributed more than I have."* Who could have asked more? Who could have been more generous than Red, admitting this, or, rather, writing it? Yet it was not true.

But as he went at the dialoging of our scenario he corrected his opinion; and as he sweated through two complete drafts of the novel, Red's memory dimmed. And so when *Arrowsmith* reached the page-proof stage in 1925, on the page after the title page there was a little acknowledgment that left not much more for me but thanks for technical assistance.

"Take it all out, to hell with it," I told Alf and Don and Ellen Harcourt. "Skip it all, I don't need it." Such was my paranoia. It was dear old Don Brace who then wrote to Red and extracted a broader acknowledgment.

Permit me here to deliver a judgment in the style of Judge Bridlegoose. This verdict has aged in the wood of my head over many years. In my own Bridlegoosean opinion, *Arrowsmith,* as a work of art, was in part improbable. All the science in it might have happened, though none of it did actually happen. The storied fictional protagonist, Max Gottlieb, was more than improbable. He was a muddy mélange of my revered chief, Professor Novy, and of Jacques Loeb, who was my master in a philosophy of the mechanistic conception of life, of God a mathematician, of God a Univac, of God a superstition, of God a childish concept, of God nonexistent. Jacques Loeb went one better than his adored Voltaire. Loeb thought Voltaire was wrong when he said that if God did not exist it would be necessary to invent him. According to good old Jacques Loeb, it was enough to say that God did not exist.

This accorded with Lewis's own philosophy, like that of all who are their own God, and it gave Loeb his importance in Red's synthesis of the mélange of the character of Max Gottlieb. I do not know if Professor Novy ever read *Arrowsmith,* but I can see him reading it and growling and in his precise, small script writing in the margin, *re* Gottlieb, one word. Bosh!

Yet Frederick Novy would have grunted approval at Gottlieb's and Arrowsmith's fanatical insistence upon controls for all experiments; and Red had written that admirably. Novy, though no bibleback, was not a man to deny God's existence. Too bad he didn't give me his feeling of God in science, when the two of us made jam sessions far into the night after our experiments were done. But I didn't feel the need of a God then and I didn't ask him and we stuck to our talk of scientific integrity—of which Novy was a master.

Of one character Novy would have approved fully. That was Leora. In her he would have detected, as many have done, a replica of Rhea. Leora was, as Lewis called her, the undemanding wife every man dreams of. "Why not end the book with the death of Leora; why not call the book *Leora?*" Alf Harcourt asked Red after reading the manuscript. Red flew into a fury. He threatened to withdraw the book before publication and said he'd sail back to England never to return. Who was Alf to tamper with this masterpiece? Then Alf took me aside. "Take Red back to town and cool him off," he said. This I did in my role of bouncer in charge of the great American novelist's unstable and capricious genius. It was a rugged job.

Why did I stick by it? Well, because Red had taught me to let my imagination go. Without that, I couldn't have begun to write the book about the microbe men. I couldn't have become a writer without apprenticeship to Red's wild genius. But then, neither could I have become a writer without severe apprenticeship to Lytton Strachey, though I had never met him. At Fontainebleau in 1923, after reading the completed first draft of *Arrowsmith* I thought it was a fine book and was proud to have had some part in it and said so with exclamation points in the margins of the manuscript. What I think of it now is that it's okay not to be more widely identified with its composition. Red did me an unwitting favor by not giving me joint top billing on the cover. Red was right, ethically. Apprentices are not supposed to have their names on a product.

CHAPTER SEVEN

Now, at the end of March, 1923, at last we were on our own in a little furnished flat in Flood Street in Chelsea in London with sight of the river in a region haunted by the ghost of Thomas Carlyle. Here, largely safe from the demands of Red's capricious affection, we were happy. Here Rhea grappled calmly with the complications of British housekeeping. While she sallied forth to King's Road to find a fishmonger whose wares stank not too much, I went off with my notebook to the British Museum where —according to Dobell's directions—search began into the life of Antonie van Leeuwenhoek and his discovery of the microbes that he called his little animals.

Gracie Lewis had made her descent upon London and she and

Red swept into a swirl of London high life aglitter with great names, celebrities, and nobby persons. Red's self-assurance was such that big names, to him, instantly became first names. Once I heard Red calling a personage on the other end of a telephone "Max"—it was Max this, Max that, and dear Max and good old Max. It was, of course, Lord Beaverbrook.

Gracie and Red dashed about searching for a suitable country seat and a nice British school where they could park their puzzled little six-year-old boy, Wells. But no sooner had they settled down than they were off to Fontainebleau, taking a château where Red would have the seclusion demanded for the first draft of *Arrowsmith*. Their rootlessness was a replica of Red's restless brain. They ran away from potential happiness.

Now that Red had the design of the novel nailed down in almost 90,000 words of scenario, the Lewis–De Kruif interfamilial relations became relaxed. They came one evening to dine with us in Flood Street. They brought along with them a distinguished personage from the groves of academe—Professor Chauncey Brewster Tinker, at whose feet Red had sat, as a student, at Yale. For once, at dinner, Red did not dominate; he encouraged the good Professor to lead the conversation, and at the dinner itself there was no obscenity—all went politely. Then came disaster. Gracie and Rhea withdrew (as stylish ladies should) to our tiny living room while the Professor and Red and I lingered (as British gentlemen should) over the brandy. Alas, we lingered just a bit too long, or so thought Gracie. She burst in on us and announced stormily that she had never been so insulted in all her life. How crude of us to exclude her so long from our cultured conversation! She poured upon the three of us a tirade eloquent in the manner of Madame du Deffand. Meanwhile Rhea was nowhere to be seen. She was allergic to all scenes and fusses staged publicly. Poor Professor Tinker bowed his head in bewilderment. Red—this was new in my experience of him—was reduced to embarrassed silence. The soirée broke up disastrously.

Our own little circle of friends was graced by Clifford Dobell and Dr. William Bulloch. Dr. Bulloch's talk belched forth in a thick Scots burr that held us spellbound. Dobell was learned and sardonic. As Dobell was the last word on the life and work of Leeuwenhoek, so Bulloch was on the lives of all the first-line microbe hunters and especially the *Abbate* Lazzaro Spallanzani —the agnostic experimenting priest who had disproved the spontaneous generation of microbes while Pasteur was still only a gleam in his grandfather's eye. "You're welcome to study all my material on the *Abbate*," said Bulloch. With Dobell he laid the solid foundation for the first two heroes of the book about the microbe men.

In contrast to Red and Gracie, Bulloch and Dobell gave not a damn about big names. On the contrary, they were connoisseurs at cutting them down to size. While Dobell was a haughty recluse, Bulloch knew everybody—including European royalty he'd been given the task of screening for absence of hemophilia in a project to find a female of blue book who was not a carrier of this blood dyscrasia—and therefore a suitable candidate to marry the Prince of Wales. Bulloch was a keen judge of the abilities of medical scientists, American as well as English. He confirmed what I'd heard about Popsy Welch. "Popsy Welch?"—meaning Professor William H. Welch of the Johns Hopkins—"As a scientist, Popsy was the greatest diner-out in medical history," said Bulloch.

At the end of one of our convivial evenings bibbing Burgundy, Rhea and I escorted our two friends down the stairs into moon-drenched Flood Street. "Stop," said Dr. Bulloch dramatically. "Do you realize where we now stand?" "Where do we stand?" To which Dr. Bulloch answered: "We stand only a hundred yards from the spot where Dante Gabriel Rossetti had improper relations with Algernon Swinburne."

"Paul Ehrlich," exclaimed Bulloch on another occasion. "There was a gay and witty dog. He came prancing out of his bedroom in nothing but a skimpy shirt when I came round to take him out to dinner. 'Do you know what my discovery of 606 amounted to?' Ehrlich asked. 'My dear colleague, for seven years of misfortune I had one moment of good luck.'"

Red generously tried to introduce Rhea and me to a British

literary and political *haut monde*. This was before Red had entered Lord Beaverbrook's charmed circle. Red and Rhea and I were invited for a weekend to the home of H. G. Wells at Easton Glebe in Essex. I was curious to meet this remarkable man, who way back in 1912 had been my first hero in the world of letters. Rhea danced with Ramsay MacDonald, who was soon to become prime minister, and she had the honor to sit across the dinner table from the magnificent immensity of the Countess of Warwick.

Rhea and I were asked to stay beyond the weekend after Red had departed. Then Mr. Wells drove us back to London in a little motor car—his first one. He asked me to sit in front with him but I had to refuse because Rhea was in agony with cystitis and I sat holding her hand, helping her against her pain. How she stood the long ride into London without asking Mr. Wells to stop I do not know. I was stupidly too bashful to tell him her trouble and I lost my one and only chance to ask the great man questions saved up for many years.

Then his new little car—of which he was very proud—developed a flat tire just as we pulled up before our Flood Street apartment and Mr. Wells and his son Gyp knew not what to do. While Rhea fled upstairs I changed the tire quickly. "How did you get to be so expert?" asked Mr. Wells. "Working at Ford's in 1906," I said. "Oh," said Mr. Wells, "then you're not the mechanical genius I thought you."

A pleasant memory of Red Lewis is his kindness to my mother and sister, who visited us on their way back from Brussels to America. Arriving at our humble Flood Street home in a magnificent open rented Daimler, he took us on a personally conducted tour of Burnham Beeches and Stokes Poges, immortal for Gray's *Elegy*.

"Don't you think the *Elegy* is great?" my mother asked Red. Then Red delivered a disquisition. Reciting, he proceeded to take Mr. Gray apart, dissecting him poetically limb from limb.

"The curfew tolls the knell of parting day," Red began. What was that but a cliché?

"The ploughman homeward plods his weary way," he intoned. Gray made you think all plowmen plodded and were weary at the end of work. "A cliché!" Red continued.

"The moping owl does to the moon complain." How did Gray know owls mope? "Sheer nonsense," Red explained.

Red seemed happy that day at home with our Midwest family and he came up for a drink and a snack in our apartment after we'd ridden our weary way home in the elegant Daimler. On our arrival at Flood Street mother offered to pay the rent for the Daimler and Red allowed her to.

That 1923 London summer was halcyon. Our funny little Flood Street home became a pleasant mecca for a few visiting firemen from America. Donald Brace, the artistic balance wheel of Harcourt, Brace, came to make serious talk about my microbe men and he offered me a generous contract which he signed without batting an eye and thus began his lifelong brotherly love for both of us—thirty years of friendship unmarred by a single word of misunderstanding. It was Don who gave the book its title, *Microbe Hunters*.

On hours off from the microbe men I set out to get an insight into the souls of these wild Karamazov brothers; and I got to understand their sensuality—so much like my own. At the end of the first reading of the mighty book emotion overwhelmed me. Face down on the bed I cried and cried and cried, and knew not why. "Why do you cry?" asked Rhea. "Alyosha tells those young boys they'll all meet with him at the resurrection. They answered 'Hurrah for Karamazov!' "

"Why should that make you cry?" she asked me. "I don't believe in immortality," I replied.

At the end of that London summer we went to Paris to see Emile Roux and to dig into the original publications of Roux's boss, Pasteur. We spent many hours in the Louvre and Luxembourg galleries, where Rhea was at her happiest. On a memorable midnight we walked between the flowers fragrant on the Pont des Fleurs to watch the hurly-burly of the truck farmers bringing their spinach and carrots to Les Halles. We ate the strong onion soup at the Chien qui Fume where two ladies, dancing, made eyes at Rhea. In the dawn we climbed Montmartre, exchanging badinage in our funny French with bands of mingled roisterers weaving home from what must have been a notable *bombe*. We climbed past the Moulin de la Galette made famous by Vincent van Gogh; and ended at the Church of the Sacré Coeur to watch the sun rise over Paris.

Presently to our little Left Bank hotel, grandly called the Trianon Palace—our bathroom had a bidet but no biffy—came wonderful news from Red Lewis. He had finished the first draft of *Arrowsmith*. Here it was only September and he'd started it late May. Would we come out to Fontainebleau to read the manuscript?

It took parts of three days and two nights at Red's grand château to get through the manuscript, word by word. It was a thrill to find how Red had not loused up the science and how he'd used it all as we'd brewed it up in the Caribbean and to see how he'd got it straight as if he himself was Novy and Jacques Loeb and Arrowsmith rolled up together into one. It seemed to me that it was good blood-and-thunder adventure too.

"You've done it, my boy. It's great," I told him. "What's wrong with it?" he asked, his pale-blue eyes suspicious. "I'd change only one word in the last sentence where Martin and his friend have gone to the bush to make science on their own." I said. "How'd you change it?" asked Red. "Those last words—'and probably we'll fail'—" "What would *you* say?" "I'd suggest *possibly*, not probably, we'll fail," I said mildly. "That shows you've missed the whole meaning of *Arrowsmith*," Red said, shaking his head sadly. That was the difference. He was for the down-beat—I was for the up-beat.

It seemed to me that "possibly we'll fail" would have been a bit more true, psychologically. Of course searchers do fail far more often than they succeed. They mostly fail forward. Yet it was my belief deep down that the thought of failure is not in the heart or brain of any searchers worth their salt at the outset of any project. Or they wouldn't have started it. But Red had come a long way from our knock-down-drag-out arguments in the Caribbean. Red was in command, magisterial, the sole author now. He'd asked me a thousand questions then. Now he knew the answers.

"How to sum up this Institut Pasteur?"

Emile Roux repeated my question in his slow, precisely spoken French. "We have absolute anarchy here—" he hesitated, and then finished with a smile: "tempered by a benevolent despotism." Emile Roux was the Institut's director and hence its despot and never was there a tyranny more gentle than that of this greatest of the disciples of Pasteur.

Roux had mammoth modesty. "A worker proposes a research idea to me. It is my first reaction that he is crazy—his notion seems so wild and new. Then I have a second thought—it is maybe me that's insane. So I tell him to go ahead and try it."

Roux had not forgotten Pasteur's mad originality and he remembered his own. It was an unforgettable interview, observing the amused self-honesty of this hawk-faced, bearded, ancient pupil of Pasteur. "For example—who could have been more foolish than Yersin and I were, when we were trying to demonstrate the toxin of the diphtheria bacillus of Löffler? We couldn't find that poison. Nobody had been able to find it. Everyone knew it had no soluble toxin. Yersin and I couldn't find it. We knew it must be there. We found it because we were foolish."

I hadn't yet studied Roux and Yersin's original report of their immortal discovery. "Why do you say you were foolish?" I asked him.

"Study the protocols, and look at the enormous amount of broth filtrate of a diphtheria culture that we had to inject into guinea pigs—to prove there was a soluble toxin. Thirty-five cubic centimeters into one small guinea pig! We had almost to drown the little beasts in filtered broth before we found any toxic effect," said Roux.

"But we now know that only traces of a filtrate are enough to kill a guinea pig," I said.

"But Yersin and I did not know that in 1888," said Roux.

"We had to give that enormous dose—" Roux hesitated, "because we were idiotic. You see, it wasn't experimental insight that led us to the really powerful poison. No, it came from neglecting, yes, forgetting. We succeeded by doing nothing. You see, the poison was so weak because we'd only waited four days after seeding the broth to let the microbes make their poison. Then— it must have been an accident?—we tested the toxicity of a broth that had stood in the incubator *forty* days. And there was the poison, killing guinea pigs with a fraction of a cubic centimeter!"

"But who could have known—"

"Nobody. It was not knowledge. It was only our stupidity to try everything. It was only our faith. How often is faith foolish and how often sagacious? It was our faith" (today it would be called a hunch) "that it is not the microbe itself but its toxin— nonexistent according to all knowledge—its *toxin* that killed children with diphtheria."

"You must have had to kill many guinea pigs to find it," I said. "A veritable army of them," Roux replied.

"And that was not the end of our stupidity," he went on. "We had the powerful toxin; we hadn't the insight to inject small bits of it into animals to see if their bodies would make an antitoxin to neutralize it. In our ignorance we left that discovery to a German," said Roux regretfully. "To Monsieur Emil Behring."

"But look what's coming of it now," I said. "Right now, in your institute, Doctor Ramon has tamed your diphtheria toxin. He's got rid of its poison without destroying its power to immunize children. You can guard all the children in the world from diphtheria. You can wipe it from the world," I said, enthusiastic. "We may hope," said Roux.

It was a great day. Emile Roux had taught me what would be fundamental to my projected history. Its theme would not be "let us now praise famous men." Its watchword must be that the celebrity usually claimed by eulogistic biographers for their subjects is largely an *arrière pensée*. Actually the so-called heroes are human. When too busy to go to the biffy, they make water in the laboratory sink. In their adventures they are brave, sometimes; they are stupid, often; they have good hunches and a few brilliant intuitions; they are, above all, lucky. Emile Roux was all of these, but differed from most celebrities in that he admitted it. He was all these things and then he was what most celebrities are usually not. Roux was first, last, and always honest.

Toiling through the tomes of *Oeuvres de Pasteur* in the library of the Institut, Pasteur's precisely written comments on the margins of these mighty volumes made him come alive. Never lived there a genius who took such good care that posterity would realize that, in every one of his controversies, it was Pasteur who was right—even when he was mistaken.

But his comments revealed Pasteur wouldn't let it go at that. It was not enough for him that he should be a saint of science. At the end of Tome II, *Fermentations et Générations Dites Spontanées,* far from being uplifted, I sank back exhausted and a little sad. How he fought for sick humanity, this great man; how he loved humanity and how he loved himself.

What disturbed me was an item at the end of his collected studies, devoted to jumping up and down upon the grave of his old friend Claude Bernard. In the twilight of his days, Bernard, that most eminent physiologist, had made certain grossly heretical experiments—blasphemies against the sacred science of Pasteur. Bernard when he made them was old, and, as Pasteur hinted in print, perhaps a bit dotty. How otherwise could he have called Pasteur's proof of the nonexistence of spontaneous generation in question? This posthumous publication by Bernard was mild and tentative. Pasteur in ignoring it would have helped it fade into oblivion. But Pasteur demolished poor dead Bernard by a brilliant series of experiments. Then, alas, the distinguished scientist, Monsieur Berthelot, used Bernard as a club to hit Pasteur, who had published his refutation of Bernard's critical researches. Pasteur was frantic in his fury. He used Bernard to hit Berthelot, in turn, in a series of indignant discussions before the French Academy that left its venerable savants aghast. It was not enough for Pasteur to disprove in the laboratory—as he brilliantly did— Bernard's experiments. Against poor dead Bernard he employed the *argumentum ad hominem,* the kind of argument that shows an opponent not only to be wrong, but suggests that he might have beaten his mother.

In these discussions, to the horror of the Academy, he scolded Berthelot and Bernard's other friends for daring to publish researches that questioned his, Pasteur's, own theory. Pasteur published an unfortunate pamphlet against poor Claude Bernard, who could not answer it from his grave. It hinted that Bernard in his last days had lost his memory. It supposed that Bernard had become tainted with mystical ideas by associating too much with literary lights of the French Academy. In his last days Bernard, perhaps, had lost the sharpness of his famous observer's eyes. "I'll wager Bernard had become so farsighted—*presbyte*—that he couldn't see the yeasts that were there," said Pasteur.

In his fourth and last rebuttal in his discussions with Bernard's defender Berthelot in the *Comptes rendus de l'Académie des Sciences,* Pasteur disposed of both these disbelieving dogs, Bernard and Berthelot, with a testimonial to his own achievements. This had been pronounced long before, in 1861, in this very Academy. eulogizing Pasteur as a savant of rigorous judgment and perspicacity.

Why was I sad and depressed? It was at the prospect of having to write all this if the book about the microbe men was to show a portrait of Pasteur the man. Knowing all this, how could I write about him *con amore?* God love Pasteur, he could not help it. In his grand career he'd got to be a genius long before he was dead and this was not so much his fault as the merit of his greatest contribution—namely, to tell the world that microbes are a menace.

Who'd read a book treating Pasteur as human, all too human? Who, among our living microbe men, would recommend it? I'd need testimonials. To this day in the groves of our medical academe Pasteur can still do no wrong. When you write about Pasteur, you should rave about him. If you wanted to be a respectable historian of the golden, blooming times of bacteriology, you started off by adding an infinity of years to Pasteur's already excessive immortality. It was absolutely safe to praise Pasteur, just as Matthew Arnold was on perfectly sound ground praising Shakespeare. But how was I going to confine myself to praise alone? I could not, if I was going to be a real writer.

And what did that demand of me? It would require the possession of an instrument the use of which is hazardous in the extreme if one wants to make a living in beautiful letters. What I would need is an apparatus described to me not long ago by Ernest Hemingway. A good writer, says the forthright Ernesto, has got to have a built-in, shock-proof detector of what's left in stables by horses. He used the four-letter word.

Those last days in Paris our book about the microbe men had a great success before I'd written a line of it. I talked it. Norman Hapgood, my old editor, hearkened in a little Paris restaurant, all attention, to my telling about Pasteur. He saw the whole book as a fascinating example of a new art of debunk, in an untouched field. Pasteur as the master of a new medical PR— public relations—was as amazing as the news that General George Washington enjoyed wenches. Norman made me happy: "We'd like it serially for Hearst's *International*," he said. But on Norman's return to the States he gave the news to his boss, the master buyer of big literary names, the thin-lipped editor Ray Long. Norman then manfully wrote us the sad news of the book's rejection by Hearst's *International*.

Norman had suggested we get material for articles before returning to the States, so we went to the slope of a mountain in the sun near Leysin in Switzerland to meet Rollier, who was the high priest of the healing power of the sun for TB of the bones; we got the strange, little-known story of his tanning these tuberculars back to strength and vigor. Then in the last days at the Institut Pasteur I met the Russian brain man, Ivan Petrovich Pavlov. He started us off digging into the weird, complicated story of his discovery of conditioned reflexes in dogs. This was the beginning of the penetration of the mystery of the mechanism of the cortex and hypothalamus of the human brain.

Pavlov was terrific just to look at. He didn't speak English.

My Russian was limited to *da* and *nyet* and *nitchevo*. The old gentleman was honesty, with a beard, as he sat there serenely answering my questions translated by his physicist son; and Pavlov seemed pleased that the questions were solid. I'd come armed by study of the Oxford University Press edition of his *Lectures on Conditioned Reflexes,* and by a briefing in their abstruse science by Pavlov's pupil, Anrep. Pavlov did more for me than merely getting me a magazine story for Norman. He immunized me against the peril of what I came to call the analism promulgated by Sigmund Freud, just then beginning to taint American psychiatry and even psychology.

What if the book about the microbe men should turn out to be a bust? The possible popular success of the articles I was writing on Rollier, Banting, and others was in itself a menace to the book of the microbe men. We had not much money. Rhea kept me unscared. Her faith kept me unperturbed by possible failure. We both of us felt strong, armed with energy and astonishing facts and by our always deeper love. Then came bad news for the project of the microbe men.

A cable from Norman asked us to hurry home. We were all in trouble. A vaccine maker in Detroit had filed suit against Mr. William Randolph Hearst, Mr. Norman Hapgood, Heart's *International Magazine,* and Paul de Kruif for damages in the amount of one million six hundred thousand dollars. For an article by Paul de Kruif, 1922, in a series known as "Doctors and Drugmongers." The charge? That my story had in effect called the manufacturer a murderer with vaccines alleged to kill the sick people they were designed to save. Would we please hurry home to collect evidence that would disprove the charge. If I could do that, Mr. Hearst was all set to fight. If I'd been wrong, well, if I'd been wrong, where would I be as a writer?

Now, for sure, hopes of soon beginning the book about the microbe men went glimmering. On the one hand I was sure of not having made the accusation that the vaccines were fatal, only that they were phony in their claims of cure. On the other hand how did the vaccine maker have the nerve to file such a suit if I hadn't damaged his business? In the sinister secrets of the law I was a suckling. Mr. Hapgood assured us that Hearst's would pay our "expenses" in such an investigation and I sank into indigo gloom—foreseeing myself spending years as an antilibel leg man, interviewing physicians from coast to coast, a series of disdainful doctors who didn't care a damn if I was being sued for crusading against vaccines that really good medicos did not use. The book was white hot in me now. I had to return home, but I had to write the book.

CHAPTER EIGHT

I WENT home into an atmosphere of the gay, golden 1920's when America was a gigantic poker game with deuces wild. Ours was a country aglister with prosperity built on the blown-up values of securities, some of which were sound. These were the doubtful days when Albert Einstein and Sigmund Freud propounded their profundities to a nationwide obbligato of "Yes, we have no bananas, to-day." They were topsy-turvy times when America's most publicized spiritual leader was the Reverend Aimée Semple MacPherson, boffing out her four-square gospel till the very rafters rumbled in her Angelus Temple. It was the frivolous decade that saw justice meted out by A. Lawrence Lowell, who was not a judge, to Sacco and Vanzetti. It was the Utopistic 1920's when Mr. Herbert Hoover prophesied automobiles and chickens for all.

We had the luck to have Henry Mencken for a mentor in matters mundane outside our own science. A Rabelais redivivus, with hair parted almost in the middle and high-buttoned shoes, he taught us that these gods of the golden 1920's were more than merely phony—that would have roused our indignation—he showed us that beyond their spuriousness they were funny—and that sent us into belly laughter. Then too, Menck was our guide in music, the most consoling of the arts.

All suggestions for amicable settlement of the suit against Hearst and me had been rejected by the plaintiff. Preliminary study of the complaint brought us the cheering news that the plaintiff was not claiming that my story had implied that the vaccine maker was a murderer; the story was confined to demonstrating—by heavy documentation—that the vaccines were *not* cures as claimed. In the article his wares had not been my only target. I had attacked another manufacturer's vaccinelike remedies —"phylacogens"—and these had actually sent certain unfortunate patients to their reward. And these deaths had been published medically; and we quoted the disasters; and then Hearst's *International Magazine,* for illustrations, published advertisements of both products, side-by-side. The make-up man had switched the captions—calling the plaintiff's relatively innocuous product murderous; and letting the sinister phylacogens off as ineffective but harmless.

It seemed as if the magazine's editors had made what might turn out to be a million six hundred thousand dollar blunder. Let them try to get out of it, let us get on with the book about the microbe men. But Rhea said no—"You wrote the article and you should have seen it through right out on to the newsstands. You didn't. Don't alibi."

What to do? Would any reputable doctors back up my attack on the useless vaccines—would they testify to the article's truth—excepting its caption? I scouted about. Not for free they wouldn't. Not for anything they wouldn't. There was that name Hearst—in those days not savory. In this desperate situation there was one man—just one—who might come to our rescue. He had been my mentor in the series on doctors and drugmongers. He was a Galahad against quackery. This was no less than Dr. Morris Fishbein of the *Journal of the American Medical Association.*

"Mr. Hearst will have to hire the best available experts, Paul," said the Prolocutor. "I can get them for you, but Mr. Hearst will have to pay," said Dr. Fishbein.

"Who are they and how high do they come?" I asked.

"The men who might help you—if Mr. Hearst will pay—are Dr. Ludvig Hektoen and Dr. Ernest E. Irons." Dr. Hektoen was not only a celebrated pathologist; he was the director of a distinguished institute, he was a medicolegal expert as well. "They will have to be approached as consultants on this case. Before they'll consider such a delicate matter—remember the plaintiff has been accused of murder—they should ask a retainer of ten thousand dollars each."

Old Doctor Hektoen became my kindly guide. "Look for possible deaths among patients, who might have lived if they'd got proper medical care instead of the plaintiff's bacterins," he said in his slow-spoken judicious manner with a charming Nordic accent. Dr. Hektoen radiated benignity. Nights working at the microbe men I dug through heavy tomes of the *Oeuvres de Pasteur*, brought back from Paris.

At first in Chicago we had no social life at all. But early that 1924 we did acquire a little friend. It was an ikon. We were wandering down the Boule Miche and passed a toyshop and in its window among expensive baubles we spied a tiny wooden duck scarcely two inches long. "Buy him for me, Dassa," said Rhea. "He might bring us luck." This little duck had wheels. He had staring eyes. When you pulled him along on a string his neck rose and fell and his beak opened and closed pompously and we bought him for six bits and baptized him "Oskar." Years later he was to calm a most dangerous burst of turbulence that threatened to part us forever.

Then we gained two friends on the frayed fringes of Chicago's cultural bohemia. That winter and spring marked our education under the tutelage of a remarkable character, Charles Neil Thomas and his beloved Lida. He had been retired from the materialistic world of commercial paper banking and with Lida presided over a literary salon, on a capital sum gained from the sale—in dribs and drabs—of his vast prewar liquor cellar, possibly the finest in then dry Chicago. That cellar, like the biblical widow's cruse, kept Tommy living like a slightly drunken lord and at the same time delighting visiting celebrities—among them Sinclair Lewis —keeping them in a state of pleasant lubrication. Their every word seemed a brilliant bon mot in the fog of Tommy's booze.

Tommy Thomas as a *literateur* surpassed most of his visiting literati in wit and brains and especially buffoonery and he might have been a real literary critic but for his Lucullan love for foods, wines, liquors, and Havana cigars. He declared himself proudly to be a parasite on what he laughed at as our decadent economic order, akin, he said, to the last days of the Roman Empire as described by Gibbon. He hooted at all economic soothsayers, fiscal and professional. He loved lugsury, as he called it. He deplored his own decadence. He was a sybarite and a devotee of literature and the seven lively arts. To Rhea and to me he brought the Dublin world of James Joyce, of Oliver St. John Gogarty, of AE, and Yeats. He loved *Ave atque Vale* by George Moore and was indignant when I said Moore's *Hail and Farewell* gave me the impression of cantaloupes slightly overripe.

Then all at once—it was like diving into fifty-degree Lake Michigan water—I was writing the microbe book. One day it seemed to explode out of my typewriter as if without preparation —on the same day we watched the Gold Cup speedboat races on the river in Detroit. I was on the big writing sprocket at last and knew it and Rhea knew it as the romance of Leeuwenhoek, the first of the microbe men, poured on to the paper. . . . Leeuwenhoek, so Dutch, so quaint, so innocent, so ignorant, so different from today's professors in their cozy colleges, and far above them in his naive originality.

Then, happy day, who but Red Lewis appeared to give the book a boost along. Like a raffish, pock-marked Providence, he swooped with *élan* down upon Detroit from far Saskatchewan, bringing a bunch of celery picked up in Kalamazoo as a present for Rhea. "Where's the press?" he asked in disappointment when I met him at Michigan Central depot alone. I apologized and he telephoned all three of the newspapers from our apartment. After the press conference, punctuated by his escorting sundry newspaper sob sisters one by one to his own apartment for personal conferences, at last Rhea, Red, and I were cozy and alone.

Red's bloodshot light-blue eyes darted over the typescript pages of Leeuwenhoek, first of the microbe men. "It's magnificent, Paul," he said. "By God, you're a *writer*." This sent tingles down my spine. "But there's one spot where you should soup it up— a spot that yells for a purple patch. You've missed it," said Red.

"Where?" I said. "Right after old Antonie calls out to his daughter: 'Come here, Maria, look what I've discovered!' You have him showing Maria the little animals no eyes have seen in all history—"

"What's wrong with that?" I asked, a bit testy. "Everything. You've left out the real punch paragraph—it would be a terrific exordium. Could be the big scene of the whole book maybe. . . . The opening up of a new, marvelous, terrible world. . . . "

Red was right. And that instant his purple patch exploded in my brain. Red and Rhea were as if nonexistent as I hurried to the typewriter. The passage came out onto the page in spurts and jets:

Caesar had gone to England and come upon savages that opened his eyes with wonder—but these Britons were as ordinary to each other as Roman centurions were to Caesar—

Huge elephants amazing to Alexander the Great but commonplace to Hindus—

The Pacific Ocean astounding Balboa but ordinary to Central American Indians—

. . . But Leeuwenhoek? This janitor of Delft had stolen upon and peeped into a fantastic sub-visible world of little things. . . . Beasts these were of a kind that ravaged and annihilated whole races of men ten million times larger than they were themselves. . . .

This was Leeuwenhoek's day of days.

These fragments tumbled out of the typewriter crudely. Red looked at the page, rough with typos. "You've got it," he shouted. "You know what you've done?" I asked him. "Now the book takes off from way up there," and I pointed out the window to the sky. "Now it opens up key of C major, presto."

"Purple patches can't come too often," warned Red, "and keep them short."

The book about the microbe men was born without benefit of checking by bacteriologists or physicians. I discussed my work in progress with but two such persons and they were two of the book's main characters still living. One—a memorable day with serene Theobald Smith at Princeton—telling me how he found the tick transmission of Texas fever. "This made mankind turn a corner"—these were his words. The only other was one great day with fierce, mustachioed, growling Sir David Bruce—David the Bruce—and his lovely Lady Bruce in Toronto. "Why, there's one! Right on your neck," Lady Bruce recounted, pointing to the tsetse fly about to bite her burly man and—maybe—kill him with its sting deadly with *Trypanosoma gambiense.* "We'd been hunting the tsetse for months—that's the way we found it."

All the latter half of 1924 and till 1925, October—when the last words of the last chapter about the magic bullet were written on the shore of Lake Michigan—we moved about, but not grandly. "Keep your basic expenses low," said my publisher, Alf Harcourt, and we finished the first Pasteur in the frowzy second story of a coaldealer's house in Mount Vernon in New York. "This is something elegant," said Henry Mencken. "This is period furniture—early North German Lloyd, you know that, Rhea?" He pronounced it "Ray-ah."

Fiscally we sailed close to the wind. "Come write at our house while we're in England," said Alf Harcourt kindly. "Come write at our house while we're in Italy," said Don Brace later, with equal kindness, and Rhea mothered the beautiful Brace daughters Kay and Donna while I wrote the hilarious saga of Elie Metchnikoff, who religiously swallowed cultures of his Bulgarian bacillus to give himself eternal life but kicked the bucket, alas, at the unripe age of seventy-one.

Alf and Don watched over us like foster fathers. Fortunately, we owed them nothing. The big advance on *Arrowsmith* had been repaid by our share of that book's serial rights. There was a race between finishing the microbe book and using up our dwindling funds. Then Alf and Don came to the rescue. To the *Country Gentleman* with the help of Ann Watkins, the vivid literary agent, they sold the chapters on Pasteur and Koch and Theobald Smith for serialization—after all other big magazines had turned the book down as ridiculous. Now with us safe in the black, I tore into the last chapters with unleashed fury, in a tent on the shore of the Tittabawassee River back of Rhea's home in Freeland and then on the shore of Lake Michigan where we walked many miles every day and swam in the rough, cold, autumn water. It was past midnight in the early morning hours of October first. "It's done," I shouted.

Now in early October in New York Don Brace said the book was marvelous. Alf Harcourt said he liked it, even though my prose didn't "parse" in some places. They were going to send the book to the printer right away to get it ready for publication in March, 1926. Alf was oracular. "I believe it just might sell out its first printing," he predicted judiciously. I hadn't the nerve to ask him what the first printing would be.

"Somebody has phoned," said Alf. "There's her number."

I called, and who was it but the dark lovely lady from Reno. For three years, to me, she had been gone and forgotten. It was one of those dirty kismets that can ruin your life. That part of my life, thank God, was over, I thought. But now this day and the next and the next I saw the dark lady and she was as lovely and sadder than ever yet strangely wild, and seemed quietly desperate, in an abandoned love. Now Rhea was about to join me and I told the dark lady we must not see each other any more, ever. I explained to her that Rhea in our three years of marriage had become my one and only. "Just once more," murmured the dark lady, pleading, and we were lost again, and then she went away.

Now, waiting eagerly for Rhea, I rationalized my infidelity. I was not promiscuous, which means engaging in sexual intercourse indiscriminately or with many persons. One slice off a cut loaf is never missed, as Herman Bundesen, Chicago's public health czar, said. It was only an episode of a double life led by many men. It was a peccadillo. It was only a bit of a binge. It was not disloyalty. It was dragging my ashes, as Roy Fritsche used to say. Hadn't I needed it after the long strain of the writing of the microbe men? (What rot, this rationalizing. It had been no strain; it had been a joy.) The irresponsible imp in me said for me to forget it, to act as if it never had happened; and that seemed easy —because in fact I wanted Rhea more than ever. I'd only been temporarily a bit Turkish.

Meeting Rhea at the Grand Central Station was a grand reunion and her eyes shone with love and with quiet pride at the good news I now told her. Don believed the book had a real chance to go. Royalties were rolling in from *Arrowsmith,* now a best seller. More good news. The *Country Gentleman* wanted me to do a series of science adventures—offering $1500 per article. We were so happy. We were as if newlyweds with financial worry away. Our success seemed to cancel out my infidelity—wasn't it only a peccadillo—a slight offense, a petty fault? Not a sin? We settled in a little furnished apartment in Bronxville. Cheap. "Keep your basic expenses low," warned Alf Harcourt, businessman that he was. He liked his writers to be artistic—and frugal. "I've always found it useful to have from five to ten thousand in a savings account," said Alfred.

Before the publication of *Microbe Hunters* early in March, Alf Harcourt gave Rhea a kindly warning. We must not hope too much. The book trade was showing not much interest in my offbeat opus, said Alf. We'd be lucky if it sold out its first printing —2800 copies.

Immediately upon publication the sales of the book exploded in our faces. "One of the noblest chapters in the history of mankind," wrote Henry Mencken. "A book for those who love high adventure, who love clear, brave writing," reported William Allen White. "Accurate as to facts, absolutely," pronounced the good gray pathologist, Dr. Ludvig Hektoen. In his colmun in the New York *World*, day after day after day, big, amiable Heywood Broun beat big booms on his influential drum and all these raves combined to rouse a demand.

It must be admitted there was a certain important medical dubiety. Dr. Morris Fishbein questioned my calling the book a history. Hardly a history, protested the Prolocutor. History? History only for readers who wanted their science sugar-coated, he said, authoritatively, but his reservations failed to stop the book from shooting up in the nonfiction best-seller lists in the summer of 1926. It shortly passed one hundred thousand copies in sales, and before its great day was over—though it sells steadily today, not really slackening its pace in thirty years—it became one of the big nonfiction books of the decade.

CHAPTER NINE

I BEGAN our new work by going against the sage counsel of Henry Mencken. To celebrate the success of *Microbe Hunters* Henry took us by ferry to a German genuine-beer bootleg restaurant in Hoboken and when we were knowing no pain he regarded me owlishly, head cocked to one side and one eye half-shut.

"You've hit the jackpot, my boy," he said. "You're all alone in a new field."

Then Mencken proceeded to expound upon the possibility of my doing a series of sure-fire sellers. A book on physiologists beginning with William Harvey's *"De Motu Cordis."* Look what a sap the scientific sages of his day thought Harvey was to think of the heart as a pump for blood. A book on surgeons. There was bushy-bearded Theodor Billroth of Vienna, famed not only as a knife man but for being the best friend of his fellow musical beaver, Johannes Brahms. There was William Halsted of the Johns Hopkins who became the slave of cocaine while perfecting it as a pain killer. Real romances!

"Trouble with surgeons is they're already too celebrated," I said.

Think of the hilarious histories I could write about the early therapists, urged Mencken. There was Doctor Theophrastus Bombastus von Hohenbeim who gave himself the nom de plume of Paracelsus. He was half-quack, half-genius. Paracelsus had found that the old rover—syphilis—was amenable to mercury, though that drug had its drawbacks, killing some people instead of curing them, and then too, despite mercury, many sufferers lamentably lost their noses or perished paretically in asylums. "This fellow Bombastus, we've got to admit it," said Henry, "was the founder of chemotherapy. . . . "

"Write this row of books, my boy," urged Henry, "and you'll make Rhea a rich woman."

Of Mencken's advice I took a dim view, though it would have been well to heed him. "They'd all be cast in the stereotype of *Microbe Hunters,*" I protested. "Funny, yes. But I'm not out to be a medical Stephen Leacock." Henry was not to be denied. "You're throwing away a potential potful of money," he said, specifically adding an adjective that made the pot a container not used in cooking. And it wasn't only the money, said Menck. Writing such books I'd be on safe ground. Mencken took me atop a figurative mountain. Maybe half-spoofing, yet partly serious, he hinted that such a series of Stracheyan histories might land me a chair in the biography of science in a university. He wobbled me a bit. Wouldn't it be wonderful to sit in a professorial chair in a cozy college and make big money writing learned, albeit raffish and gay, popular science on the side?

I believe Rhea deep down was on Mencken's side of the argument, though she never admitted it. She was a woman and does not every woman want security? Not for possible children. She had denied herself that. I was her child. Yet wasn't her security my sacred obligation? In short, now that *Microbe Hunters* had made me respectable, shouldn't I do that kind of thing over and over? No—by God—no, never.

At this moment I hadn't the faintest notion what the next work would be. I only felt vaguely about wanting to dig up men against the prevailing *Zeitgeist* of the miserably materialistic 1920's, but I didn't think about this as a unifying theme. I wanted to find brave, honest people, not brave in battle but bold in a fight for a little bit better world. These characters had got to be without pretense. Then to write about them with some emotion, maybe to give them a touch of immortality though they were public nonentities today. I proudly fancied myself a vagabond from science, a brother of others derelict from respectability and contemporary fame.

I told Alfred Harcourt these projected stories might turn into a book with vagabond in the title. Alf was dubious and looked at me as if to ask me did I actually want to try autobiography on the basis of just one success? How right Alf was to pour on the cold water! This problem was taken care of for us by Loring Ashley Schuler and Philip Sheridan Rose, editors of the *Country Gentleman* at the Curtis Publishing Company. Among all the many magazine editors to whom *Microbe Hunters* had been submitted for serialization, these two were the only ones who didn't return the manuscript indifferently or nonchalantly or with derisive laughter at its uncouth vernacular. In 1925 Loring and Phil had bought five chapters of the book and so had helped keep us in groceries. They thought I could write, if not English, at least American.

Now they proposed to turn me into a reporter. They knew, through their editorial grapevine, that there were unfamous yet fascinating figures in the Government Bureaus of Animal and Plant Industry, the Hygienic Laboratory of the U. S. Public Health Service, in medical schools and cow colleges from coast to coast. Phil and Loring told me I might be the one to make readers realize how come America had a glut of wheat, how come we had too much maize and too much beef, how come we were a fabulous land of plenty, how come we were leading a new death fight. So they sent me out to wander in a wide new scientific world.

This assignment shifted gears for us into a new life on a big sprocket. My first hunting ground was Washington. We set up two criteria to spot our men against the materialistic times: they had to have done their bit to build a better, stronger humanity; for this their reward was anonymity. Their faces had not been on the the cover of *Time* Magazine or in the New York *Times* rotogravure section.

We shuttled happily back and forth between Fleetwood, New York, and Washington in our two-tone blue Buick roadster—Adoline Bublitz, we called it—and on our first trip it was for me as if for the first time I had discovered spring. The swamp maples were red among the surrounding new green; the cardinals whistled in full song; the robins sang "kill 'em, cure 'em, give 'em, physic"; the basin by the Potomac was afoam with the pinkish white of cherry blossoms.

We found Washington exciting in those days of the 1920's; a simple little city where plain men of science lived. One memorable evening we dined with a scientific patriarch, Dr. Erwin F. Smith. I wanted to write the story of how he'd found the microbe of crown gall, a cancerous malady of trees—he was the first to discover that microbes could cause disease in plants as well as in animals and men. "I have a better story for you than my own," said Dr. Smith. "You should write about a curious character—his contribution to agriculture was immense. His end was tragedy."

Good gray Dr. Smith held us enthralled by the sad saga of Mark Alfred Carleton, a wheat dreamer from Kansas. Carleton had revolutionized American wheat culture and the Government had kicked him in the teeth for his pains. As a dreamy exploring cerealist Carleton had studied the miracle of the Kubanka and the Kharkov wheats on the steppes of Russia.

"It isn't what a wheat will yield in the best years; it's what it can stand in the worst years." That was Carleton's watchword and he became the mad, humorless, enthusiastic prophet of the suitability of these sturdy, drought-resistant, rust-resistant grains, and their adaptability to our Midwest American land. For years Carleton—a man for the hard sell if there ever was one—carried his Kubanka and Kharkov gospel to wheat farmers, grain men, millers, bakers, dieticians, housewives across mid-America. Even to the cookbook lady, Mrs. Rorer.

He was promoted to be Cerealist in Charge of Grain Investigations in the Bureau of Plant Industry by our grateful Government and his salary was three thousand dollars a year. One of his daughters became crippled with polio while the life of his son hung by a thread with mastoid disease and while another daughter died from a quick infection. Medical bills got him up to his neck in debt. That was of no concern of his bureaucratic bosses.

But his Kubanka and his Kharkov wheats took hold and spread like a fire across the American prairies. Half the yield of hard red winter wheat of the nation was Carleton's Kharkov; the yield of the Kubanka jumped to seventy million bushels yearly on our northern plains. Meanwhile the mortgage was foreclosed on Carleton's Washington home and he moved what was left of his family to a shack up the Potomac River; through its chinks blew the wintry winds.

And now the acreage of hard red winter wheat had reached twenty-one million, by far the greater part of it sown with Carleton's Kharkov—one third of the total wheat acreage of our country. It vastly boosted the yield of wheat. This was owing to Carleton's genius as an explorer, an experimenter, a salesman, and a fanatic.

Busted financially higher than a kite, Carleton struggled pitifully to climb out of his fiscal morass. He borrowed small sums of money from grain men and other sums from friends to buy his family groceries and to start a little fruit farm in Florida and a dry farm in Texas to try to make money to repay his debts. Pretty soon he found himself no longer Cerealist in Charge of Grain Investigations in the Bureau of Plant Industry. Then Carleton, outcast, drifted from one hot steamy little job to another in Central America and Panama and during the last seven years of his life certain banks that held his notes received checks in partial and even in full payment of his outlawed debts. Mark Alfred Carleton died in 1925 of acute malaria in Paita in Peru. He was clean forgotten by the Government he had served so well and by the wheat farmers and the grain men and the millers whose industry had been revolutionized by his Kharkov and his Kubanka.

Despite my story, today few remember Carleton. For me he will remain the first and best and bravest of the hunger fighters. He was a game fish who swam upstream.

That story helped me fundamentally. It put me in touch with botanists, plant explorers, veterinarians, nutritionists and microbe hunters who were making a new America, rewarded by pittances of a few thousand dollars yearly. It was not so much the publicity given them in the *Country Gentleman;* it was a new technique of reporting that intrigued them and opened us a sesame among them. First I begged them for reprints of all their scientific publications. I took this material back home to Fleetwood, studying every word of it right down to the ground. Then I went back to them and asked them endless questions—some wise, some foolish.

This genuine interest in their work gave them a glow. Then I'd go back to Fleetwood and take weeks trying to turn their humdrum science into romance. Then, before submitting a story for publication, we'd take it back to each character for scrutiny and correction. "You have the veto on all mistakes or misinterpretations," I told them. Often they'd shudder at my vernacular. Always they liked the story's respect for facts.

In chiaroscuro to poor Carleton stood Dr. John R. Mohler, chief of the Bureau of Animal Industry of the U. S. Department of Agriculture. There was a man for fundamentals, a big, slow-talking, severe veterinary scientist, the first of all men to confirm in part Pasteur's woolly prophecy that it was possible to wipe microbe maladies from the face of the globe; Mohler had done just that in America for the frightfully infectious foot-and-mouth disease of cattle. Mohler's science was as deep as it was simple. There was no cure or any preventive vaccine for this vicious virus. He'd confessed it by ruthless killing of countless thousands of cattle who were infected, or merely suspected of infection, or cattle who'd only walked along roads previously traversed by infected animals. Mohler furthermore made massive slaughter of more than twenty thousand deer, many infected, in the Sierra Nevada. He drove every subvisible, submicroscopic trace of the sinister sickness underground and clean out of continental United States.

Farmers and stockmen denounced Mohler and it was said that his life was threatened. Mohler merely tugged at his goatee, a funny little wedge-shaped beard beneath his lip, running into a point at the crack of his chin—it was an absurd little facial adornment of the kind than Mencken called a "sonofabitch." Mohler merely tugged at it and sucked at his battered pipe and, imperturbable, went on killing more countless thousands of cattle. There was a bit of General Grant in Mohler.

To infuriated farmers in defense of this butchery he quoted their fellow farmer Brown. "It's impossible to have foot-and-mouth disease unless there *is* foot-and-mouth disease," said that sententious stockman. There was Pasteur's disbelief in spontaneous generation, more clear than the master himself had said it.

By 1926 Mohler had wiped this curse out of America by killing cattle, quick-liming them, and putting them underground. And alone among all civilized countries it has remained away from us right down to this day. But at what a cost? By what murder? Mohler gave the answer: "Losses under quarantine, slaughter, and disinfection, including indemnities, operating and all other expenses, have not been so great in suppressing all the outbreaks in this country in the last forty years as those losses would be in one year if the disease became established in America."

Mohler warned me: "Don't make *me* the hero." He explained it was his cattle-killing myrmidons of the Bureau who'd won the battle. For months and years they'd sweated in rubber suits from dawn until dark, evenings they breathed the poisonous fumes of formaldehyde to rid themselves of the invisible terror they might otherwise carry to far-off cattle. . . . Their hands became horrid to look at, cracked into open sores by constant baths in chloride of lime. They hadn't killed among hoorahs, like soldiers. They did their bloody work to the tune of ranchers' tirades and in spite of children's tears at loss of their pet calves. And for their final victory there was no medal, not a parade, and certainly no bonus.

Then came good news, by way of Alf Harcourt from Red Lewis. To Alf he wrote: "I have read *Microbe Hunters* at last, and I am quite daft about it. I have never read finer drama, finer sarcasm, clearer exposition, deeper perception of human purposes; and those things must be in the writing as well as in the thought."

Then in April and May came an event that should have taught us a public relations lesson by two past masters in that mysterious art—Sinclair Lewis and Alfred Harcourt. "I have been watching the Pulitzer Prize business all winter, and I'll bet about eighty to twenty that *Arrowsmith* will get the prize this year," wrote Alf to Red.

Whereupon Red wrote—"confidential"—to Alf: "I hope they do award me the Pulitzer Prize on *Arrowsmith,* but . . . I have planned that if they ever did award it to me, I would refuse it, with a polite but firm letter which I shall let the press have, and which ought to make it impossible for anyone ever to accept the prize (in the future)."

Then to Red came the great news. "My dear Mr. Lewis: I take very great pleasure in notifying you, in confidence, that the prize of $1000, established by the will of the late Joseph Pulitzer for the best American novel published during the year 1925 has been awarded to *Arrowsmith*. . . . "

Now Alf showed his public relations wizardry. To Red he wrote: "It would be even better if the press carried the announcement that you had won the prize for a day or two, and *then* the announcement of your refusal." Alf's sense of timing was terrific. Red felt the historic significance of his refusal of the prize. To Alf he wrote, with selfderogation: "An asinine, useless, expensive gesture, refusing this prize. But"—and now he compared himself to Martin Luther—"I can do no other."

The plan worked perfectly. The award of the prize was announced and the literate part of our population cried huzzah for Sinclair Lewis. Then came the AP announcement of Red's noble rejection and the literary uproar—pro-and-con—hit the newspaper front pages from coast to coast and across the oceans.

The rejection was hardly an expensive one; it meant untold thousands of dollars' worth of free publicity—only deducting the thousand dollars Red turned down. Now to me Red made a gesture, magnificent in its magnanimity. "By the way, of course $250 of the prize would be coming to Paul, and if he wants, I'll pay him that right now, or you are authorized to do so for me." So wrote Red to Alf Harcourt. To Red by way of Alf, I said thank you, but we wish in our obscure way to join you in your gesture of disdain. We are not having any of the $250.

We, not Red, were the asinine ones. Our rejection of one quarter of the Pulitzer Prize remained unknown and got us no publicity at all. It did give me a little hypocritical satisfaction. Over the years I've been asked: "Why haven't you got a Pulitzer Prize?" I have on occasion, without explanation, answered, "I did get one quarter of the award in 1926 but turned it down."

Now that we had a bit of money, with or without a prize, Rhea had made us our first home, a little apartment in Fleetwood near Bronxville, and here we worked and ate and drank and were merry and loved each other. After hard writing all morning I sallied out in a sweat shirt, denim pants, and sneakers for three miles of daily road work, jogging along the Bronx River Parkway. Afternoons we'd walk or drive north into upper Westchester County. In the late winter we'd stop to listen to the tinkle of ice thawing and melting into the Sawmill River.

It was my instinct that there would be no mass market for the stories I was writing unless they were primarily about people. What our heroes had in common was that they all were honest and all were as if game fish who swam upstream. Of all of them perhaps the most memorable was Dr. Edward Francis. He was an obscure denizen of the dirty old Hygienic Laboratory of the U. S. Public Health Service in Washington in the happy but now bygone days when its research men were not working primarily for huge Congressional grants of research money but for truth.

Unlike Carleton, who dreamed wheat under Kansas and Russian skies, Eddie Francis was a picturesquely dirty-talking scientific anchorite who toiled with his hands in a stinking little den in that Hygienic Laboratory—the red-brick building on the hill over Foggy Bottom looking out over the Potomac in Washington. Here Eduardo worked from six in the morning till six in the evening daily, three hundred and sixty-five days a year for many years. His one goal was the elucidation of the mystery of tularemia, a plaguelike disease of rabbits. First finding it in Utah in people who'd been bitten by deer flies, nearly killed by it himself, its microbe, *Bacterium tularense,* became his one enemy and one friend in all the world. On every visit to Washington, I paid my respects to Francis. Like a profane, honest, free-thinking monk in his smelly, cluttered little cell, his object was to accumulate masses of fact that might defeat the danger of tularemia to rabbit hunters and housewives who cooked rabbits for their families and their hunter husbands.

Francis became my mentor in his unique, lonely, peculiarly individual method of hunting microbes. He had disdain for scientific theory. "Don't think too much, don't reason, don't use your brain too much—work with your hands," that was his watchword. "Try everything," he said. He brought out his admonitions in jerky jets, sententious, aphoristic, contemptuous of academic scholarship, squinting, throwing back his balding head, making strange, twisting gestures with his hands and movements of his whole body.

In his cubicle, paper-littered and no bigger than a bathroom, in a fog of smoke of his cheap cigars, Francis hoarded his facts. At this job he toiled like an automaton, piling up mountains of data magnificently accurate no matter whether they seemed significant or not. From this giant jumble Francis wove a design of simple truth that told plain people how to foil tularemia and how to duck its death. "You see, the trouble is," said Eduardo, "we try to look at nature with our brains instead of our eyes."

Like a spider in a web Francis collected hundreds, then thousands of cases of his new sickness, under the title, "Tularemis, Francis, 1921, a new disease of man." It became known in the vernacular as rabbit fever, from coast to coast. Every one fact about the sickness was greeted by Eduardo with joy and laughter.

As rabbit fever grew in public health significance, Hygienic Laboratory director Dr. George McCoy—famous as the one laboratory director in the world who did not direct—gave Francis helpers. What ho, here, those poor boys all began to come down sick and had to go home. Their duty had only been to hold rabbits, shave them for inoculation, take them to the incinerator after Francis had set down the last precise autopsy of their death.

Francis found these boys had all come down with tularemia. "What kind of damned bug have we got here?" asked Francis. "Can it crawl through glass, did it hop onto my boys through the skin of sick animals? Seems as if you can't come within a yard of the damn germ without getting bit by it," said Francis, chuckling with fiendish amusement. Down in the rabbit hutches in the smelly basement of the Hygienic Laboratory Francis put up a big sign in bold letters before the rabbit cages: TULAREMIA! KEEP AWAY! Having had the disease, he was immune, and did all the work himself from then on.

From British bacteriologists came gibes that Francis and his men must be sloppy, careless technicians to become infected. To the Lister Institute in London Francis sent cultures of his mysterious microbe. Bang!—down came three Lister Institute scientists with tularemia's aches and fever and its tiredness in their backs and in their bones. "By a brave discretion," said a British medical journal, "the authorities in England have decided to close down all work on tularemia." Eduardo showed us this statement with a guffaw.

With savagery, Francis double-checked and superchecked all claims that tularemia might be cured by serums or prevented by a vaccine and blew all this pseudoscience to smithereens. Of all the facts this automatic man had piled up, here was the grain of life-saving truth his work had boiled down to—let him tell it in his own plain words: "If all cooks, market men, hunters, housewives, and others who dress rabbits, would wear rubber gloves when doing so, they would not contact tularemia. It should be remembered that thorough cooking destroys the infection in a rabbit, thus rendering an infected rabbit harmless (and safe) for food."

Many years after my story had been published in the *Country Gentleman,* came a pleasant aftermath. A schoolboy came excitedly waving a soiled, ancient, torn back copy of that magazine, to Dr. Clifford Caudy Young in Portland, Michigan. "My dad's been sick with what his doc calls typhoid fever. Read this. Here's what he's got. It's tularemia discovered by Dr. Francis."

It was just that, Cy Young found when he checked the boy's father's blood at the Michigan State Health Department Laboratory. "That's the way your work is striking fire," said Cy.

It was an exciting life on the new big sprocket. All of my heroes were different from each other—the lives of all of them seemed books in themselves. Rhea, though sharing my excitement at the new work, was worried at the turbulence stoked up in the new environment. Subtly now she began preparing to move us away from Fleetwood and the fleshpots of Park Avenue and the world of Washington. These were not the places to write the book that threatened to grow out of the hunger-fighter stories.

In the early summer of 1927 we drove heigho and happy away to western Michigan to spend the summer with my mother at her little house, Blue Water, on Lake Michigan's shore. Together we rafted big driftwood logs from miles away through the cold water to Blue Water's beach. We cut the logs up with a crosscut saw and split them into fireplace wood with a maul and wedge and double-bitted Michigan ax. Rhea could swing the maul like a man. I swam far out in Lake Michigan daily in a crude free style and taught Rhea to subdue her fear of rough deep water.

Back at Blue Water I wrote conscientiously about the honesty of selfless men. Along with austere Edward Francis, a hero among my hunger fighters was a soft-spoken, brave man, a gentle Jewish desperado, Joseph Goldberger of the U. S. Public Health Service. Goldberger was earning an obscure immortality by his long fight to prove that the disease, pellagra, was not caused by microbes—as was conventionally believed—but was in fact a dietary deficiency disease, a hidden hunger.

In many sessions at the red-brick building on the hill in Washington, in a little office close by that of Edward Francis, Goldberger told me the story of his battle to prove his then off-beat science. Committees and commissions of serious scientists were hardly prepared to disbelieve that pellagra was infectious. With a resigned sad smile Goldberger told how—he seemed quietly infuriated—he at last demolished all criticism by experiments as awful as they were fundamental. If pellagra was indeed infectious, its alleged microbe cause should be found in the blood of pellagrins and especially in their excretions—because it was by this latter route that authorities believed it passed from one human being to another.

Alone in the washroom of a pullman car, in a bit of flour he rolled the intestinal discharges of a dying pellagrous woman into pills and swallowed them. Over weeks and months he repeated this self-experiment seven times over. And seven times he injected himself with the blood of desperately sick pellagrins. And along with him his wife, Mary Goldberger, and his colleagues from the red-brick Hygiene Laboratory—including Edward Francis—all repeated these experiments on themselves, in support of their friend. None developed pellagra.

In prisons and insane asylums in the pellagra-riddled South Goldberger found the red rash flaming only among poor people living on diets of the three M's—meat (salt pork), meal, and molasses. These victims he cured by copious meals of milk and lean beef—not common in the poverty-stricken South. Then finally he spotted a cheap preventive and cure in plain brewer's yeast. Statistically Goldberger and his men proved what they were already sure of. Among relatively prosperous Southern families with good incomes of, say, a thousand dollars a year or more, there was none of this red death. "Give poor folk an extra dollar," said Goldberger, "and they can be taught to buy fresh meat and milk for their kids and themselves."

If they only had a bit of land and a little daylight in the evenings, they could till truck gardens and eat their greens that were also antipellagrous. But where were the teachers, and where were the dollars, and where was the land, and when was there daylight? Pellagra is only economics, said Goldberger. "But now your brewer's yeast does the trick, why not see they all get yeast?" I asked the day I left him to go back to Michigan to do the story. "Who's going to see to that?" asked Goldberger forlornly.

He bid me good-by and good luck at the front door of the laboratory. Just before he turned to go back into the red-brick building he repeated his pitiful theme. Pellagra is only ignorance; pellagra is only poverty. Curing those ills was not his job. It was to be the last time I saw him. His last words to me—he died of cancer soon after—I remember best of all. "You understand, De Kruif," he said. "I'm no economist. I'm only a doctor."

Soon after this I found myself in the pseudoscience of economics, way over my head. Phil Rose had sent me out to Ames, Iowa, to interview a very deaf professor who hadn't the faintest idea who I was or what I was after till just before we bade each other good-by. The professor's pitch was to make wallboard of all cornstalks, thus getting rid of the corn borers then menacing the

American corn crop. It'd work if you picked up all the cornstalks.

Next day I met as complicated a human creature as any in all my experience. This was Henry Agard Wallace of the great democratic dynasty of Iowa Wallaces: the editor of the farm paper, *Wallace's Farmer*. All day, in flashes of sardonic humor but with hardly a smile, he discoursed on the economic martyrdom of the tough men of Iowa's black soil, the mysticism of Krishnamurti, the theosophical ideas of Annie Besant, the virtues of McNary-Haugenism, the skulduggery of capitalists in general, the folly of trying to defeat the corn borer by turning all cornstalks into wallboard, the pseudobenevolence Herbert Hoover was exploiting to get set to run for President; and coming back to it again and again —the science of genetics.

He spoke modestly and there was iron under his gentleness. Henry Wallace looked quizzically at me with his mystic gray questioning eyes from under an unruly shock of hair. He was first, last, and always *against* city slickers and *for* the embattled Iowa corn and hog men; and rural revolution smoldered in his mild conversation—he was a low-keyed John Brown. He was the prophet of a fight against the enslavement of the Iowa corn and hog men, the loss of their cornland by foreclosure of mortgages by the city money-masters. His remedy? The one hope of the farmers to lick the new frontier of hard times was to raise the greatest number of hogs off the least number of acres of land by the least number of hours of human labor. It all boiled down to yield, yield of corn per acre, biggger yield from smaller fields. And for that Henry had the answer—hybrid corn.

From boyhood Henry had dug deep into the genetics of the Abbé Gregor Mendel, the Dutch biologist; Hugo de Vries, and Professor George H. Shull of Princeton. He'd experimented with tall and short varieties of peas, with evening primroses, and with the hybridization of pure inbred lines of maize, and he had emerged with a systematic, practical crossing of inbreds to produce enormously greater yields of corn. Henry combined his genetic savvy with capitalistic cunning and the product of his

Hibred Corn Company was already revolutioning Iowa's maize. He was on the way to big money.

"That goes for corn all over—outside Iowa?" I asked. "Without a doubt," said Henry. "I'll ask Phil Rose to let me write it," I promised. "The *Country Gentleman* will never print the hybrid corn story," he professed. Henry thought the Curtis Publishing Company was dedicated to a Pollyanna worship of America's golden industrial calf.

On my return to Des Moines with Phil's okay to go ahead, Henry, delighted, became my professor of the age-old mystery of maize and the marvels of modern corn genetics. We talked corn corn corn till the subject got us groggy and then we went off for slogging walks over the soggy Iowa prairies—twelve miles one afternoon—running up the last hill, over our shoetops in the sticky gumbo—having ranged over everything from the philosophic necessity of atheism—my view—to the theosophic consideration of reincarnation of souls—Henry's interest. In short, we became friends. And the hybrid corn story got published in the *Country Gentleman,* the first nationwide recognition of Henry's back-yard genetic science.

Within six years he was a big man in the New Deal in Washington and I did not dream that deep within Henry Wallace there smoldered the ambition to become the leader of the Century of the Common Man. That was the John Brown in him—a gentle, peaceful John Brown without the night of the long knives. Bad psychologist, I didn't detect it. To further the Century of the Common Man, he'd have to play with the long knife. He was a most complicated man.

Even in those early days of our friendship, where he left me was in his mathematics. As to Henry's economics of bigger yields from smaller fields, I simply swallowed it hook, line, and sinker. His terrifying abundance turned him into a sorcerer's apprentice. In a few years it had poor Henry thinking of having to plow under his too abundant corn and he actually had to kill the resulting too many little pigs. His complicated mathematics made everything too simple. Nature's own mathematics was too deep for both us.

Nineteen hundred and twenty-eight saw what at first seemed to be a triumph for our stories of these new obscure and honest men. Don Brace thought they were good enough to put together in a book—*Hunger Fighters*—and in the 1928 summer he came to Blue Water with the news that the Book of the Month Club had bought it. First printing—91,000 copies. Then came a letdown. The prospectus to the Book of the Month subscribers was written by one of its editors, the literatus, Dr. Henry Seidel Canby. His praise of the book was phrased in words like those of a Christian Scientist writing advertising copy for a new drug. Members of the Book of the Month Club are wont to place their orders with the idea that they are purchasing works of art and Seidel apologized for the book as "journalism." Seidel's authority and prestige were enough to keep Book of the Month members away in droves and Harcourt was stuck with more than 40,000 copies of its huge first printing on his hands. Yet the book slowly, and in the form of cheap editions, managed to sell out. Dr. Canby was right, the book was journalism and not a work of art. The writing was overdramatized and what came to be known as "breathless," even those parts of it that were written when I was hardly breathing at all. This tag is tied to my writing by many reviewers, including those who do not read the books.

Phil Rose had a theory that we in America had arrived at our present glory not by Mr. Lincoln's oratory, or by the generalship of U. S. Grant and W. T. Sherman, or by the deeds of our pioneers with hairy ears, or by free enterprise, but as a consequence of a concatenation of impersonal forces—of a geology beginning aeons ago in the past. "You write that, Paul," said Phil. "Tell how we've been lucky to take advantage of the ore in our mountains, of our rivers and great lakes and the big pines and black soil." It sounded epic as all hell.

It would be fun. We'd be alone, away from everybody; which was our dish. We vanished from the world of books and our friends knew not where we were or what we were up to. It was another of many honeymoons. "Paul and Rhea?" roared Henry

Mencken. "They're running rum across Lake Huron." Henry was only partly wrong because we did not run it to sell it but to drink it in secret, enchanted conviviality.

I dug into the geology of iron but could make little of it. How it got there was God's business. I was distracted by stumbling upon the story of seven forgotten pioneers who had made and lost fortunes developing the greatest of all America's deposits of iron.

It was Phil's theory that America's magnificence had not been built by merry Andrew Carnegie, or his big tough ironmaker, Charlie Schwab, or his cold-eyed hatchet man, Henry Clay Frick. America's industrial age might not have happened if the cosmic forces of the environment hadn't set Lake Superior down in a vast rim of iron, so that from the big Gitche Gumee down the St. Mary's River and down Lake Huron and Lake Erie and down Lake Michigan a parade of big long boats could cheaply float red ore to Gary, Detroit, Cleveland, and Ashtabula—to be turned into money for libraries for Mr. Carnegie, into money for fun, fun for Mr. Schwab, and into money for Rembrandts for Mr. Frick (who showed his artistic insight by calling railroad stocks the Rembrandts of investment). And finally to make possible the U. S. Steel Corporation as a monument to the optimism of John Pierpont Morgan, the head bull financial operator of American history.

In my iron research my first briefing officer was one of the last of America's real pioneers, Chase Salmon Osborn. In build he was a miniature Paul Bunyan, and he was proud of having killed a man in his early days in Florence, Wisconsin. Osborn was a successful Sault Ste. Marie newspaper publisher. He had slogged through northern forests hunting iron to work off his energy and as a hobby; had made millions at it; and in a lordly gesture he had given those millions away. He had been a fighting governor of the State of Michigan and had been considered for the Presidential nomination in the little smoke-filled room when the boys handed it to Warren Gamaliel Harding in 1920. He had even dabbled in the chemistry of what made fireflies turn on the little torches in their tails in the early summer evenings. Now, a legendary figure, he lived on a modest annuity in a little log cabin on his island, Zheshebe Minis, in the St. Mary's River. Osborn was the one rich man we had ever known who disdained big money; he had no regard for his own philanthropic insight that would have been a phony excuse for piling up more money; and best of all he deeply understood money's power to corrupt.

Chase Osborn was locally known as the Ogemaw—Ojibway for "chief." Past seventy, he was straight and tall and very strong and his dark eyes looked through us and ten feet into the ground behind us. He loved a fight and believed in universal peace. He was a practical joker. Welcoming us, he casually handed me a chunk of glittering grayish rock, obviously hoping I'd unguardedly drop it on my toes. I managed to hold it. He frisked my shoulders and upper arms and said, "You should have been a heavyweight prize fighter."

"D'you know anybody in Duluth who'll give us the lowdown on the discovery of the Mesabi iron range?" I asked. "The Merritts," said the Ogemaw, "they're famous." He gave us a glowing letter of introduction—"To whom it may concern."

At Duluth a speedboat operator took us to view the giant ore docks, already inactive and portending the crash of 1929. "Do you know the Merritt family?" I asked. "The iron people? They must be big shots in your town." "Big shots hell," the boatman answered. "They went busted higher than a whole flock of kites way back in 1893." "But didn't the Merritts discover the Mesabi iron?" "Sure," said the boatman. "And they owned it, but then John D. Rockefeller heard of it."

That afternoon in a great office building in a small smoke-filled room I met three survivors of the ancient Merritt magnificence. In their headquarters of "The Northwestern Exploration Company," three of them sat tilted back on their chairs, their hats pulled low over their faces, aiming expertly at a communal spittoon, otherwise doing absolutely nothing at all. Their active lives had ended long ago. Late that afternoon I came back to the Hotel Duluth, myself excited, furious, anxious to tell Rhea the fate of the Merritts. It was a Horatio Alger yarn in reverse.

In the beginning 1890's—landlookers, timber cruisers, bush-whackers—the Merritts, four brothers and three nephews, stumbled upon what seemed enough high-grade Bessemer ore to keep the nation in iron for many years. But they needed cash to build a railroad from the Mesabi down to Lake Superior. They borrowed it on disadvantageous terms—times were tight, pre-panic of 1893, but praise the Lord! a finger man—sniffing at the rumors of a vast iron find—hinted Mr. John D. Rockefeller would help them. To the Merritts he seemed providential. The great philanthropist confirmed his finger man's offer and Mr. Rocke-feller helped them, all right, and the Merritt boys within three years lost all their iron.

I didn't realize you don't battle a public relations machine backed by a billion dollars. Yet those were the days, the days of that 1928 autumn in Duluth and on the Mesabi. They were the salt of life. We had fun that autumn. We drove again and again up the Grandmother Hills to the Mesabi. We gawped goggle-eyed into the enormous holes in the red earth that for almost forty years had disgorged iron to be converted into gold. Iron that Mr. Rockefeller had bought from the Merritts for a song and sold for sixty-eight million dollars to enable Mr. Pierpont Mor-gan to start the U. S. Steel Corporation. (Poor Mr. Rockefeller had in turn fooled himself, alas, driving a soft bargain—the ore he'd sold turned out to be worth more than a third of a billion dollars.)

These were the last of our really carefree days. Having ex-plored the Mesabi battleground where the Merritts met their fiscal doom, we drove through Lake Superior National Forest and the needle of the compass in Rhea's hand whirled madly as we went past deposits of hidden magnetite. "What a kick it must have been for those Merritts when they first found it," said Rhea. Back East, Phil Rose listened dour-eyed to my recital of the rise and fall of the Merritt iron men. Here he'd sent us off to write about geology and we'd come back with a sad, forgotten human story—not appropriate for the *Country Gentleman* in a company, The Curtis, that specialized in happiness, not tragedy.

Actually, I was ill-equipped to find my way through the pious, perilous thickets of high finance. On the contrary, it was easy for me to follow the narrative of that surviving iron man, John E. Merritt, because in a minor way I'd been lost myself in the deep bush and in danger on white water. His story roused great *cafard* in me and stirred in me a partiality for the Merritts. I mastered the six big Merritt scrapbooks and formed an awe for mighty Leonidas Merritt, bushy haired, with an explorer's squinty eyes, the leader of the Merritt clan.

From magnetic surveys made by his brother Cassius, Leonidas predicted vast iron hiding close under the pine needles in enormous basins. The Merritt boys soaked every cent of their savings as timber cruisers into buying their hoped-for ore-rich hills in the Mesabi. Carrying a hundred-pound packsack through shin-tangling bush with no tumpline on his forehead to ease the burden, Leonidas bulled at the head of the Merritts in a hunt for theoretically nonexistent ore, and after twenty years the Merritts stumbled on the bonanza of the Mesabi iron and, by god, they owned it.

Local magnates offered the Merritts nine million dollars for their Mesabi holdings but Leonidas turned the offer down and threw in all the Merritt chips with Mr. John D. Rockefeller, putting up the enormous Merritt holdings for a modest loan to build the ore road from the Mesabi down to Duluth.

And here was where I went wrong myself in wanting to write the ensuing tragedy. In America you do not muckrake a saint, and Mr. John D. Rockefeller in 1928 was well on toward sanctity. Still, I went on writing the quaint story of how—within three years of their discovery—the Merritts were relieved of all their iron. Yet I was hardly objective. The trouble was that I had become emotionally committed to the character and the fate of brash and bold Leonidas; we were fascinated by his blend of pioneering competence with fiscal foolishness. What I should have seen was that poor Leonidas had no business to be in business. When the 1893 panic hit, the Merritts had no moolah. They were lacking in Mr. John D. Rockefeller's greatest of all business virtues—for him it was axiomatic always to maintain a strong cash position. At the Stanley Investigation of the U. S. Steel Corporation's origins, before Congress in Washington in 1910, Leonidas, testifying, made a *maxima mea culpa,* taking public blame for the loss of the Mesabi.

"I was to blame," he said, recounting the Merritt disaster in the autumn of 1893. Leonidas told Chairman Stanley and his committee: "I could not conceive that I could have gone down to New York with millions, absolute millions of my own and my brothers' money. I could not conceive how in hell, within those few months, I could have gone to New York and lost all those millions."

"And then you went back to the woods?" asked Chairman Stanley.

"Yes, sir, after one thing and another, I went back into the woods in the snow and the cold and tried to forget all these things," said Leonidas. "My brother Cashie"—that was the great iron explorer Cassius—"had more nerve than I had. It killed him."

Leonidas was at his best that day. He did not accuse Mr. Rockefeller or the blessed Reverend Mr. Gates. That day Leonidas forestalled Ernest Hemingway's apothegm—"Every damn thing is your own fault if you're any good." Thus had Hemingway corrected himself for his attempt to alibi his gut-shooting a kudu.

I wrote *Seven Iron Men* in Fleetwood in the winter of 1928–29. As a book it turned out a flop, not even *d'estime.* "So you've taken up muckraking?" said Carl Sandburg. "It's the most cruel book I've ever read," said our Wall Street friend, Tommy Thomas. "Cruel to whom?" I asked. "To Mr. Rockefeller, of course." Mr. Rockefeller had done our country a great service. He'd got the Mesabi iron into orderly, businesslike hands, ready for the U. S. Steel Corporation. His ethics in so doing? Ethics are not in question in the great epic of American business, explained Tommy. "Before you started the story, you should have realized that, in times of financial stringency, many properties inevitably change hands." Tommy's economic insight was simple and profound.

Right now in a futile moment I wish the clock could be turned back, to give me a chance to take a second whack at this seven-iron-men story as it might have been told—with the writing savvy picked up in the thirty years that have gone by. The trouble with the book was I didn't know how to write it. I overwrote it, attempting to make myself a belle-lettrist, trying to create even a musical movement in it, naming parts of it *andante, allegro, più presto* and *fugato*. This was phony. What came out was pseudo-music all in a high key and all in the same rhythm and hysterical. If I had only been enough of a writer to have written it straight and plain and deadpan, it could then have had humor. The facts behind it were so bizarre that, if they'd been underwritten, readers might have thought what funny, contrasting characters go to make up our wild, woolly land.

I slanted the yarn to make it come out my way, not God's. Before ending this *arrière pensée*, let me take a last look at the book's two protagonists, John D. Rockefeller and Leonidas Merritt, as they appeared in photographs long after the knock-down-drag-out battle for the iron of the Mesabi. Scanning a portrait of Leonidas, at 82, the year he died, you'd swear life had been kind to him. He had just retired after many years of honorable service as commissioner of utilities and finance for the city of Duluth; it seemed the citizens had trust in his honesty if not faith in his financial genius. His face was strong, serene, though a bit battered, as would be expected of a man who'd been to hell and back. At his death he had no debts. By his heirs his fortune was stated to consist of $1500 worth of household goods, $800 miscellaneous, and $150 in cash. Over his grave sounded the volley due to a soldier of the Civil War and as his body was lowered a bugle blew taps. It was noted that some mourners shivered and that in their eyes were tears. The City of Duluth went into official mourning for Leonidas Merritt for a period of four days.

Over the face of John D. Rockefeller, in a contemporary photograph, the years seem to have taken a mysterious revenge. Mr. Rockefeller's face seems to have become mummified into a set smile, as if he were remembering the many hundreds of millions of dollars he had lavished, trying to satisfy his Reverend Mr. Gates's passion "to bring far-reaching benefits to mankind." Mr.

Rockefeller must be pitied as the reincarnation of poor old King Midas. As the steward of God's gold—which he esteemed himself to be—Mr. Rockefeller's success had been mystical because the more gold he gave away the more he got. It kept coming back to him and to his children and to his children's children right down to this day.

The portrait of Mr. Rockefeller must arouse our sympathy. His fate seemed worse than that of mythical King Midas who merely died of acute starvation because the very food he touched turned horridly into gold of no caloric value. Mr. Rockefeller was in a curious way less fortunate than Midas. His medical scientists—paid handsomely—were able to keep him living to a great age on a low-calorie diet—so it is reported—consisting of next to no food at all. This anticipated today's nutritional science that proves half-starved white rats live twice as long as their well-fed litter mates. Mr. Rockefeller could have amply afforded the most dainty, tasty, succulent foods three times a day.

In the 1929 autumn when *Seven Iron Men*'s critical and commercial failure made it apparent that the silk purse of its magnificent material had turned into a sow's ear, as a work of art, came encouragement from an unexpected quarter. On a train on the way home from Florida, having covered the Bureau of Plant Industry's fight to eradicate the Mediterranean fruit fly, I picked up a copy of *Scribner's Magazine* and began, at first idly, to read an installment of the new novel, *A Farewell to Arms*. I'd never before read a word of Ernest Hemingway. To me it came as a *coup de foudre*. In a blinding flash it taught me that I did not know one damn single solitary thing about how to write a story. It stirred in me a little impulse to emulate Hemingway. Knowing well my capacities, that would have been ridiculous. It was that here at last I'd found a teacher. Not of a writing style that is the greatest of our time, inimitable despite its horde of imitators. It was not at all the style that I aspired to learn. It was the mysterious alchemy of its profound effect upon me as a reader, an effect achieved by little words that were so simple yet so true—not in a photographic sense as true to life—but true in a sense that gave emotion that was the far side of so-called reality.

From my earliest writing days I'd felt the need of teachers. I'd begun by aping authors who seemed to talk my own innate language. H. G. Wells was the first of these but I'd had to leave him when he became preoccupied by what he thought was the desperate need of our all clubbing together in a world state. This seemed to me to destroy his knack of telling a true story. Then Henry Mencken's boisterous demolition of political, ecclesiastical, and academic dignitaries held me enthralled, and I tried to apply Henry's unique technique to the deflation of the prevailing poopdom among doctors. The results of my attempted imitation of Mencken were not outstanding. I didn't know all the good and bad about that most wonderful profession. It must be admitted that Sinclair Lewis taught me technically while I was aiding him with *Arrowsmith,* yet that great satirist's contempt for certain human weaknesses among plain people was something I could not imitate because it was something I did not feel.

For a moment I had luck, kicking free of all literary influence to tell in my own way, and in my own style, reeking with rhetoric, stories of the only men I truly knew, certain microbe hunters. But when that vein ran out, where would I go from there? Nowhere, so it seemed, excepting back to the bleak life of a "feature writer." But I didn't want to be a feature writer. I wanted to be a writer. And I was hell bent to be a writer no matter how long it might take me to get down what I secretly believed was in me, if only one book that might have a chance to live as a human story. From Ernest Hemingway I learned that I'd have to start from scratch, to begin all over.

CHAPTER TEN

I<small>T</small> was an ominous morning toward the end of October, 1929, when our beachmaster, William Deplidge, came in reporting: "All our summer's work's wiped out." His face was despair. It had been a rugged summer with the level of Lake Michigan rising to the highest in its recorded history, chewing out our broad sand beach below the bank of Blue Water. Deplidge was a small gnomelike man, twisted with bad arthritis, eating quantities of aspirin to hold down the pain, walking with a shuffle, like Charlie Chaplin. That summer Deplidge had determined we would subdue Lake Michigan. Afternoons, Deplidge, Rhea, and I worked to foil the mean, cutting surf of the rising lake. We were ridiculous. Deplidge had devised his own system of riprapping, laying saplings side-by-side, butt ends to the bank, with their branches just in the water. To hold them in place we begged and bought hundreds of used burlap feed bags. Deplidge holding them, Rhea and I filled them with sand, then Rhea tied them shut with twine, then Rhea and I dragged them, laying them flat, just in the water, on the branches of the saplings to hold them down. Not to build a wall. But Deplidge's sapling-sandbag system slowed down the waves so they dropped their own deposits to build up new beach, bit by bit.

Deplidge was proud to have fooled Lake Michigan. Now this October morning the northwest gale and the pounding surf shook our little shingle house. This morning Deplidge reported all our new beach swept away. The five steps down the bank to the beach were gone. The combers were chewing at the main bank.

"Don't worry, William," I said. "We'll start over." "The car ferry *Milwaukee* went down last night with all hands—fifty lost they say," said Deplidge. "Downtown they report the stock market has gone to hell." "Forget all this bad news, William," I said, cheerfully forgetting he was way past sixty while I was only thirty-nine. That wild morning I'd begun writing, asking, "How long can we live?" The story opened with what for me were strange words. "I don't want to die." "I don't want to die," I wrote. "There are too many birds left that I don't know the songs of."

That wild morning we went to the edge of the bank to watch the combers threatening to chew the bank out from under the little Blue Water cottage. "Let's find some place where we can build further back from the shore," said Rhea. It seemed she'd made up her mind to move us into the woods in the dunes close by Lake Michigan to stay.

My writing was now taking a new turn. I began to look for a single simple characteristic that might be common to a few contemporary pioneers in medical investigation. My search was offbeat as usual. It wasn't mentality, brains, that I looked for in these men primarily. It had been my long experience that medical men may be mental as hell yet come up with no science that will make the difference between life and death. It was now only such science that interested me.

Right then in these 1920's a new kind of man seemed to have come to fight hitherto inexorable diseases. Frederick Banting was saving the lives of diabetics far gone in coma; George Minot was rescuing victims hitherto absolutely sure to die with pernicious anemia. About these searchers I'd heard the remark: "They aren't deep thinkers, they just stumbled on their discoveries." Defending Banting and Minot against some medical friends, I said hotly: "They may not be brilliant, but by God, they're honest." They had to be because they asked about any patient only—does he live or does he die?

What did I mean by honest? And how could I understand the essence of these maybe not brilliant honest men without myself being through and through out in the open? "We are all dishonest," says the lie-detector expert, John Edward Reid, of Chicago. Reid says that if we were all completely honest, human society could not exist. I was convinced that Banting and Minot had reached their Promethean heights not by their intellects but mainly by their honesty.

But to get back to Banting. In the spring of 1930, having soaked myself in the history of his discovery of insulin, proud and confident, I went to see him in Toronto. He was hatchet-faced and severe, looking like a man who had been to hell and back. It was obvious that Banting did not like me.

"What's wrong with me, Dr. Banting?" I asked, coming right out into the open. "Well, if you want to know," he answered dourly, "I did not like the way you ran down Pasteur in *Microbe Hunters*." He regarded me as a mere debunker of the greatest hero in all medical science. Then I had luck.

Banting happened to be on a Canadian committee for the study of undulant fever—Brucellosis—and he mentioned that the committee considered this a public health enigma. "Maybe getting rid of Brucellosis shouldn't be too difficult," I said. "The Bang bugs are shed in the milk of infected cows—what you should do is Pasteurize it." Immediately Banting asked me many sharp questions and my answers convinced him I really knew my onions and he thawed toward me and took me out to lunch and all of a long afternoon he told me the rugged time that he and Charles H. Best had been through in 1921 and 1922, first to prove that there was such a hormone as insulin at all; and then to keep a scientific eminento from swiping their discovery. Through all his story there gleamed a simple, devastating truthfulness. He called them as he saw them.

His story had grim humor. He admitted he had no business to discover insulin, let alone try to. He was a Canadian war veteran, trying to eke out a living as a surgeon in London, Ontario, and after waiting twenty-four days for his first patient to come and ending up the month with only four dollars on his books, he landed a job as demonstrator in Western University, so he could eat. His brain fallow, in his idle time in the night he evolved a hunch that diabetes could be controlled if he could extract a sugar-burning hormone from the pancreases of dogs. Many better men than Banting had tried that and failed miserably. He hied himself to Toronto to explain his theory to the distinguished Professor J. J. R. Macleod, a blood-sugar authority. The good Professor demolished Banting by a Schopenhauerian *argumentum ad hominem*. How could *Banting* hope to accomplish what the highest-trained physiologists in the world had not succeeded in establishing or proving? Macleod couldn't shake Banting off. What did Banting want, really? "I'd like a bench in your laboratory this summer and ten dogs and an assistant for eight weeks," said Banting. To get rid of this importunate nuisance, Macleod said all right, all right, and went off to Scotland for the summer and forgot about Banting.

It is history how Fred Banting and Charles Best sweated through the 1921 summer. They quickly used up their ten dogs. They killed many more dogs in vain. "We got the dogs, all right," said Banting with a reminiscent smile. By late autumn they'd kept a completely diabetic dog—deprived of its pancreas—alive and healthy and happy on shots of a crude extract of pancreas for seventy days. A dog that should have been dead in ten. There was *insulin!* And it set the world of medical science into an uproar.

Professor Macleod came back to realize that Banting had pulled off what other physiologists had failed at, utterly. Now the professor dropped his own work on anoxemia and began to supervise the efforts of Banting and Best to perfect a safe, effective insulin. What bothered Banting and Best was trying with feeble bits of their still dangerous medicine to save desperately sick diabetics now pouring into Toronto begging for this almost nonexistent hormone. Macleod having taken over, Banting was lost in the shuffle. "I had no job," he explained. "I was four thousand dollars worse off than a beggerman." He consoled himself on laboratory alcohol. "It was Charlie Best who saved me, getting me back to work to help find a safe insulin. I would have gone under if it hadn't been for Charlie," Banting explained. They found the insulin, but now the tremendous discovery—exciting physicians world-wide—was no longer theirs. It had passed into more highly scientific hands.

Professor Macleod appeared before the Association of American Physicians and gave them the great news. "I move that the Association tender to Dr. Macleod *and his associates*"—italics are mine—"a rising vote expressing its appreciation of *his*"—the italics are mine—"achievement," said Dr. Woodyatt of Chicago. "We are all agreed in congratulating Dr. Macleod *and his collaborators*"—italics once more are mine—"on their miraculous achievement," said Dr. Frederick Allen (of the Rockefeller Institute), who had perfected a low-calorie treatment that starved poor diabetic devils half to death though they did live somewhat longer.

It was a great day for Professor Macleod. "I wish to thank the Association very much in the name of my associates and myself," said the Professor. It will remain forever mysterious what exactly Macleod had contributed to the discovery of insulin except that he gave Fred Banting and Charles Best the ten dogs and the eight weeks' use of the little laboratory.

"How come everybody now knows that you and Best really did it?" I asked Banting. Banting looked at me with a slow smile. It happened that honesty was highly esteemed among certain principal citizens—medical and lay—of the city of Toronto. Some of Banting's friends who'd seen him through his private hell laid the facts before Canada's grand old man, Sir William Mulock, Chancellor of the University, famed for integrity and for drinking a bottle of Scotch every day. Not long afterward Professor J. J. R. Macleod was no longer seen in Toronto. He had returned to Glasgow for good and Banting and Best finally got universal recognition for their discovery of the medicine that has since saved thousands of diabetics doomed to death.

What made his friends stick by him was their awe of his stubborn desperation. They knew he wasn't brilliant—just obstinate. He'd come back from the war with a very deep ugly scar from a battle wound on one of his forearms. "I'm going to keep that arm," Banting told the surgeons who said he'd die if they didn't amputate. It was this arm that later helped him to vivisect those dogs that led to the discovery of insulin. His bravery was at the bottom of his honesty—though at this time I did not realize that honesty and bravery are synonymous.

In these late 1920 days I came to know George Minot because Banting's insulin had saved his life. Insulin had made Minot, who had been half-dead on a starvation diet, strong enough to make a tremendous life-saving discovery all on his own, as a practicing physician in his private office. In its early stages Minot's discovery seemed too strange to be credible academically, even in such a scientifically openminded institution as Harvard Medical School in which Minot was a professor. In many long jam sessions— once he was convinced I'd mastered his scientific publications— Minot told me the inside story of his adventure.

What George Minot was obsessed with long before he came down with severe diabetes was pernicious anemia, so-called because its victims invariably died. Way back in his intern days in 1912, George Minot had scrawled on the chart of a dying patient: "To be sure, what we need to know is the treatment of pernicious anemia."

That was what all doctors needed to know but didn't, yet from all other doctors Minot was different: he had no notion that it was impossible to know it. Minot was an admirer of the great pathologist, Dr. James Homer Wright, who, when asked what he thought was at the bottom of this fearful thinning of the blood, roared impatiently: "Dammit, Minot, can't you see it's the bone marrow that's sick?" Minot kept bothering Dr. Wright. "But what do these megaloblasts"—young immature red blood cells that refused to develop—"what do these megaloblasts mean in these pernicious anemia patients?" "What ails you?" asked Wright. "Can't you see the bone marrow is chock-full of cells that can't grow up? If we only knew how this happens! Can't you see pernicious anemia bone marrow's like a tumor; embryo stuff overgrowing the marrow fat, overgrowing everything . . . but not developing. But get out! What the devil do you bother me for?"

For years Minot tried many remedies to save these anemic people, especially transfusions. "Inside a few weeks there was definite improvement in about fifty per cent," he said. "But they all died finally." Minot shouldn't have been so raw-nerved about them. He should have taken comfort from the great Dr. William Osler, who had proclaimed: "To accept a great group of maladies, against which we have never had and scarcely ever hope to have curative measures, makes some men as sensitive as though we ourselves were responsible for the maladies' existence. . . . We should not bring the art of medicine into disrepute by quacklike promises to heal, or by wiredrawn attempts to cure in what old Burton calls 'the continuate and inexorable maladies.' "

Minot was only thirty-four when diabetes hit him—pre-Banting —and when you got the sugar disease that early you were as good as a goner. Every moment hunger gnawed at him and he knew that giving in to it would kill him. Then Banting's insulin brought him back strong, swiftly, magically. His own necessity to diet had made him a nut about diets for all sick people and he kept edging toward a certain diet for pernicious anemia people, all of whom were peculiarly pernickety eaters. At last, in 1925, he made the discovery that pernicious anemics about to die were brought back to life by eating liver. He was a tall, thin, precise man whose gray eyes burned with sincerity as he tried to defend to me the rhyme and reason of his curiously irrational science. His ratiocinations ran this way: it's in northern countries that most pernicious anemia is found, and in northern countries there is the greatest production of dairy products.

"But millions of people in these dairy regions eat a lot of other things besides cream and butter," I protested, "and they never show a sign of pernicious anemia."

"Pernicious anemia," said Minot, "is a lot like pellagra—sore mouth, upset digestion, nervous troubles." "But didn't Goldberger show pellagra could be controlled just by eating enough lean meat and milk?" I asked. "And didn't you feed lots of lean meat, protein, to pernicious anemia people and didn't they die anyway?" "They all died," said Minot.

Meanwhile Minot edged toward liver. In a book, *Newer Knowledge of Nutrition,* Minot had come across certain obscure virtues of proteins—*in liver.* Liver whooped up the growth rate of white rats. Minot remembered old Doctor Wright's saying, "In pernicious anemia it's the bone marrow that's sick. It's those megaloblasts in the sick bone marrow that can't grow up into adult red blood corpuscles." "Then I remembered about baby lions," said Minot. "Zookeepers tried to raise lion cubs on lean meat but they got rickety—their bones no good." But the same book said that when lion cubs are fed on liver, fat, and bones, they grew up strong and beautiful animals. There it was again. Bones bad when no liver. Lions eat liver and develop fine bones. The marrow of the bones is sick in pernicious anemia.

Another bit of science that should have stopped Minot's liver theory. Three Rochester, New York, doctors had bled healthy dogs, bled them and bled them and when they fed those dogs liver, their blood came back. But this wasn't pernicious anemia, only secondary anemia from repeated hemorrhage having nothing to do with pernicious anemia. Then I thought I had Minot. "Dr. Whipple [head man in the secondary anemia dog research] stated that beef heart and beef muscle could cure that dog anemia too." As well as liver. "But all the beef muscle in the world won't help your pernicious anemia folks," said Minot.

In his private practice, Minot began feeding a few pernicious anemia patients liver, gobs of liver, as much liver as they could stand. Pretty soon two of his pernicious anemia patients came back to Minot. He told me his surprise. "Hello, by jingo, here were both of them feeling much better. So it went all during 1924 and 1925, with my not thinking much of it," said Minot, but presently here were not two but ten patients in his practice that Minot was cajoling into eating so many grams of red meat, just so much fruit, such and such quantity of green vegetables

151

"and at least a quarter of a pound of liver every day," insisted Minot. Some of them loathed liver. Minot looked in cookbooks to find tasty ways to prepare liver and he wrote out elaborate directions for their diets. "And by jingo, none of them died," he said. Yet Minot was still lukewarm about it. He did not believe what he saw.

"I did not talk about it at that time because I didn't think it was anything to talk about," said Minot. He just kept feeding all ten of them more and more liver. Minot recalled that it was Dr. William P. Murphy—a young physician only five years out of medical school—who exhibited the first real enthusiasm. Minot, offhand, asked Murphy to try a special diet on pernicious anemia patients then in a bad way at Peter Bent Brigham Hospital. After eight months Murphy was as excited as such a slow-talking phlegmatic man can get. People he knew should have been dying, should have actually been dead, but they began to get up and walk, began to beg for more liver because they themselves felt it was liver.

Respect for hard facts, that was Minot's scientific religion, and now Murphy's independent results gave him a perfect check on his own first astonishing observations. Murphy had done his work not knowing about Minot's first ten patients so miraculously alive and healthy—on liver.

Rumors began to get around. Minot's friend Dr. James Howard Means of Massachusetts General Hospital came to Minot asking him: "Have you heard of the remarkable work someone is doing with liver feeding for pernicious anemia at the Brigham?" Yes, Minot had heard of it and knew it was true. Now sick people came to the Brigham *in extremis,* with blood ten times thinner than it should be, or with next to no blood at all. Minot and Murphy sat by their beds pouring fresh pulped liver down them through stomach tubes. They fed liver and more liver and saw life come back into these lost ones whose eyes opened and they said they felt a little bit better. In less than two weeks they were wanting to walk and on the heels of a first whisper of new strength came a great surge of red corpuscles in their blood.

Finally Minot's discovery came out of the fogs of the primitive into the bright glare of the scientifically respectable. Before the Association of American Physicians—the same body Macleod had set afire by his description of Banting's discovery—Minot reported how he and Murphy had saved dying people simply by feeding them liver. Minot had wanted to call his report: "Treatment of Pernicious Anemia with Liver." His academic colleagues got him to tone down his forthright title to "Treatment of Pernicious Anemia by a Special Diet." No mention of liver in the title. At the end of Minot's address there was a rustle of decorous excitement. Minot slipped out of the meeting in a hurry up to his hotel room to his wife. "I grabbed my figures and charts. I went all over them," said Minot. "I could hardly believe, myself, that all I'd told them was true." His genius was his insight that what is simple may also be deeply fundamental. What he did was to make his observations over and over and over and to get Murphy to make them over and over not knowing that he, Minot, had made them, at last arriving at such massive confirmation that what had seemed silly, was not.

CHAPTER ELEVEN

ON June 7, 1930, we shoved off from Cherbourg in the Buick roadster, driving slowly with the top down along the Norman hedgerows and spending the first night at Caen. Next morning we drove east through Pont L'Evêque where we asked the road from an enormous old farmer lady loaded down with the famous cheeses of the region. It was nice to find that she understood my rusty French. Next day we stopped at noon at a prosperous-looking, well-kept, stuffy-seeming Flemish town, Tournai. "This is where my Grandpa de Kruif was born," I said. I asked the maitre d'hôtel of the restaurant what people did here for a living and he answered, "Not much of anything." Rhea said: "Gosh, they all must be born rich here." "All excepting my grandpa," I said. "His folks were indentured, practically slaves."

At Brussels we celebrated an uproarious reunion with André Gratia, who'd been my comrade at the Rockefeller Institute in 1920. He took us to a hole-in-the-wall restaurant, Grégoire, where Rhea—herself a noted cook—pronounced the *entrecôte gran'mere* to be out of this world. From a neighboring table a man got up to study the label on our Burgundy bottle and then went back to discuss our taste in wine, seriously, with his companions. "You understand," said André, "Grégoire is what we call a serious restaurant. No music."

André and I recalled our 1920 Rockefeller days when we were young and poor and gay and did not give a damn and made cynical jokes about what we called the prevailing pseudoscience. Gratia was now a brilliant Belgian bacteriologist. He'd studied the bacteriostatic action of molds almost simultaneously with Alexander Fleming. This was ten years before Fleming's mold product, penicillin, came to be. He took us to pay our respects to old Professor Jules Bordet—the same who'd stoked me up to do *Microbe Hunters* long ago. He was littler and wispier than ever but in full possession of his marvelous marbles. Bordet was an immunologist's immunologist and though he'd won the Nobel prize, his fame in medicine was esoteric. You ask almost any doctor about Bordet and the name means nothing. He apologized for the appalling sloppiness of his laboratory. "It doesn't matter," he explained, "so long as it's clean inside the test tubes."

It had been clean enough inside his tubes to permit his discovery of the great Bordet-Gengou phenomenon, progenitor of blood tests. "Why did Wassermann—not you—apply it to the test for syphilis?" I asked. "Maybe I was too busy arguing with

Paul Ehrlich about his side-chain theory," apologized Bordet, who lived in a realm above the practical.

It should have been called the Bordet-Wassermann reaction. Bordet was the real originator of the blood test that could prophesy doom in the bodies of victims of syphilis long before they broke down with incurable paralysis of the insane. It was this that had brought us to Europe, to talk to Julius Wagner von Jauregg in Vienna, who'd found a dangerous, fantastic trick of burning syphilis out of the brains of paretics—and better still out of victims in whom it lay dormant. This doom could be foretold by the Wassermann reaction. It was exciting to be going to see Wagner-Jauregg.

Gratia, who hated all things German, told us to be on guard crossing the border. "Your car has a French license. The crazy German kids will throw rocks at you." They did just that. Excited at the prospect of seeing Wagner-Jauregg, we drove through the Ardennes and down past the Bernkasteler-Doktor vineyards in a crashing thunderstorm, down toward the Rhine where legendary Lorelei lured stupid sailors to their death. In Mainz we saw why André Gratia feared Hitler—three years before he came to power. We were blocked at the main street for almost an hour watching a fierce parade of German *Jugend*—already Hitler *Jugend*. In shorts, and marching to a high wail of reed pipes and the beat of drums, thousands of tough, tanned youngsters celebrated the French evacuation of the Ruhr. Toward Stuttgart our car was stoned by Hitler teen-agers who snarled, *"Franzozen!"* Dining that night at the Schlossgarten in Stuttgart we were appalled by the energy of the prosperous German eaters.

In Stuttgart it appeared that all was not well for me, deep in Rhea's heart. A cable had come from the secretary of one of my editors hoping she might see me in Paris. It was stupid of her not to have addressed it to both of us. For the first time in our life, Rhea broke into a storm of jealousy, though my relation with this young lady was platonic; but it seemed now as if Rhea hated me. The injustice of her suspicion smashed me—she was suspicious of the wrong person, for I had, once again, been unfaithful during our stay in Michigan—and I wept and she was silent, sadly, for many hours, till at last we made it up in each other's arms.

Reaching Vienna all was good again between us and Vienna was a contrast to Stuttgart; Vienna was gentle, its glory gone, yet gay. Herr Gabriel, the head porter of the Hotel Bristol, was a bug about Beethoven and we got him the German edition of Thayer's *Life of Beethoven,* translated by Deiters and Riemann. Gabriel promised to direct us to all the master's rural haunts around Vienna, and got us a carriage to the Zentral Friedhof and on the way we bought a little bouquet of yellow roses and in a private ceremony we laid them on the grave of Beethoven.

Now came the day that marked still another turning point in my working life. This day I first saw Julius Wagner von Jauregg —he'd dropped the "von" and shortened it to Wagner-Jauregg now that Austria had become a republic. He received me at Landesgerichtsstrasse, No. 18, in a high-ceilinged, old-fashioned study entered through a door decorated with a brightly polished plate asking one please to wipe one's feet before coming in. There was something craglike about this hairy, lean old man. He was tough, as you'd expect he'd have to be, saving the sanity and the lives of paretics by endangering them with the dangerous fever of inoculation malaria.

In slow, precise French with a German accent he told how he had groped forward for thirty years from his original observation that feverish infections—like pneumonia or typhoid—seemed to heat mental fogs out of certain crazy people. He saw naturally contracted fevers—occasionally—and unaccountably—reverse psychotics of all types back to mental health. Way back in 1887 Wagner-Jauregg had reported these experiences in a scientific paper in which he recommended that hopelessly crazy people be infected with erysipelas or malaria, and the medical world's reaction seemed to be that Wagner-Jauregg must be a bit balmy himself. There was too much danger of letting erysipelas and malaria loose around the city, said the doctors.

Wagner-Jauregg was mulish. He found a way to stoke up pretty fair fevers in crazy people without infecting them with dangerous diseases. He injected them with Robert Koch's tuberculin, in longer and larger doses, though tremendous tuberculin, as a remedy for TB, already had a bad name because it didn't often help consumptives, and sometimes killed them. For ten years Wagner-Jauregg slogged at this tuberculin-fever treatment. It mostly failed to help psychotic victims though it gave them really good fevers. Yet this was tantalizing: there were a few, whose families had tried to forget them because they were worse than dead, who'd gone home sane after the tuberculin-fever ordeal. "But I had to admit I'd failed. It was *comme ci, comme ça*," said the old psychiatrist, with a grim reminiscent smile.

"Here's where I went wrong," he explained. "I was trying the tuberculin on all kinds of dubiously classified psychoses—dementia praecox, paranoia, melancholia. All with cause unknown. And all with duration that varied. They might end in recovery without any kind of treatment at all." He showed a lacerating self-honesty. At last he cleared the decks for an experiment based on one stern proposition. In all the jumble of mental diseases there was one malady that had a sure, clear-cut diagnosis and outcome. Its definition was agreed to by all authorities: "General paralysis of the insane"—paresis—"is an incurable sickness, which in the course of a few years leads to imbecility and death." This was the ultimate fate of countless thousands of victims of syphilis, the old rover.

From now on out he'd fever none but this type of the surely doomed. He stuck to the tests for eight years—on sixty-nine paretics he used long bouts of tuberculin fever; sixty-nine he left without treatment. At the end of the eight years, five of those not fevered were still living; eight of the fevered ones hadn't died. Negligible. He stuck to it. He added the traditional old rover remedy, mercury, to the tuberculin fever. He started the treatment on paretics still in the early stage, called nervous breakdown. In 1914 he reported results on eighty-six early paretics treated with tuberculin fever plus mercury during the years 1907–1909. *Twenty-six* of them who should have all been dead were actually alive in 1914; seven had returned to work.

In high psychiatric circles this news caused hardly a ripple. That got Wagner-Jauregg into a smoldering fury. He asked whether the chance of *any* paretic as to life were so brilliant that you weren't justified in trying *anything*? The sand in his own hourglass was running low and he knew it. Then, on a fateful morning in 1917, he growled guttural orders to his assistants. During the next two months they inoculated nine paretics with acute, red-hot malaria. All of them were maniacal or demented, on their way to the madhouse, all with hope abandoned.

Ten years went by and in 1927 what had happened was unbelievable. Of those nine doomed, three were completely sane, all by their clear brains earning their own bread. Cured. All the nine had got dangerously sick with the malaria microbes multiplying in them. And then, just when those first three had got so brilliantly well, came disaster. Enthusiastic with his successes, he'd shot what he thought was safe, benign, tertian malaria into four more patients, but the blood he'd used turned out to have hiding in it the deadly half-moon parasites of malaria tropica—aestivoautumnal. Three out of four of those patients died from malaria.

But good news again. Give your paretic the right kind of safe malaria and, though it burned them, it was easy to cure by quinine, much easier than malaria naturally acquired from mosquitoes. Yet alas, only three out of the original nine were saved. Then he got hold of old rover victims not yet crazy or paralytic, but who by spinal-fluid Wassermann tests were known to be hiding the pale spirochete in their brains and who had the first faint evidence of nervous breakdown. Then malaria inoculations. And now not three out of nine, but eighty-three out of every hundred were well and working, years later.

It had taken him hours to tell his story and it grew dark and I could just see his rugged silhouette against the window. His voice came through the dimness a bit unreal. He stopped talking and rose and groped about with a long stick, like that of an old-fashioned lamplighter, and reached for the gas jet high above him. "Of course, what is most important is to *prevent* general paralysis," he said, and he admitted his original malaria treatment was not widely applicable. "Too many preparalytic people don't think they'll need this severe treatment.

"You may come back any afternoon," he said as I took my leave. "Just give me a day's notice. We're now making progress with malaria for *early* syphilis." "In America there's the beginning of development of a new kind of fever—safe—that might replace malaria," I said. His old mountaineer's eyes gleamed: "You must tell me about that. It would be wonderful, *ausserordentlich!*" he said. It stirred me to hope to help bring that about.

Beethoven, who in his own way had been a fighter like Wagner-Jauregg, was in counterpart to our work with the old psychiatrist. Many days we went out to Baden, to Mödling, to Heiligenstadt and to Ober-Döbling—where Beethoven had composed out of doors in the summer. We wandered hand-in-hand in the Wiesenthal along the brook where he sketched the Pastoral Symphony. We ate at the little tavern, Zur Schönen Aussicht, where he lived while writing the mighty Eroica.

We visited Beethoven's haunts around Baden and had schnitzels at an inn that had a few bars from a Schubert song painted on its front and we tried to sing it and afterward shot with an air gun in the inn's outdoor shooting gallery, fat ducks running on a rail. When Rhea beat me as a marksman it made her proud. In the nearby Vorderbrühl we demanded seltzer water with our Schlivovitz to the indignation of the *Oberkellner*.

In the late afternoons I went again to pay my respects and talk into the deepening twilight with Wagner-Jauregg. He told me how his friend Kyrle, a bearded, Bohemian-looking Viennese with a broad-brimmed hat, on a mountain-climbing trip, had revealed a great new advance in the malaria fever treatment of the old rover. To preparetic people Kyrle had given six shots of Ehrlich's salvarsan—606—then right after that, malaria, then curing the malaria with quinine. Then six more shots of salvarsan. That was all. Wagner-Jauregg's voice lifted, exultant in the semi-darkness of his study. "On hundreds like that Kyrle tried his combination malaria-salvarsan. Not one of them—it's eight years now—not one of these has come to the psychiatric clinic with general paralysis." Would our American syphilis experts have the nerve to try that, I wondered. "Too bad for their patients, if they're frightened to try it," said Wagner-Jauregg.

We came toward the end of a short European stay in a haze of high living, happiness, and hard work. "Let's live it up," I said. "Let's spend the dough we'd saved to stay a year." We drove toward Denmark across the Lüneberg Heide at the top time of the blooming of the heather. In Copenhagen I dug into the deeds of Niels Finsen, the first to win the Nobel Prize in medicine for his carbon arc ultraviolet cure of skin tuberculosis. Finsen was a primitive. On his way to his slow death he'd got his first hint of the life-giving power of ultraviolet by watching a mass of sick and dying angle worms come back to life in the strong rays of the sun.

"Aren't you proud to have won the Nobel Prize?" the newsmen had asked Finsen. "No," he said. "He lives best who lives unknown." The world of big-time medicine has taken him at his word.

Our last two weeks before sailing we spent, happy, in England, dining every night with Clifford Dobell and one night adding Dr. William Bulloch, who thrilled us when he said, "My boy, I've just been writing a short history. It's for the Medical Research Council's *System of Bacteriology*. You picked out the right men for your *Microbe Hunters*." Bulloch generously forgot he'd told me who they were, years before. We dined another night with Dobell and great old Sir David Bruce and his great lady, the co-discoverers of *Trypanosoma gambiense,* the cause of fatal African sleeping sickness. Both of them were almost at the end of their tether, past eighty. "When I get up there," growled Sir David in his deep Scottish burr, pointing up to heaven, "I'll say to God, 'let's have a couple of cocktails and talk it all over.' "

We drove, heigho for Lake Michigan, back to my mother's cottage at Blue Water to begin to try to write the mystery of the characters of Wagner-Jauregg and Finsen. One golden autumn afternoon we walked along the shore watching an endless, mysterious migration of big hawks, hundreds and hundreds of them with black wing tips, sailing along southward in a strange procession, each bird about a hundred feet behind the one in front. "They're American roughlegs, I think," said Rhea. What had made them make a rendezvous—and where—to sail away from the coming cold weather? How would they know to disperse when they got to where they were going? Nobody in all the world could tell us. In awe we watched that majestic, utterly enigmatic migration that afternoon and though we looked for it later every October along Lake Michigan's shore we never saw it again.

"Let's look for a bit of land on this shore, away from everybody," said Rhea. "Let's build a shack where you can work with nobody to bother you, just for us alone. We'll find a spot in the woods in the dunes where there are hepaticas and Dutchmen's-breeches in April and wake robins in May," she said. "Where we can learn the spring flowers and watch the spring warbler migrations. And where you can teach me to swim better in the rough water in the summer." It sounded like heaven and so it became.

In an early November snowstorm in a big surf kicked up by a northwest wind we bid a wild farewell to Blue Water at Lake Michigan. Dressed in nothing and covered by terrycloth bathrobes we ran down the steps to the Lake. Naked, we hit the surf that was so rough it didn't seem too cold. We hurried back up to the cottage wrapped in our robes and warm from the sting of the less than fifty degree water, and before the fire blazing on the hearth we drank a big whiskey-soda and I was proud of Rhea—what a tough girl and so beautiful. It was the salt of life.

Next day we went through a valley between two high wooded dunes. Big beechwood trees made it seem an outdoor cathedral and between the beeches there were black and white oaks and maples, virgin timber. "This is it," said Rhea, and that was the beginning of what was to become Wake Robin.

That early winter of 1930 a strange unforeseen working life began. We drove to Dayton, Ohio, to visit our friend, Dr. Walter Simpson, the brilliant pathologist. I told him about the possibility of artificial fever—to hook up to Salvarsan—Ehrlich's 606—the combination might just possibly be used to cure the old rover in its early stages and so prevent general paralysis of the insane.

"It would be a natural," I said. "You see, malaria can't be used to treat syphilis simultaneously with arsenicals—they knock out the malaria. If we only could develop a safe artificial fever—we could give it a one-two punch."

Walt Simpson took fire. "You should get to know Boss Kettering," said Walt, and presently he introduced the Boss to me on the long-distance telephone and that unorthodox genius talked to me from Cleveland for almost an hour. "Sounds like you and Walt have really got something," said Kettering. And five days later in New York that open-minded wizard and I had lunch together in his apartment in the Park Lane—not leaving the table from twelve-thirty till nearly five in the afternoon. He was research, walking. He seemed to care for nothing else.

"The docs tell us about certain diseases being incurable," said Kettering. "D'you know what an incurable disease is?" he asked. "It's one the doctors don't know anything about." Then he chuckled. "The disease has no objection to being cured at all."

Boss Kettering's optimism made everything seem easy. Boss Ket listened with genial impatience to my account of the dangers and difficulties of the already existing artificial fevers. Chief among these was a fever stoked up by a contraption called the radiotherm, evolved by General Electric's Dr. Willis Whitney. The discovery had been accidental. While tinkering with a short-wave broadcasting gadget, two of his engineers had got hot, got bothered, had shot high fevers—just working in the same room in the invisible field of the machine's short-wave energy. Such was the origin of the radiotherm.

"What's wrong with that, why don't the docs get busy and use it on paretics?" asked Kettering. "One of them, Dr. Leland Hinsie, has, but the hell of it is the machine burns them," I said. "The only patients who don't mind it are the paretics too far-gone, too blank to care. When they get that radio fever," I said, quoting Hinsie, "they sweat in rivers. Then the short-wave energy arcs across the sweat pools and burns the be-Jesus out of them."

Kettering chuckled. "That should be easy to fix. You say these people lie in a box between the short-wave electrodes? We'll just blow hot dry air in there. That'll evaporate their sweat. That'll cool the outside of them down. The fever'll go on inside them." Now Ket, too, was afire. "We'll get Doc Whitney to sell us a radiotherm. Then we'll see if we can make it practical. We know some fellows in Dayton who'll try it at Miami Valley Hospital." Ket never used the first person singular.

Boss Ket—Charles Franklin Kettering—of General Motors was a freak and there'll never be another like him. Where many men of science tend to be stiff, Ket was relaxed and salty. Where the merriment of most men of science tended to be measured, Ket's gags were Will Rogersish. Where the usual men of science seem contented with their contributions to knowledge, Ket lived in a perpetual state of amazement at his own ignorance. He made light of his inventions and discoveries—among them the automobile self-starter, high-octane fuels, and the modern Diesel engines that were right then getting set to make steam locomotives things of the past. In 1930, when we first met, he was in his early fifties and at the top of his form. "We haven't done a goddamn thing," Ket said.

In the early spring of 1931 I began to make payments on Wake Robin and to make trips back and forth to Dayton, to help lay plans for a safe, practical, powerful machine fever, to be combined with arsenicals and bismuth, to fight the old rover in all its stages. Walt Simpson and Fred Kislig were the doctors who had the guts to try it, backed spiritually and financially by Kettering, to whom nothing was impossible. Walt Simpson was learned in the perils of the old rover to heart and brain. Outwardly Simpson was hardboiled but his rough-talking, profane exterior camouflaged a human heart. He was that rare thing, a combination of laboratorian and doctor and he was, when necessary, a martinet. Fred Kislig understood and was skilled in the standard chemical treatment of the old rover; better yet he understood and loved human beings. Kislig had affection for the least of people, for incorrigible sinners and outcasts of humanity. To him, victims of the old rover were not sinners. This preference for mankind's underdogs kept Kislig poor. No time was too much for him to take to fight last-ditch battles for the lives of those wretched with whom more stylish doctors might not want to bother.

Such then were the pioneers with whom we got ready to embark on a quest for a new hot fight for life. Expensive science—but for wherewithal we had the backing of Boss Kettering.

In Dayton that autumn thoughts of our trouble all seemed wiped away in a fury of launching, along with Simpson, Kislig, and Kettering, of the first clinical tests of artificial fever combined with arsenicals and bismuth—on far-gone victims of the nervous complications of the old rover. Kettering was confident that just blowing hot air into the fever cabinet would evaporate sweat and cool the outside of patients down and prevent their burning. But it turned out that the short-wave radiotherm was exasperatingly uncertain. The fevers it stoked up were now feeble, now ferocious, generally unpredictable and invincibly uncomfortable.

How could those first patients of ours take their torture? Only because for them all other hope was gone. They'd all been treated to no avail with arsenicals and bismuth; they'd been poisoned and not cured and were all at the end of their tether. How did we dare to go on shoving these wretches into that dangerous coffinlike contraption? We were driven on by the miracle of resurrection in our very first patient. He had come to us after attempts at suicide because of the lancinating pains of locomotor ataxis. Maybe the fever machine would kill him? He bitterly asked, so what? But presently his pains faded before the arsenic, the bismuth, and the fever; and his eyes were doglike in gratitude and he began to gain weight and grow strong and came back slowly from one hundred and ten pounds to his old one hundred and ninety. He was happy with his family again and with the job he'd had before his illness hit him.

Even so, Kettering and Simpson and Kislig together could not have induced the patients to stand the long, hot, uncertain torture of the radiotherm. It was fever nurse Florence Storcky—kidding them with gaiety and kindness—who cajoled them. Have you ever seen cheerfulness walking? That was Storcky.

It was Storcky who was alert to protect the hot spots burned on her patients' bodies despite the air conditioning. She iced their hot brows. She watched their bounding pulses for signs of possible failure of their hearts. She told them stories. She kidded them back and back into their experimental hell. She led them through many ordeals toward strength they had not felt for years, to a surge of energy that made them forget their suffering. "You fools," Storcky told them. "Don't you *know* you're getting better?"

Even so, Storcky must have given up this hot science—it was so utterly impractical excepting that it cured them—if it hadn't been for Edwin Sittler. Eddie was a brilliant engineer that Boss Ket had brought us from Frigidaire. This youngster was joined by young Dr. Worley Kendell, fresh out of medical school—it was a brash pioneering that could only be done by youngsters. Storcky, Worley, and Eddie slept little, snatched quick meals— and worked and worked desperate months till they stumbled by accident upon a fever machine that had a chance to become safe and practical. One day the radiotherm, the short-wave broadcasting gadget, went "Bs-s-s-t" and gave up the ghost in the middle of a fever treatment. Storcky, Worley, Eddie, all were quietly frantic. These breakdowns were bad for the morale of patients already halfway up to a fever of 105 degrees. Now here the man lay, nothing but hot, slightly humid, air playing over his naked body.

But what was this? The man's fever kept going up anyway without the short waves from the radiotherm. Just from the hot air blowing over him. That night the three young fools worked till dawn, Rhea and I watching. With just the right proportion of moisture in a current of hot air, they lit a beautiful fever in Storcky's friend, Nurse Kate Rife. Good-by to the short wave. Such was the accidental origin of the Kettering air-conditioned hypertherm. The nightmare of skin burns worried the experimenting youngsters no longer. The terrific blasts of hot dry air were no longer needed. The moister the air you blow around the patient the less hot it needs to be to heat him safely to any safe temperature his sickness demands. To hold the fever precisely at a given level, for hours, you circulate around him moist air not quite as hot as a hot day in Arizona.

Now the Dayton fever doctors and nurses were set for what turned out to be ten years of clinical experiment—amid skeptical sniffs of many venereal disease authorities. They set out on long clinical tests on hundreds of patients. They gunned for an arsenic, bismuth, fever cure of the old rover, of earlier and earlier stages of the old rover long before its clinical nervous phase. They shortened and shortened the fever till total fever-chemical treatment was taking just over one day—twenty-nine hours in all—including six hours of fever at a temperature of 105–106 degrees, Fahrenheit. This was the goal of the Dayton men—to find a substitute for eighteen continuous months of big doses of the then standard arsenic and bismuth treatment, so often poisonous and always so uncomfortable that the majority of the sufferers quit before the end of it, preferring to take a chance with their sickness.

CHAPTER TWELVE

I WAS now deep in the book *Men Against Death,* and we took the manuscript to Florida where I wrote furiously and where, afternoons, we walked miles along the beach in the sun north of the Hillsboro Light and swam far into the surf and became brown almost like Indians and for me there was no woman other than Rhea.

There was a change in Rhea, post 1931. She became—who could blame her—suspicious of me, somewhat severe of me, a little less tender. On the way back north in the early spring of 1932 we just escaped death in an automobile in Tennessee. At the top of a hill, on a curve, Rhea driving over sixty miles per hour, the accelerator stuck on the floorboard and the big Buick roadster went into a dry skid, bumping over low rocks and bringing up against a rock face. Rhea was thrown out through the door and I was severely cut by the rear-vision mirror. Bleeding heavily, I helped her—I can see her now, her gray eyes unfrightened under her scarlet beret. She wiped the blood from my face and scrutinized the wound. "It's nothing," she said. "Get out the iron horse," she ordered. From this white metal flask we both took big slugs of whisky. We looked at the car, a total wreck, its engine jammed back through the firewall. How could we be alive?

That evening in Nashville after buying a new Buick we faced each other across the dinner table in our hotel room. My head was bandaged and it made me feel a bit dramatic. She had no words of pity but smiled and said: "Isn't it good we're alive?" "You like?" I asked, pleased she made it plural. "Yes, I like," she answered, "I love you." "It must mean there's something left for us to do together," I said.

That 1932 saw the beginning of Rhea's really effective therapy for my turbulence. We bought twenty-nine acres of deep wooded dunes we had found on the shore of Lake Michigan. This hide-away was ten miles from Holland, Michigan, and our nearest all-year-round neighbors were nearly two miles distant. I'll never forget our first walk alone through that forest toward the big lake. The hills were dotted white with three-petalled trillium wake robins. "Let's call it 'Wake Robin' " said Rhea. We walked as close together as if newly wed. By the lake shore as we loved each other we listened to the cheerfully raucous song of a crested fly-catcher above us, himself in love. This became the site of the Wake Robin house.

Together, under the direction of our beachmaster, old William Deplidge, we cut a clearing in the woods two hundred feet from the edge of the bank above Lake Michigan's shore. Together we cut down the big trees with a crosscut saw. With a wedge and maul and a double-bitted Michigan ax we cut the big logs into firewood. Rhea learned to swing the maul and the ax like a lumberjack. Then that early summer there arose a little house, the first we could call our own. Rhea called it "The Shack"—it had one room with a lean-to for an in-a-door bed and another lean-to for a kitchen and our facilities were a simple outdoor Chick Sales from which it was pleasant to regard the blue of the lake in the early morning.

Mornings I worked outdoors in the sun-dappled shade of oaks and maples. Afternoons we walked many miles in the sand under the strong summer sun on the lake shore and swam in the cool water of the lake and explored the dunes for miles around. Thus began a magic routine that lasted twenty-five years, becoming deeper as the years went by. My dangerous, sentimental sensuality had vanished. What was left of this infirmity petered out into minor fickleness such as that of glancing surreptitiously at ladies' bottoms. Rhea's fierce possessiveness was my discipline, the green peace of Wake Robin was a medicine. Rhea was the doctor and she began to reward me with her smile again and we loved each other and I felt it was going to be never-ending.

In 1933, Rhea—her own architect—began to design and expand our shack into a split-level, low, rambling house; its gray-green hand-split shakes made it look as if it were part of the woods. That year she had to face in me another type of turmoil; it was not sensual but mental. About a year after the publication of *Men Against Death* came a letter from the cantankerous and powerful poet, Ezra Pound. His letter assured me *Men Against Death* displayed honesty and sincerity, despite its economic ineptitude. Why did I persist in writing success stories about many medical achievements, with never a mention of a man-made cause of death more murderous than all the billions of microbes put together?

Pound pointed out it was poverty that was the big killer. Despite our knowledge of the microbic and metabolic causes of human suffering, the trouble was that there was not enough money to make that knowledge operative and to enforce it. He was far from a communist but he had an economic panacea for poverty, namely Social Credit as expounded by the Scottish engineer, Major C. H. Douglas. I'd never heard of Douglas but if Pound said Social Credit was the answer, that was enough for me. I was that suggestible. I bought and studied all the writings of Major Douglas. A parable by the good Major excited me. He asked me to imagine a company of people crossing a desert. Some few had big water bottles but the great majority were equipped only with little ones. This was our economic order. The throats of those with the little water bottles became parched; their lips became cracked and black. Yet there were, potentially, water and big bottles enough for everybody.

That's humanity today—when power to produce anything for everybody is limitless. At Wake Robin life seemed to me to be as simple as that.

In 1933 in the beginning of the deep depression I was dominated by the economic philosophy of Boss Kettering, who seemed convinced that what America mainly lacked was enough science. All we needed was more research to stimulate more industry to give more men work for greater production. So in 1934 it came about that my writing took a fundamental turn. We began to search out and report upon the misery of a part of humanity that could not be blamed for its suffering. Rhea and I began to study the needless sickening and dying of children. Here is our Simple Simon economics: little rich girls and boys didn't have to be deprived of a single calorie or a solitary unit of vitamin to give enough death-fighting food and vitamins to all spindly-legged undernourished poor little boys and girls.

Many letters came to me as answers to my celebration of the hope of medical science for children and their mothers and fathers. They'd read of some medical discovery I'd glorified, but they hadn't the railroad or the bus fare to get to the hospitals administering it. Many were too proud to ask for charity. This avalanche of letters elated me because it meant my work was striking fire.

I studied the proceedings of a conference in Harrisburg, Pennsylvania, in March under the chairmanship of Dr. Samuel McClintock Hamill. He advocated that the medical profession band together voluntarily to search out the sickness, to build up the strength of children whose upkeep under our economic order could not be industry's headache. The spirit of this conference was its determination to start giving Pennsylvania's children a solicitude long shown by our Government for the well-being of its pigs and cattle. Dr. Hamill, together with devoted men and women, jarred many prosperous Pennsylvanians out of their complacency about the state of health of the state's poor children.

The state of the health of the children in our neighboring small western Michigan city of Holland was not much better. It was a prosperous town and as well-painted as any in America and now, in the springtime, it was about to burst into beauty with the bloom of a million tulips. The tulip was the living thing the burghers tended with the greatest solicitude for its nutrition. Nothing was too good for the tulip. Now Holland's infant death rate, which had got down to 20.9 per thousand live births in 1926, as the wages of the workmen began to dribble down to nothing—now that death rate had trebled, reaching 64.2 per thousand.

I made a private inquiry into the purchasing power of the Holland factory payrolls—the city's chamber of commerce hadn't made the investigation and who blames them? We found that hard workers who'd worked at one job in one factory for thirty years were now drawing pay checks averaging from seven to ten dollars a week, the weeks they worked. "Who's going to take the rap for caring for the children—somebody's got to pay the shot," the lady county welfare director said. The mothers themselves couldn't pay, the doctors couldn't be asked to do it for nothing. The state had a law adequate to care for the sick children but (as is common in the rich state of Michigan) the state had not much money. Sixty-four small white caskets were now being carried annually to the cemeteries where only twenty had gone in the days when the workmen's families could afford something more than salt pork and potatoes.

I was told that when you begin to be bothered by the passing away of children who don't have to die, your worry may be assuaged by biometrics. My friend, the distinguished biometrician Dr. Raymond Pearl of the Johns Hopkins, proved to me that this parade of more and more little white caskets has its bright side. Dr. Pearl was such a physically huge man and so judicious in talking that he made you believe him. He pointed out that biometric science only concerns itself with the fate of the human race *as an animal species.* Forget that those little white coffins hold somebody's hopes, somebody's baby son or daughter or brother or sister. That is sentiment, but not science. Didn't I realize that it has been proved by slide-rule biometric science, that when you cut down the dying of small babies, if those babies hadn't died when they were very tiny, then more of their cohort, born that year, would be sure to perish in the years to follow? You only postponed the job of the undertaker by cutting down infant mortality.

Did this hold for older children as well? I dug back into Michigan records of young lives that had begun in the boom days. Here were three miserable little brothers. They'd been born in '22, '24, and '26 amid the bull market uproar when Detroit promised to be permanently hard, bright, and dynamic. We probed into the lives of these three little boys in 1928. They were certainly not fit to keep living. Their father was a victim of paresis; their mother had broken down with dementia praecox. If you'd entered the shack where these three wan waifs lived, you'd have found the spindly-legged, rickety boys gnawing at crusts of moldy bread.

Now it is 1930 and the three little boys must surely be dead because of their deplorable heredity. Now they have the luck to come to the notice of the Children's Aid Society of Detroit, which has money to help maybe one out of every thousand children who are forlorn. When found by the Aid Society, the three little boys had the color of fungi. If saved now, they'd surely die later! But the workers of the Children's Aid Society were ignorant of biometrics.

Now it is 1934, and when you see these youngsters you'd swear they were not the same children at all. They live on a farm under care of a foster mother and father. They raise garden crops on their own plots of ground. They're hungry all the time but it's from fishing and swimming in the summer and sliding downhill in the winter and they have all the milk, meat, green vegetables, and eggs their stomachs can hold. The kindness of their foster parents has built this food into their straight, strong, tanned bodies. Who's going to say they'll die next year because they were saved three years ago?

It was wonderful to watch, in the days of the early 1930's, how our good Americans took this semistarvation that resulted from the breakdown of our money system. Among them I found one, a pipe fitter in a foundry, who'd had the luck and the skill to work all through the Depression. His slant was philosophic:

"We workmen are beginning to realize that we can produce enough for everybody, more than enough. But somebody's keeping the dough out of our pockets. If the big shots who control the wherewithal, instead of making that money scarce, would take all the wheat and meat and wool and cotton we need to feed us and keep us warm, and if they'd put these necessaries in a great pile and throw the troops around it to keep those things from us—we'd mighty soon go and get what we had a right to. But that isn't the way they keep the stuff from us. The power to *buy* the stuff is what they keep from us."

I began to see red. Old Otto Carmichael, a rich and shrewd man from Muncie, Indiana, told me: "Take it easy my boy. You're impatient. A change in the money system is going to take years."

I kept turning away from visions of the semistarvation of children. Back at Wake Robin, returning from our grim investigations, I breathed the air washed clean by the lake and drank good whisky and chopped wood and rejoiced in the feeling of my bare feet in the sand and we washed down imported Döhveziener sausages with Rhine wine in our canoe far out in the quiet lake and swam and listened to Beethoven's strong music as we sat before the fire in the evenings in our new homestead. Yet Rhea kept prodding me to go out and look for pain, for physical suffering, for death, especially that of children, because of want of the fundamental necessities of life and then to tell about such events in the strongest words possible to as many millions as possible. She asked: "What could make Americans more angry than this—that they were being made to suffer and die in the midst of a land where the chance for life should be limitless?"

We visited the nearby Ottawa County welfare where the welfare workers used the Government pittance they were allowed skillfully to half-fill the bellies and half-clothe the bodies of the county's children. We found these officials deeply worried about whether folks getting help from welfare should be allowed to keep and feed their dogs. They asked whether it wasn't our main economic trouble that there were not only too many children but too many dogs to feed. All that afternoon we listened to a questioning of the good of life not only for dogs but for children. The welfare people were neo-Malthusians.

The welfare workers put us on the trail of cases of rheumatic fever and heart disease, notoriously an ill of those who were poor. They sent us to see the mother of a little four-year-old girl, named Joan, in Grand Haven, Michigan. In November, 1933, Joan's mother had begun to worry over certain peculiar symptoms in her little daughter. If in their beginning Joan's father and mother had then known us and asked us: what can we do to save her? we could have told her that she seemed to be suffering from rheumatic heart disease. Dr. Alvin Coburn had not long before proved that this ill was triggered by a streptococcus throat infection and I had written the story, telling its now possible happy ending. He had taken rheumatic children to Puerto Rico and under its balmy sun the streptococcus had vanished from their throats and along with it their rheumatic misery. Joan's father, who was getting twelve dollars a week on the CWA, could not be told to take Joan to Florida, California, or Puerto Rico.

Coburn had found other expedients against the rheumatic terror. Among families with good food high in protein, especially eggs, the disease was rare. With Joan's family the trouble was they had no money. The economic explanation was that American people then couldn't buy what they were collectively able and willing to produce and they couldn't buy because they hadn't the money, because of low production. Joan's God-fearing, gaunt-faced mother didn't put it that way when she told us the story of Joan's final heartbreak. She told it with the stoicism characteristic of a Frisian woman and only at the end got up, turned away, wiping her eyes on the corner of her ragged dress. At the end she questioned her own religion, saying it was a shame to bring these children into the world when you weren't allowed to feed them.

Joan's father was your best type of hard-working Dutchman, and her father and mother began to taste the torture of not knowing what they were going to feed their children and Joan's father looked at his hands, wondering why there was no work for those strong hands to do. They both of them dimly felt the bitterness of life under a system that forgets a family can't eat enough one month to last them through the next one.

One evening, undressing her, Joan's mother said, she noticed big, strange black and blue spots on her little daughter's legs. Next morning Joan started to play but got tired right away. The doctor said it looked like scurvy and that Joan should have plenty of milk and oranges—all she could eat. Joan got tired quicker and quicker and her color became a bit bluish. One afternoon she began to cry, her mother said. It wasn't natural in her, she had always been so happy and cheerful. She said it hurt her so, right here, and she put her hand over her heart. "I felt there, and it was pounding terrible hard—too fast to count it."

Joan was white and lay in her mother's arms, quite still, and suddenly started writhing and screaming. Then her nose began to bleed and there was no stopping it. Again the doctor was called and said she should be taken to Ann Arbor, to the University Hospital, where they would transfuse her for free. At seven this cold snowy night, Joan, in the arms of her gaunt-faced father, in a car driven by her uncle, started out through the whirling snow one hundred and seventy miles to Ann Arbor. Her father said Joan seemed so happy to be going on this auto ride except when those sudden pains made her scream. Then, when the pains eased, she looked up at her father and smiled. In Battle Creek Joan screamed for the last time. She stayed quiet for a long time and her father took her in his arms out in the snow in front of the headlights. She opened her eyes and looked up at her Daddy and gave him what was her last big smile. It was one thirty in the morning now and very cold and, there now being no need of a transfusion of the blood that could have been got free at the University, they started back to Grand Haven in the snow.

Stirred up with Joan's needless death—it was only one of thousands—I wrote to Boss Kettering describing it. I wrote to him and told him how such infamies in our land of enormous wealth, in a country with unlimited requisites for good living, how this poverty causing the death of children like Joan, *nauseated* me. It made me sick at my stomach to go on telling about life-saving science. Couldn't there be a science against poverty? Mr. Kettering wrote me back kindly. He told me not to be impatient. He said that millions of children had been dying for thousands of years and we couldn't save them all at once, right now. As for my nausea, he prescribed a dose of bicarbonate of soda.

Ket's jolly admonition made Rhea see red. We were sitting round the big hexagonal table in front of the Wake Robin shack with June Simpson and her husband, Walt, who was Ket's medical adviser. Walt, who adored Ket, was expostulating on the Boss's versatility—science, economic, industrial, and then too he was such a wonderfully kind man. I agreed. Then Rhea told Walt the bicarbonate-of-soda story. "It's always, 'Yes Boss, that's right Boss.' You both act like he was God." If there was one trait in me, aside from my sensuality, that Rhea disliked, it was my awe of rich men and occasional sycophancy toward them.

I was not, finally, patient, and I published in 1936 the book about forgotten children under the title, *Why Keep Them Alive?* It set fire to many critics and reviewers.

"Every decent man and woman in the whole world should get De Kruif's message. . . . This book tells what is the matter with the world in a new way," wrote Lincoln Steffens.

"Paul de Kruif's book, written out of a Niagara Falls of impassioned emotion, starts one off on contemporary indignations of one's own. . . . And the thought of paying farmers not to produce milk and potatoes, when thousands need milk and potatoes and can't pay for them, rouses Paul de Kruif to his superbest heights of scientific indignation," wrote Lewis Gannett.

In the *New Republic,* R. A. Kocher wrote: "A tale that lacks nothing in the way of substantial corroboration. It is, in truth, so overwhelming that it would be impossible for anyone to challenge any essential feature of it."

In the *New Yorker,* given to ironical indignation, Clifton Fadiman said: "This book is a heartbreaker, a combination of report and exhortation, full of fighting anger. . . . There is no doubt that rugged individualists will attack his book on the ground that it is propaganda in favor of human life."

Men of medical and public health science paid little attention to the book. They did not attack it. They ignored it. And the top politicoes of the New Deal—right up whose alley it should have been—seemed unaware of the book's existence.

CHAPTER THIRTEEN

I**N** these same mid-1930 years I became involved in a possible research battle against infantile paralysis, the enigmatic illness now known as polio. My interest was stoked as a result of acquaintance with a wonderful man, the late Arthur Carpenter. Himself a serious polio cripple, he was manager of President Franklin D. Roosevelt's foundation at Warm Springs, Georgia. The activities of the Warm Springs Foundation were devoted to the treatment of polio in warm water, with no accent on research that might lead to the prevention of the crippler. Money for the support of the Warm Springs Foundation poured in from parties celebrating the President's birthday, each January 30. When the public danced and made merry on that day in 1935, the total take amounted to around one million dollars.

"Why do you use all that dough to dip cripples in warm water?" I asked Carpenter. "That doesn't cure them any more than it cured you or the President. Why don't you ask the President to devote a part of that big dough to research on polio *prevention?* Nobody knows a thing about that!" Carp lighted up at my suggestion. He consulted Mr. Keith Morgan, then a most devoted friend, even a worshiper of Mr. Roosevelt. In less than no time the President's Infantile Paralysis Research Commission had been appointed, financed by nearly a quarter of a million dollars from the 1935 Birthday Balls for the President. This was big money for polio searchers, who had been poorer than church mice. The Commission consisted of the usual eminent laymen. Its chairman was Mr. Jeremiah Milbank, outstanding in his knowledge of polio history. To my amazement I was appointed the commission's secretary with the job of spotting virologists, neurologists, and epidemiologists who might be interested—now that at last there was a bit of money—in research on polio prevention.

This work began to take a lot of time away from my proper job of writing. My friend and publisher, Mr. Alfred Harcourt, was worried about me. "You're going to have to choose between staying a writer and becoming a public health organizer," he said, with a critical gleam in his dark eyes. As for myself, I was flattered.

The Commission, for all its distinction, knew next to nothing (with the exception of Mr. Milbank) about polio science. I was flattered upon being asked to suggest a scientific advisory committee to counsel us on how to spend the $240,000. This committee had as its chairman famed Dr. George W. McCoy, director of the Hygienic Laboratory of the U. S. Public Health Service. Its personnel gained distinction by the appointment of virologist Dr. Thomas M. Rivers of the Rockefeller Institute for Medical Research. Again I was flattered when Dr. Rivers solicited my influence in getting him this post. I was pleased because of my long ago having been fired from Dr. Rivers' Institute.

Our first attempt to use the President's birthday money ended in a deplorable debacle. Our champion was the noted Dr. William Hallock Park, director of the Bureau of Laboratories of the New York City Health Department. It was Dr. Park who had exposed the folly of trying to use convalescent serum in the cure of cases of epidemic polio. If serum couldn't cure the terror, mightn't there be hope of a vaccine to prevent it? Dr. Park thought so. He told our scientific advisory committee of monkey experiments in his laboratory. His assistant, optimistic, hard-working Dr. Maurice Brodie, had the idea of turning deadly polio virus gentle by treating with formaldehyde the spinal cords of monkeys dead of polio. Dr. Brodie fooled himself—and poor Dr. Park—into believing that his formaldehyde vaccine protected monkeys against the paralytic infection. Dr. Park assured our advisory committee that this vaccine was ready for human test.

I admit that, influenced by Dr. Park's hope for the vaccine, I fought hard against scientific skeptics, notably Dr. George McCoy (who took a dim view of it), to make possible the experimental test of the Park vaccine upon children. Dr. Edwin W. Schultz, of Stanford University, had already made monkey science that should have blasted hopes for the success of this human polio vaccine test before it was started. Schultz injected many monkeys with a vaccine brewed à la Park and Brodie. But when he dropped a bit of the dangerous polio virus into the noses of allegedly vaccinated simians, they all went limp and died—as promptly as not-vaccinated monkey controls.

Park and Brodie grabbed for a straw of hope. They believed they'd proved their formaldehyde vaccine set up virus-killing power in the blood of the children they'd vaccinated. But this hope, too, was dashed when North Carolina children—every other child in a series—were vaccinated by U. S. Public Health Service experts. Testing the blood of the vaccinated children, observers found that the blood of the *not*-vaccinated children was also immune, spontaneously.

What was worse, the Park-Brodie vaccine, as given to children, turned out not to be safe. Some little ones were made alarmingly sick by it. There came reports from California that one or more people had died from polio as a result of the Park-Brodie vaccine. Investigation showed that Brodie, in his eagerness to make a truly powerful formaldehyde vaccine, had shortened the exposure of the polio virus to formaldehyde, so that the vaccine was not totally dead. A result was that the Park vaccine had actually become an immunizer because of its contents of more or less live polio virus.

I'll never forget the afternoon when Dr. George McCoy had to tell Dr. Park that the President's Commission could no longer support his human experiments financially. That was a blow from which Dr. Park did not recover. And not long after, Dr. Brodie committed suicide.

In the late summer of 1935 it was clear that the Park-Brodie vaccine had been a failure. When polio virus is safely killed by formaldehyde, it is a feeble immunizer. But when the vaccine contains living virulent virus, it may sicken and even kill some children it aims to immunize.

What's more, children had died following an attempt to guard them with another vaccine devised by Dr. John A. Kolmer of Philadelphia. Against infantile paralysis there seemed still to be no preventive hope at all. Then came a new gleam, based on a new explanation of the way the polio virus sneaked into children. It seemed possible that it made its entry only by way of the nerve endings of the sense of smell high up inside the nose. Dr. Charles Armstrong of the U. S. Public Health Service devised what he hoped would be a chemical blockade against this portal of invasion by the polio virus. A combination of picric acid and alum sprayed into the noses of monkeys protected them when the paralytic terror was later sprayed into their nostrils. But when this trick was tried on threatened children in three Southern states hit by epidemic polio—on about two million youngsters—the protective effects of picric-alum sprays was by no means clear-cut.

Then hope for a far more powerful chemical blocker was put before the advisory committee of the President's Commission for Infantile Paralysis Research. It was a cheap and simple chemical, zinc sulphate, first tried by Dr. Edwin Schultz. The Commission advanced to Dr. Schultz what seemed to be lavish money for needed experimental monkeys. His results with the simians seemed too good to be true. To me Dr. Schultz wrote, "somewhere the light must be shining for children threatened by infantile paralysis. Will zinc sulphate be the answer?"

The Commission's advisory medical committee pondered well this powerful zinc sulphate monkey science. Here was the question: is what's true for monkeys true for man? The experiment might be feasible, if the zinc sulphate could be made to cover completely the delicate endings of the nerves of smell. Could this be done so that it would not be harmful? And would it be sufficiently comfortable to insure parents bringing their children back for as many treatments as might be necessary while the epidemic threat of polio was present?

The Commission granted the money needed to answer these ifs to experts at the University of Michigan Medical School at Ann Arbor under the direction of the famed neurosurgeon, Dr. Max Minor Peet. Dr. Peet's plan was to insure complete zinc sulphate coverage of the endings of the nerves of smell by a long-tip atomizer. Dr. McCoy took a dim view of this procedure. "When you try to put it way up in their noses, the children will wiggle." The experimental children did more than that. They fought and squirmed and twisted like embattled eels. They bellowed. They complained of headaches. And older children reported that the zinc sulphate caused a loss of their sense of smell.

That day Armstrong's face was a study as he saw the chance of a preventive spray going aglimmering, this year of 1937. Then Armstrong smiled. "I've got an idea," he said. "You might be able to hold those kids still if you put each one of them in a plaster cast while you did the spraying." His ridicule of our hopes and his own laughed away our disappointment.

This is an example of the resourcefulness of the infantile paralysis virus. Zinc sulphate blocks it. But why did the virus have to choose such an infernally un-get-at-able corner of the human anatomy for its path of entry? That, in those days, was thought to be the one path of entry of polio.

Late in the afternoon of that depressing day in Ann Arbor, I drove home to Wake Robin, too fast, into the setting sun. Far too fast, but not caring because here was the defeat of a deeply held hope. Despite the money, it turned out to be a flop.

President Roosevelt was most kind to his research committee despite its apparent failure. In November of 1936 he gave us a luncheon at the White House. Rhea showed solicitude. She took me out and bought a hat for me saying: "You can't go to a White House luncheon bareheaded." It shook me up to be in this fast company—nabobs including Chairman Jeremiah Milbank,

Edsel Ford, Mrs. Nicholas Brady, Felix Warburg, and certain other eminentoes whose names I do not now remember.

The affair began impressively. The Research Commission stood in a loosely deployed circle in a big room the décor of which I do not remember except that on one wall there was an impressive oil painting of the first President Roosevelt. Then came a solemn moment, the entry of President Franklin D. Roosevelt, walking painfully, supported by the arm of his great friend, Keith Morgan. It hit me deeply the way he walked despite his disability. One by one our circle advanced to shake his hand. For each member of the Commission, when introduced by Keith, he had a smile and a quip and a kind word—though the great majority of them were Republicans. He held my hand in an iron grip. He looked at me and said nothing, then gave me a knowing wink.

At the luncheon he asked me to make a report of our Commission's activities. "How long do you give me, Mr. President?" I asked. "Will fifteen minutes be enough?" he asked, smiling urbanely. God knows that was long enough to relate the next to nothing we had so far accomplished.

Never before had I seen a man who radiated such confidence, such power, such urbanity, and such charm. Though the majority of his guests were his political and economic enemies, he called them by their first names, asked solicitously about the children of some of them he knew. His humanity, his obvious bravery, and his suffering dominated all of them. He said nothing about the continuing enigmatic nature of polio. He encouraged us all, telling us that infantile paralysis research *must* go on. He disclosed nothing about how he was going to arrange this in terms of economics. His smile was as kind as that of any man I'd ever known.

That evening I got to know more of him. He gave three of us a little dinner in his study—Arthur Carpenter, his Warm Springs Foundation manager, Otto Carmichael, a Hoosier Rabelais from Muncie, and myself. He introduced us to his special cocktail. "When you shake it, you remind me of Henry Mencken, Mr.

President," I said. "Oh, you're a friend of Henry's?" he asked. "He's a great fellow!" Henry Mencken was his most bitter critic.

Otto Carmichael, the old Muncie margrave, was the star of the evening. Though apolitical, he worshiped Mr. Roosevelt as one of the greatest of our presidents. Otto had made a deep study of the history of the Roosevelt family and told the President stories of one of the buccaneering Roosevelt forebears that the President himself had never heard. He threw back his head with guffaws of delight, saying, "Tell us more, Otto. I love it, I love it, I *love* it." "What are your politics, Paul?" he asked me suddenly. "I've got no proper politics, Mr. President. I believe in production for use." "How many Americans know what that means?" he asked.

Just before we left, it was after eleven and we were in a daze at the intimacy of that evening, the President invited us down to spend Thanksgiving with him at Warm Springs. I had to give him my regrets. He looked up at me from the little wheel chair in which Gus Gennerich was about to take him out. "Please come to see me often, Paul," he said. "I'll not bother you," I said. "I'll ask to come when there's something only *you* can do to help us in public health."

In 1937 The National Foundation for Infantile Paralysis was announced by the President. Mr. Basil O'Connor, the President's former law partner, became president of the new foundation. Mr. O'Connor in my opinion was second only to the President himself in political acumen and sagacity and he turned out to be the greatest raiser of research money for a specific cause that the world has ever known.

With finally adequate sinews of war, the new foundation was to set out to fight the paralytic terror on every front; to finance the discovery of science for its prevention; to broadcast to doctors knowledge of modern treatment that might prevent the horrible deformities visiting those maltreated when they are stricken; to help communities organize themselves to make self-supporting citizens of those wrecked by the paralytic aftermath of the pestilence. It was to be planned, co-ordinated by the best scientific brains in the nation. And when a polio epidemic loomed, the new foundation would instantly pour in money to pay the experts, the community's physicians and healthmen and its nurses to co-ordinate (this had not yet become for me a dirty word) to make a field test of a preventitive (if any) upon all children whose parents might demand it.

Mr. Basil O'Connor asked me to become secretary to the general scientific advisory committee, to choose the chairman of the general committee's special committees—for virology, neu-rology, epidemiology, et cetera. He gave me carte blanche to select them. I pinched myself to see if this was a dream or actually was happening.

"When are you going to find time to write?" asked Rhea, when I plunged up to my neck in committees. It took me a number of years to be saved from ruin as a writer. If you aspire to be a real writer, Ernest Hemingway says you must be equipped with special apparatus to detect what is finally not true and good. As the National Foundation flowered into financial magnificence, it turned out that this was the equipment that I lacked. To my chagrin, in the early 1940's, Dr. Karl F. Meyer, closest of my scientific friends, told me that the Foundation should change its name. Karl said the National Foundation for Infantile Paralysis was privately being called "The Infantile Foundation for National Paralysis."

In the middle 1930's the failure to find anything hopeful against polio was counterbalanced by the progress against other forms of human misfortune. In 1936, Dr. Thomas Parran, who had just been appointed Surgeon General of the U. S. Public Health Service, asked me to help publicize his fight against venereal disease. That year Tom Parran had dared to speak out from his position as generalissimo of the nation's healthmen. In the *Reader's Digest* he wrote what before had been only hinted at in the halls of science. He risked censure because what he sought to fight had been in itself shameful, unmentionable. In his *RD* article he stressed an important fact: that the American people are not stupid if only you do not act as if you so regard them. Parran at last said to millions of readers: LET'S CALL IT SYPHILIS AND LET'S GET RID OF IT.

"How do I go about helping you?" I asked Dr. Parran. "Get hold of Dr. O. C. Wenger of the Public Health Service. Attach yourself to his coattails—and hang on. . . . Wenger has taught me almost everything I know about venereal disease," said Parran.

Wenger was a fighter, but gay and Rabelaisian. Wenger had eyes that were sometimes gray, sometimes china blue; his hair was a stubbly crew cut. He had temperament resembling that of welter-weight prize-fighting champion Ace Hudkins, a willingness to take six punches in order to give one. Wenger had a way of leveling with his VD patients that made them love him. "I've never had syphilis," he kept telling them. "But only because I've been lucky."

For years he had dreamed of devising a syphilis dragnet. In 1921 he had gone to Hot Springs, Arkansas, to make a venereal disease survey that might take him ten days, maybe. He stayed there sixteen years. Here he didn't have to roam around to find the secret sickness. At Hot Springs a parade of victims came to Wenger. Hot Springs was a mecca for sufferers from the sickness of the sinister name. They came in Pullmans, by motor, by blind baggage or hitchhiking. It was only the lowly victims that concerned Wenger. At the Government Free Bath House he took up his station. He quizzed a bedraggled procession of sick people, pilgrims all to the alleged magic of hot water. Here came cripples from all causes, wretches twisted with arthritis, rubbing elbows with the tuberculous and an occasional leper. None could afford a doctor. The ticket of admission to the bath house was the pauper's oath. Here Wenger found syphilis.

Building his own lab benches, with one lab man, one clerk, one nurse, and Miss Charlotte Reamy to help him, Wenger organized a mass production of spotting and treating syphilis that was one of the wonders of the medical world. His dragnet was nothing but the blood test. Though at this time most of the poor people came for hot baths for sickness not venereal, Wenger's blood test found thirty-three out of every hundred to be syphilitic.

Twenty-seven Hot Springs doctors became Wenger's devoted unpaid assistants. To mass-treat his horde of sick ones, he devised a long table. Over it there hung, from a long pipe, a battery of fifty glass cylinders in a gleaming row. From the cylinders through rubber tubing there flowed the clear, yellow, dangerous 606 Salvarsan—into the arm veins of fifty people at one time. So he toiled for seven years, his intensive treatment slowly cutting down the incidence of the disease among Hot Springs paupers. His clinic solidly established, Wenger ranged out from Hot Springs over the South. With money furnished him by the Julius Rosenwald Fund, he got permission to sweep a blood test dragnet over one entire Mississippi county. Of course his test had to be confined to Negroes since it was the tradition that nice white people do not have this sickness!

FREE BLOOD TEST BY GOVERNMENT DOCTORS AND FREE ICE WATER. This sign on Wenger's auto brought the black people in swarms. On Sundays Wenger and his crew marched into Negro churches. In the middle of the service Wenger asked the pastor to step down from his pulpit, had this shepherd of the flock roll up his sleeve as an example. In that county, Wenger found one out of every four colored people infected. This sensational field test dragnet petered out because there was no more Rosenwald money available. And Dr. Thomas Parran, in 1931, then chief of the Venereal Disease Division of the U. S. Public Health Service, had a budget of only $80,000 yearly to fight venereal disease that was costing America annually hundreds of millions of dollars. "What we did in those days," said Wenger, "was like taking a teaspoonful of water out of the Atlantic Ocean and carrying it coast to coast to pour into the Pacific."

It was difficult to daunt O. C. Wenger. Back at Hot Springs he devised an intensive, continuous treatment of syphilis, condensing an ordinary year's treatment into three months. The free hot baths that all the patients took probably made the powerfully poisonous arsenical treatment safer, while this heat very likely enhanced the chemical treatment's power. Deep in his heart and brain Wenger knew that his long VD fight, from a point of view of prevalence nationwide, had accomplished next to nothing.

Burned into my memory is Wenger talking at Hot Springs to a pretty seventeen-year-old girl, who was at the clinic for treatment for her combined syphilis and gonorrhea. He kindly quizzed this bit of human flotsam. To this interrogation Rhea listened with especial attention. The girl had been a waitress in a restaurant in a little Oklahoma city. Total take, including tips, not more than a few dollars a week. Despite her sickness she had a defiant flippancy about her and gave the eye to the orderlies and even the doctors. Wenger turned from this little slipshoe lovy to Rhea. He seemed to forget that the girl was there. "Look at this kid," he said to Rhea. "What chance did life ever give her to be self-supporting and decent? We'll treat her here. We'll cure her. She'll be well fed and have a good clean bed and shelter out at the camp while we're fixing her. Then what'll she do? She'll wrap up her toothbrush and nightie in a bath towel. She's got no money and no place to go. We've cured her. But who's going to make a decent citizen of her? She's well built, pretty, and she's got some brains too. But when she's cured, what'll she do? She'll stick her bath towel under her arm, and hit the highway, to go—"

Suddenly the forlorn subject of Wenger's discourse startled us. She burst out crying. Her tears stopped Wenger's philosophizing and he put his arm around her shoulders while she kept on crying, incontinently. Rhea understood that her tears were not those of self-pity. She'd get along somehow, get men again, get syphilis again maybe. "You awakened her, you stirred her up emotionally," Rhea told Wenger later. There were tears of indignation in Rhea's gray eyes. And this episode stirred her to become a collaborator with Wenger in his quest for a wider VD dragnet. Rhea's fury resulted in Chicago's becoming the first of all American cities to take up Dr. Parran's challenge to smoke out hidden syphilis. This campaign began not in Chicago but in a little city in Arkansas in the foothills of the Ozarks. To this town, June, 1937, Wenger had taken us to a conference he had arranged with health officers, nurses, physicians of the county's medical society, the state health commissioner of Arkansas.

With Wenger urging her, Rhea for the first and only time in her life, spoke up in meeting. "What would happen," Rhea asked, "if all the people of this county were asked, by a referendum, whether they'd be willing to have a free blood test for syphilis taken, *in strict confidence,* by their own family physician?" To this innocent question there came no answer. Except from Wenger. He forgot about the Arkansas backwoods county and hurried us all away from the meeting. Early next morning back in Hot Springs he stormed up and down our hotel room. He said, "Rhea, we'll put your question to the people of Chicago."

Two days later the three of us were in Chicago, Wenger putting his audacious proposal before the city's famous health commissioner, Herman Bundesen. Herman's answer was affirmative, quick, and bold. The referendum, okayed by the U. S. Public Health Service, the Illinois State Department of Health, and the Chicago Board of Health, read: "In strict confidence and at no expense to you, would you like to be given, by your own physician, a blood test for syphilis?"

Howard Hunter, assistant administrator of the Works Progress Administration, transformed a part of the WPA into an emergency VD-fighting army. Hunter set going the machinery to get a million of these ballots printed and produced a force of clerks and statisticians to analyze the returns on this vote submitted to the citizens of Chicago. A hundred thousand replies rolled in. The sentiment expressed was an overwhelming YES—in a proportion of twenty to one of all those voting.

Dr. Reuben L. Kahn, distinguished blood-test scientist, came from Ann Arbor, Michigan, to organize Chicago's laboratories for a giant campaign of blood testing. The Council of the Chicago Medical Society unanimously approved Wenger's project that would turn the city's doctors into public healthmen, drawing the citizens' blood in their offices. Meanwhile airplanes—it was the idea of Dr. Theodore Bauer—flew over the city towing strange banners: HELP CHICAGO TO STAMP OUT SYPHILIS. Physicians were bedeviled by patients telephoning them for blood-test appointments.

Then came what seemed a disaster. In September, 1937, Wenger, who was but fifty-two, seemed to have come to the end of his tether as a front-line VD fighter. Suddenly the heart of this never-tired man grew tired. Rhea and I watched him, gray-faced the day a letter came to him from the Public Health Service in Washington. "What the hell," said Wenger. "They're pulling me out of this. I know I may not have long to go. But I wanted to die with my boots on."

Wenger was supposed to be stricken with a type of heartwreck that gives its sufferers an average of about two years to live, if they live not generously and fiercely like Wenger but by "taking it easy." He went down South—where one might live long despite heartwreck—and organized a case-finding and treatment program among the heavily infected black inhabitants of Glynn County in Brunswick, Georgia, and its adjacent counties. Here among the live oaks with their streamers of Spanish moss and among Negro huts, in little Negro churches, and jungle dance halls, Wenger began the test of a new toy to fight VD. It was a beautiful, mobile VD clinic housed in a big trailer. He called it his "bad-blood wagon." In January, 1938, we went down to Brunswick, Georgia, to see what we could do to help him. One mysterious and hilarious Sunday evening under an enormous live oak in Darien, Georgia, Wenger's crew had parked their bad-blood wagon before an ancient and picturesque Negro church.

Wenger is shouting, like a circus barker: "Free pink lemonade and hot dogs for all who'll take a blood test!" The congregation, from fathers and mothers through swains and dusky damsels all the way down to adolescents and pickaninnies, filed through the trailer, shed their blood for the Kahn test, passed out the other door for hot dogs and pink lemonade. Now at last came the Negro parson. He was bigger than Jack Johnson and clad in a handsome overcoat though the night was balmy. "He should have special consideration," says Wenger. He whispered to Dr. M. E. Winchester, Glynn County health commissioner. "Ask the

Reverend if he'd relish a sip of White Horse Scotch, Windy," said Wenger. The black man of God tossed off an eight-ounce slug of straight Scotch without blinking an eye, gave Wenger and Winchester a courtly bow, and disappeared into the church.

"His sermon should really be something," said Wenger. "I hope he'll put in a plug for our bad-blood wagon." He did. Then we all set out from the house of God to a Negro jukebox dance hall. In its sinister atmosphere Wenger became a Dionysiac master of ceremonies. He solicited nickels from us to keep the jukebox blaring its music. He clapped his hands. He stomped his feet. In the dance hall's back room the blood of the dancers was skillfully drawn by Negro public health nurse Beatrice Johnson, her assistant recording their addresses and names.

Between the dances, couples vanished into the subtropic night and from the bushes came sighs, giggles, and wild cries of delight. "Aren't you causing more VD by your whooping them up with that hot music?" I asked O. C. "Maybe so," he said. But what Wenger really did was to win the devotion of these celebrants. They knew he didn't disapprove of their revelry. "What other outlet does Jim Crow civilization give them?" asked Wenger. In Glynn County that year Wenger and Winchester drove the syphilis rate down to an all-time low.

For all his heroic fight, Wenger's weapons against syphilis had a limitation in those later years of the 1930's. He was not armed with a truly magic bullet. Wenger's Salvarsan and bismuth shots were powerful, but they were dangerous as well as uncomfortable. They only produced spectacular results when they were directed by Wenger's special brand of enthusiasm.

Now in the late 1930's, Providence presided over the discovery of the first death-destroying sulfa. Across the ocean in Germany, France, and England, a few relatively unknown neo-alchemists were rubbing their eyes and only half-believing their discovery of that first sulfa—a first hint of the opening up of a new world of life-guarding chemical science.

In 1935 Dr. Gerhard Domagk, professor in a dye factory, in

the I. G. Farbenindustrie in Elberfeld, Germany, published a report of a momentous mouse experiment. Every streptococcus-infected mouse remained chipper if treated with an orange-colored dye, trade named "Prontosil." All not treated, the control mice, died. Domagk reported that this Prontosil was harmless in test tubes to the hemolytic streptococcus—that malignant microbe reminiscent of a chain of microscopic rattlesnake rattles. Prontosil was harmless to streptococcus when mixed with these bugs in glass dishes. It only walloped the microscopic rattlesnakes when they were already at their deadly deviltry in the bodies of mice and men.

Then in Paris, Mr. and Mrs. J. Tréfouël reported that they didn't need the elaborate, patents-applied-for Prontosil to cure mice of streptococcus infections. They took this Prontosil, broke it down chemically into a compound much simpler, para-amino-benzene sulfonamide—"sulfanilamide" for short. This was an old coal-tar chemical that had been kicking around laboratories for twenty-five years. It had been synthesized as a mere laboratory exercise for his Ph.D. degree by a young man, P. Gelmo, who disappeared into oblivion during World War I. There was then no known use for sulfanilamide and it was not patentable in the 1930's. Did the chemists of the German dye trust surround this sulfanilamide with chemical side-chains to turn it into the orange-colored Prontosil, *patentable,* which could be sold at a profit? Or had they innocently used sulfanilamide as an intermediate in the production of their Prontosil, without being aware of sulfanilamide's streptococcus-killing virtue? To these ethical questions the answers are not clear.

Dr. Perrin H. Long, of the Johns Hopkins University, brought both these marvelous medicines back to America. It was my good fortune that Rhea had known Dr. and Mrs. Perrin Long at the University of Michigan, and in 1936 and 1937 Perry Long began to brief me on the multiple marvels of this first of the sulfas. He told us how the English doctor, G. A. H. Buttle, had reported the sulfa to be powerful not only against streptococcus but meningococcus—cause of epidemic cerebrospinal meningitis. Long incited his colleague, Dr. Francis Schwenkter, to take this new jump from mice to men. Ten out of eleven youngsters dangerously sick with epidemic meningitis got spectacularly better when shot with the sulfa into their spines, and when given pills of it by mouth.

Here were children deadly sick with mastoid infection by streptococcus. The sulfa saved them. It began to make profitable mastoid surgery unnecessary. In a year's time, out of 43 proved cases of streptococcus meningitis of which Perry Long had record, 36 were now alive and healthy. Thanks to these simple sulfa pills swallowed and to sulfa solutions injected into their spinal canals. In the first sulfa days Perry Long had been smiled at as being too enthusiastic. But by 1937 in Europe and America there was no longer question that thousands of lives had been saved by sulfanilamide from childbed fever and other forms of blood-poisoning caused by streptococcus. Yet the final proof of the sulfa's life-guarding power was Long's band of 36 youngsters and grownups who had no right now to be living, but were alive and well.

If sulfanilamide cured meningococcus meningitis, why not try it on this microbe's close cousin, the gonococcus? Dr. Long was a genial kidder and spoofer and he now set about joshing urologists at the Brady Institute at the Johns Hopkins. "You might as well use dishwater as what you're using to try to cure your gon cases. The fact that there are a dozen different irrigations, alleged cures for gon, only goes to prove there aren't any at all." Thus Perry kidded Drs. John E. Dees and J. A. C. Colston, who were veterans in the futility of using any kind of chemical at all to cure gonorrhea. In June, 1937, at the annual meeting of the American Medical Association, Drs. Dees and Colston reported that, in 36 out of 47 people to whom they'd simply fed pills of sulfanilamide—no irrigations, no injections—in these 36, all painful, dangerous, gonorrheal discharge had disappeared within five days. There had been only three relapses and Dees and Colston declared themselves to be "profoundly impressed" with sulfa as a gon cure.

Through the *Ladies' Home Journal* and *Reader's Digest,* with whom I began a relationship that has lasted a quarter of a century, the work I followed was made known to millions of Americans. There were good moments, and there were bad. In 1939 in a story by Mr. J. C. Furnas in the *Ladies' Home Journal* there was a box written by Dr. Thomas Parran of the U. S. Public Health Service. The Furnas story, "That Mothers May Live," told of the remarkable drop in maternal mortality in 1937 and 1938 in our country. Dr. Parran made a statement that made us happy. The Surgeon General described studies made by the New York Academy of Medicine and subsequent reports from many states and cities.

"As a result of these studies, and as a result of the widespread educational effort, in which the *Ladies' Home Journal* through articles by Paul de Kruif played an important part, women and doctors both became conscious of our unnecessary loss of (maternal) life," wrote Dr. Parran. In 1937, the American maternal death rate dropped fourteen per cent under the previous year. In 1938, there was a further decline from the original six, to four per one thousand live births. "This represents the lowest rate yet recorded," said Dr. Parran. The Surgeon General went on to remark that this sensational result was not completely due to the *Ladies' Home Journal* stories. "It is likely that the use of sulfanilamide . . . may have contributed somewhat to this result."

In these exciting years of the late 1930's and the early 1940's, chemists, jumping off from the original sulfanilamide, began to create more powerful and safer chemical sulfa cousins. One of these was sulfathiazole, whose clinical use against gonorrhea was tested by Dr. John F. Mahoney of the U. S. Public Health Service. This story was first popularly published in the June, 1941, issue of *Reader's Digest* and for its truth as well as for its sensationalism I caught unshirted hell from eminent nabobs, as well as alarmed protests from my own friends, Dr. Bundesen and Dr. Wenger in Chicago.

It seemed that what I wrote about sulfathiazole was too, too wonderful. Sulfanilamide, first advocated by Dr. Perrin Long, cured about three-quarters of fresh cases of gonorrhea and an even greater proportion of chronic cases. But the sulfa treatment was rather rough on the latter sufferers. They had to be hospitalized for many days. Really effective doses of sulfanilamide often made them sick. There was danger that the blood of some of them might "turn to water." It was a tossup as to which was worse, chronic gonorrhea or its cure. But sulfathiazole was another matter. Doctor John Mahoney gave gonorrhea patients four tablets of it daily, one after each meal and one at bedtime. Within three days, in very close to nine out of ten cases, their discharges vanished. Mahoney's careful follow-up of his patients over a period of months proved that a cure had been effected within the first five days. As for the few who relapsed, if the treatment was resumed after a few days' interruption, three out of five of these were cured. This brought the score of success up to 95 out of every 100 infected. So little sulfathiazole was needed to produce these cures that its harmful effect was negligible; and the patients could go right on working.

While I was at Wake Robin writing the chronicle of a real dawn of chemotherapeutic medicine, little clouds began to appear upon our happy horizon. For certain physicians, big ones, high echelon, these sulfa stories were too good to be true. The sulfathiazole gon cure disturbed the eminent medical society of the Neisserians. These doctors called themselves thus—euphemistically—because as urologists they were largely concerned with the deviltry caused by the gonococcus, a microbe first discovered by a German gentleman named Albert Ludwig Sigmund Neisser in Breslau. To designate themselves and their society as Neisserian removed from them the stigma of being called "clap doctors," a name given them by raffish laymen.

Soon after the *Reader's Digest*'s announcement of the sulfathiazole cure of gonorrhea, the eminent Neisserian society passed a resolution condemning me for the story. This didn't bother me too much because of my faith in the solidity of the clinical results published by tough, skeptical Dr. John Mahoney. What's more, in their denunciation the Neisserians published no blast against Mahoney's science. They simply blasted De Kruif for his undue enthusiasm and excessive "expansiveness." The latter term had a psychiatric connotation.

Despite this Neisserian indignation, rank and file physicians were becoming authentic clap doctors, curing thousands of cases of gonorrhea with a few pills of sulfathiazole. But what truly disturbed Rhea was a telegram from Dr. Herman N. Bundesen and Dr. O. C. Wenger from Chicago. Before the story's publication in *Reader's Digest*, we had proudly sent them a copy of our manuscript with its wonderful news. We urged them to get going on a project that might begin to wipe out the curse of clap from the city of Chicago. To our dismay we received a joint Bundesen-Wenger wire, beseeching me not to publish the sulfathiazole yarn. Bundesen and Wenger were among my dearest friends and we had always been proud of their faith in what we wrote—no matter how seemingly expansive. This wire sent me deep into the blues but I had watched the positive results of Mahoney's work on Staten Island, and I could not distrust what I saw. I published the story.

The subsequent widespread confirmation of Mahoney's work restored Bundesen and Wenger's confidence in me. Wenger never lost that confidence till the day he died. Yet here was the beginning of a bitter lesson. Again and again I fell on my face, writing what was simple scientific truth. There are certain physicians who distrust good news even when it is true. There are certain other doctors—and a great portion of lay people—who refuse to believe bad news because that news is propaganda backed by enough money.

CHAPTER FOURTEEN

On a noon in December, 1939, I was asked to have lunch alone with the President in the White House. It was a little more than three years from the day in 1936 when he'd been told I'd only ask to see him when and if he alone could help on a health project. Now from the woods in the dunes of Lake Michigan's shore, from Wake Robin, I'd come to him as a courier. Surgeon General Thomas Parran of the Public Health Service had sponsored this meeting that might be momentous. Dr. Parran had the idea that the Dutch in me might click with the Dutch in the President. The Surgeon General had chosen me to put a plan for an expansion of preventive medicine before the President. In my inside coat pocket there was a two-page memo—just the length, so we'd been told, that Mr. Roosevelt would be likely to read through to the end. It outlined an expanded attack against preventable sickness and death. The plan, practical and economical, had been cooked up by Dr. Parran, by Dr. Clifford Caudy Young who'd built Michigan's marvelous health department laboratories out of money he'd saved the state by his health work, and others. A group of politically powerful physicians headed by Dr. L. G. Christian of Lansing, Michigan, believed that the co-operation of organized medicine was certain since the plan contemplated no change in the private practices of medicine. The economics of the plan had been approved by Mr. Marriner Eccles of the Federal Reserve Board.

The politics of the memo had been given the blessing of Mr. Harry L. Hopkins.

The gist of the plan was that it was immensely more costly to maintain needless illness and deaths than it would be to wipe them out. So I came into the President's office loaded for bear. We all felt our project was a natural. Just the same, as Pa Watson led me in, my mouth was dry and my forehead dampish. Here sat the man who could make our dream come true, or break it.

"Good to see you again, Paul," said the President. His head was thrown back in greeting. His close-set eyes were intense and dark-circled. He had changed from the man I'd first met in 1936. Then he had been debonair and looked the picture of bronzed health and showed charming humility, asking us shrewd questions about the fight against polio. Now in 1939 he had mutated from the man I'd known. Quickly I sensed that you didn't tell him, he told you. During the more than two hours that he talked to me, he exaggerated his old mannerism of tossing his head, especially when announcing his decisions.

In a few minutes I felt that the human first citizen of 1936 had become merely top man. It became clear to me that here was a different President Roosevelt. His former preoccupation with jobs and welfare for all Americans had been displaced by his preoccupation with his leadership in a coming battle for our survival in a world in danger. He seemed in training to become the President of the World. It was tough for me to get a word in. It was a soliloquy that I listened to. His dark-circled eyes hinted coming tragedy and flashed power, personified. My memo grew damp in my inside coat pocket.

Throughout his hard-hitting talk, telling me, telling me, telling me, I looked sharp for an opening that must come, soon or late. For a moment, while he was eating in silence, I broached the possibility of increasing our prosperity by beginning to build America over. I told him our group had a sound plan for the public health angle of this enterprise. We hazarded that, under our competitive system, much of the money needed to rebuild America would pay itself off any toll bridge or power dam.

Amortization! For a moment I thought I had him, telling him that we had concrete examples of such practical self-amortizing health projects. By spending a moderate amount of money for personnel and facilities for an attack on TB, VD, et cetera, the savings no longer having to *maintain* all this sickness would build up into a sinking fund. This might pay off the initial public health expenditures within a generation. Amortization. I hit hard with that word. The savings would retire a projected original health bond issue. "We're not talking of pain and misery," I said. "This is *economy*. It's costing us billions to be needlessly sick and to die." That was our group's slogan. "You see, Mr. President," I urged, "it's like Boulder Dam paying off its cost of construction—"

I had said one sentence too much. "Have you seen Coulee Dam, Paul?" he asked. "Yes, this past summer," I answered. "Well, we expect Coulee to start pumping water for irrigation in late 1941," he said. "You know for what? To irrigate the Quincy Plateau. To reclaim the land that's failed in dry-farming. Do you know what *I* want to do with Coulee, late '41, if Congress will let me?"

—Just a moment. Here he was telling me he was going to run for a third term. He was giving me news not known to any reporter, not known to any of his intimates, known to himself only in his unconscious, not known even to Mr. Harry Hopkins, who'd been told he was the Presidential heir apparent—

I steadied myself. I asked him, "What is it you intend to do with Coulee?"

He became animated. "I'm going to take John Steinbeck's Okies, hundreds of thousands of them now in California, and move them up there, and make a green country for them." It was a statesmanlike idea, though the President hadn't consulted the Okies on whether they would want to go to the Coulee.

This gave me a chance to expand the President's vision of rehabilitation. I got ready to pop our memo at him. "The point about our health plan," I said, "is that it wouldn't require more than one hundred million dollars a year." The President cut me short. "Such money is out of the question, right now," he said. "We're going to need all the money Congress will appropriate —for ships, tanks, guns, bombers." He accented each killer word.

Good-by to our health plan. To be sure of the needed billions for death, it would be best not to confuse our solons with a request for a hundred million for life. Despite my disappointment, it thrilled me to be taken into his deep confidence, twice. First, he was going to be a third-term President; second we were going into the war. In his third term he was planning a peaceful project of green land for the Okies. But in that same third term he was fixing to be the commander-in-chief in the coming Armageddon.

If I'd been tough enough right then, I'd have asked him: "Mr. President, are you using these two contradictory prospects to give our health plan the brushoff?" But you didn't talk that tough to the President. At least I didn't dare to.

I didn't even take our health plan memo out of my pocket. When the President saw he had me licked, his gay geniality returned. He began philosophizing about doctors in general; medicine seemed to be a profession which he didn't hold in too high esteem. He expressed himself as definitely on the side of a bold handful of Washington, D.C., doctors who were trying to establish a local, prepaid group health plan. This was being opposed by an A.M.A. group led by my old acquaintance, medicine's powerful Prolocutor. Our medical men are determined not to be run and bureaucratized by the Government. The distribution of medical care is far from perfect, but so is the distribution of houses, clothing, and groceries. There was no evidence that socializing any of these necessities would bring plenty within reach of everybody. On this issue I was on the side of the Prolocutor.

That day I saw what uses power can be put to. What good would it do to us health planners, not wanting socialized medicine, only wanting a modest expansion of preventive medicine, what good would it do us even if Surgeon General Parran did have the solid backing that was unquestionably his in the Congress? Congress wasn't running the country. The strong man sitting across from me was running it. This day I saw the degree to which Mr. Roosevelt was a coming warrior. When he spoke of guns, tanks, and bombers his face was stern, willful, and sure of power. Our pitiful plan for a fight for life, indeed! Now death had priority. He showed me clearly the manner of man you have to be to run the world in time of danger. You have to be heedless of the suffering of millions today to make possible the happiness of millions tomorrow. The President knew what side of science to use to save civilization. Our men of science and industry must produce limitless metal, TNT and future secret weapons.

This was a bad day in my life. The President had taught me to see that there were two kinds of science, which till now as a whole I had tended to worship indiscriminately as the hope of mankind. Dutifully scientists—truth hunters—were multiplying old and concocting new and horrid deaths. Dutifully too other scientists—truth hunters, too—were finding ways for our doctors to palliate the new coming superslaughter. They would staunch blood. They would mend smashed bones. They would anoint seared skin. They would calm crazed brains. Science was really a fantastic race of miracles for life against miracles for death.

What was there left to integrate me then? Tolstoy? Ghandi? Tolstoy had the most wonderful eloquence against war. Ghandi, his disciple, had remarkable personal courage to fight the imperialism that had strangled his feeble people. Religion had failed to make men neighbors. Politics was failing, even the politics of a man as noble and high-minded as our President. Beautiful words had failed.

The early 1940 years presaged the beginning of my death as a salesman of public health, which demands super politics. Yet in those years I felt we were living on the big sprocket, as the airline captains say when they gun their engines.

I was proud of these extracurricular activities, not the least of which was my post as secretary to the General Advisory Committee to the National Foundation for Infantile Paralysis. Alas, the politics in this league also turned out to be a bit too fast for me. In the first years of the 1940's, Dr. George McCoy of the Public Health Service had written to me too kindly, "You hold the scientific affairs of the Foundation in the hollow of your hand." By the end of 1941 I was out as secretary of the National Foundation.

In the autumn of 1940 I'd engineered a really big Foundation grant for the noted nutritionist, Dr. Tom D. Spies, of Birmingham, Alabama, already famous for his discovery of the niacin cure of severe pellagra. This grant did not concern polio, specifically. Its purpose was to cover Tom's researches into a possible relationship between human malnutrition and resistance to infections in general. That same autumn Tom Spies applied for another grant, from the Kellogg Foundation, for money to support an entirely different project, namely, a study of malnutrition in children and its possible effect upon their later lives. It must be stressed that these projects had nothing in common.

Mr. Basil O'Connor, president of the National Fonndation, forwarded a memo to me, written to him by the Foundation's medical director, Dr. Donald Gudakunst. This memo charged that Tom Spies had applied to the Kellogg Foundation for a grant to be used *for the same purpose for which he had already received money from the National Foundation.* "For your comment," wrote Mr. O'Connor on the margin of this memo. Tom and I asked of Mr. O'Connor a chance to clear Tom's name. Mr. O'Connor gave Tom and me this opportunity. I'll never forget how we sat across from this remarkable man in his beautiful office on a snowy afternoon. I said nothing. Tom did the talking. All we wanted was that Medical Director Gudakunst should acknowledge, over his signature, that he had known Tom's application for a grant from the Kellogg Foundation was for research in an entirely different field and of a different nature, other than that for which he had got his grant from the National Foundation for Infantile Paralysis. All Tom wanted was that Mr. O'Connor get him that little letter from Dr. Gudakunst.

Mr. O'Connor seemed to regard us as a pair of blackmailers. I was sitting on the right flank across from the President of the

National Foundation. I said nothing, perplexed at Mr. O'Connor's mounting fury. Suddenly, his visage a reddish-purple, he turned on me in a rage, denouncing me as a troublemaker who was disturbing the Foundation's efforts to conquer polio—or words to that effect. My blood pressure, though highly labile, stayed normal. The next day Dr. Gudakunst brought us a copy of the letter Tom wanted. In the letter the medical director admitted that he had known the real facts when he had written the memo to Mr. O'Connor. It struck us as curious that Dr. Gudakunst did not resign from his position as Medical Director of the National Foundation. As the months went by it appeared that all was not well. An aftermath of rumor grapevined among the B.C.M.'s—BIG COMMITTEE MEN—of the National Foundation. It seemed that Tom Spies had become controversial, disturbing the aplomb with which high scientific matters should be conducted. To certain of Mr. O'Connor's B.C.M.'s, Dr. Spies had become a "troublemaker." Also, Dr. Gudakunst reported that Dr. Rivers had said he did not agree with my high opinion of Dr. Spies as a nutritional scientist.

In the summer of 1941, it came time for Tom Spies to make application for renewal of his first year's grant. Tom's work was supervised by a special nutritional committee of the Foundation, composed of such honest men as Dr. C. Glen King and Dr. R. R. Williams. They had passed upon Tom's work as sound, and realized it would have to be long-term. But now came strange news. Tom's application was turned over by Mr. O'Connor to a committee of Foundation B.C.M.'s. Incidentally none of them had special knowledge of Tom's field of work.

The committee, though it did not turn down Tom's application outright, proposed a drastic cut in Tom's requested appropriation. Tom held out for the full appropriation or none. So it came about that he got no more money at all from the Foundation, and he had to stop his project before it had got well started. Now a little rumor began to flit about—not in writing—to the effect that Tom had not used his first year's grant for the purpose for which it was intended.

I was perplexed by this gang-up on a man of Tom's stature as a clinical investigator. He had discovered the antipellagric power of liver; had saved the lives of dying pellagrins with nicotinamide; had uncovered subclinical pellagra in little children who showed no outward sign of disease; had shown that the psychoneuroses of chemical starvation could be cured by nicotinamide plus thiamin—vitamin B_1; he had demonstrated that demented pellagrins could be rescued even after they'd been committed to custodial institutions for the insane; he had a hint that vitamin deficiencies may make human beings vulnerable to attack by certain microbes. Finally he had made it clear that nutritional failure almost never means hunger for a single vitamin. In short, lacking one vitamin, we almost always lack others. According to Dr. Wilbur G. Malcolm, honest and perceptive director of Lederle Laboratories, Dr. Spies by his deeds was really responsible for putting the beneficent power of multiple vitamins into the hands of physicians.

Late in 1941 I wrote to Mr. O'Connor, giving him my resignation. He accepted my resignation with polite regret, writing that this would be bad for the cause, *and for me.* Those last three words were ominous. I remember vividly a cordial greeting by Dr. Thomas Rivers at the last Foundation committee meeting I attended, just before my resignation. "How's politics, Paul?" Dr. Rivers asked me. I had no answer. His wisecrack was meant as an insult, though not unkindly. I was dimly discerning that "politics"—an honorable word among professional politicians— was becoming a bad word when it had to be applied to researchers and doctors.

Looking back, I'm no longer indignant at this attempt upon Tom Spies's character. Indeed I was unfair to call it "attempted assassination." Boss Kettering was amused at my simplicity in thinking that any true pioneering work should have impartial, unanimous, and immediate recognition. When I told him this story about Tom's troubles, Boss Kettering smiled benignly. "The farther a pioneer in science goes in advance of the pack," said the Boss, "the more he is in danger of attacks upon his character, especially if his work is sound."

According to the Boss, when ordinary men of the pack meet an extraordinary piece of work, they almost invariably react with a reflex of negativity. An ordinary man of the pack is for everything in his own experience and against everything he has not tried. The Boss consoled me. "You and Tom just get down on your knees and thank God for that kind of opposition. It's the best way to sharpen you. Remember, the price of progress is trouble."

It was at this time, also, that I abandoned co-operation with the lefties who had organized a united front against fascism. The distinguished Dutch documentary film director Joris Ivens had come to stay for a few days at Wake Robin. It flattered me that he'd come from Moscow, so he said, as an emissary from Dimitrov. What could the big Bulgarian want of us? Ivens said he wanted me to teach the Soviets our technique of making folks dissatisfied with their needless sickness. Ivens was a remarkable film artist and a nice Dutchman. His Marxism was so didactic that Rhea, pained with it, had left for Freeland to stay with her people, leaving me to deal with Ivens. The big film man unwittingly dampened my leftish interest when I mentioned "the Soviet experiment" in passing. He cut in, saying: "It isn't an experiment, it is axiomatic."

Ivens's dogmatism was a blessing. It ended my interest in the communist worthies, among them Messrs. William Z. Foster, Earl Browder, Bill Browder, and V. J. Jerome, all devoted to their cause. But it's impossible to be a devotee when you're fundamentally an experimenter. The books were closed on my leftist interests when Mr. Stalin got into bed with Mr. Hitler and they proceeded to parcel up Poland.

A tight bond between Rhea and me was to observe and record the blend of ferocity and loveliness of the spring at Wake Robin. March, 1941, according to Rhea's record, opened cold, plenty of ice in the lake; on the 16th we saw the first robins in the snow. On the 17th there was a savage northwest blizzard; on the 19th the balminess permitted lunch on the sun deck in front of the study and we heard the ventriloqual warble of a bluebird. March 21 there was a piercing northwest wind. On the 22nd we were moved by the springtime promise of the song of a meadow lark. On April 1 the little frogs in the back swamp began peeping with their usual punctuality. On April 3 an eagle and great blue herons were soaring over the dunes; and the crocuses in front of the Wake Robin shack were in bloom. On April 13—Easter— the jonquils were yellow flames and hepaticas were blooming modestly around them. Spring had mutated from a late one, to very early, and by April the three-petalled trillium—our beloved wake robins—were like white stars up and down the dunes.

In the peace of Wake Robin I wrote steadily and tried to keep peace with the needs the nation faced in its great and ghastly adventure of war. In 1942, *Reader's Digest* published my story: "Enter Atabrine—Exit Malaria." It really seemed, if we couldn't lick malaria, that the U.S.A. would lose the Pacific war against Japan. Quinine, the then available malaria cure and preventive, had been blocked by the Jap's conquest of quinine sources in the Pacific. Luckily for us, there now loomed a new, safer, abundant, and powerful snythetic antimalarial remedy—Atabrine.

I reported Atabrine as a hope, in the *Reader's Digest,* but the Chairman of the Division of Medical Science of the National Research Council denounced the story as "entirely erroneous." The erroneous Chairman protested that quinine was in every way a safer and more rapidly acting antimalarial drug when compared to Atabrine. The Chairman stated that the *Reader's Digest* was dispensing "misinformation potentially quite dangerous to civilian health and the war effort."

Other eminentoes joined the attack on our Atabrine story and their doubts were broadcast by *Time* magazine. The New York newspaper, *P.M.,* now defunct, dismissed the *RD* story as "sheer nonsense." Despite them, we had basic facts to support our news about Atabrine. Dr. Parran of the Public Health Service showed how there could be no major military operations in the tropics without quinine or synthetic Atabrine and there was no existing available amount of quinine; the Japs had seen to that at the very beginning of the Pacific war. All through the attempt to murder the *Reader's Digest* story, the magazine's founder and editor, DeWitt Wallace, remained imperturbable. He asked us to make him an exhaustive report on the power, safety, and availability of Atabrine. "We already had that before we wrote the story, Wally," I told him as we laid a mass of notes before him.

The yellow pills of Atabrine had been synthesized in Germany back in 1932. Fifteen of the little Atabrine pills had been proved to cure the great majority of malaria victims in five days. Atabrine brought many victims of the especially fatal form of aestivo-autumnal malaria back from the grave. Thanks to Dr. Parran's foresight, before the war began the Winthrop Chemical Company, with the help of Merck, began pouring out the powerful little yellow pills at a rate of more than five hundred million a year. The pills were cheap. They could cure the average case of malaria for a little over six cents a head.

Nearly one thousand scientific reports, prewar, had testified that Atabrine was not only a safer but a more potent cure and a more practical preventive than the old remedy, quinine. With cool effrontery, the Chairman on Atabrine of the National Research Council pronounced that Atabrine was unproved. That might have killed the little yellow hope. For a period in the summer of 1942, the U. S. Army, panicky, suspended its purchases of Atabrine. There were demands that the scientific work on Atabrine's safety and effectiveness should be done over, and it was, at a serious waste of Government money. It proved that Atabrine was indeed worthy.

Luckily, the Army had got enough Atabrine out to the South Pacific before this ruckus, so that subordinate army men could test its effectiveness during the fighting on Guadalcanal. At first, many soldiers scorned the little yellow pills. Then the men who refused their daily Atabrine ration began to find themselves chattering with chills, frying with fever, and collapsing in their foxholes.

There was a misunderstanding. It was rumored that Atabrine was not a cure but a mere suppressive of malaria. Some G.I.'s (God knows who told them) took this to mean that it might impair their sexual vigor. To squelch this rumor Lieutenant Commander J. J. Sapero reported that the officers of our armed forces had not seen this, or any type of serious reaction to Atabrine. Now the New Guinea camps put up big billboards that displayed a jolly Sultan nibbling at an Atabrine pill and smiling at a toothsome girl while remarking: "Atabrine keeps me going." The boys believed the billboards. By the summer of 1944, army medical men reported that Atabrine had cut down malaria in New Guinea by ninety-five per cent in fifteen months.

Dr. Norman T. Kirk, surgeon general of the U. S. Army, reported officially: "Acquisition of knowledge of how to produce an effective substitute for quinine—namely Atabrine—has been the greatest single contribution to the war effort."

In these mid-1940 years, I found out how straight-shooting is the one weapon against crooked medicine; and how one magnificent medical discovery nearly went into the ash can because of medical bureaucrats in the Government. It is now unquestioned and historic that Dr. Leo Loewe of Brooklyn made a discovery that transformed nearly one hundred per cent fatal subacute bacterial endocarditis into a disease that was potentially curable.

What, in 1944, nearly happened to Leo's discovery? Every dose of the then still scarce but essential penicillin was under control of the federal Office of Research and Development—the OSRD. The big medical wheels of the OSRD had tried out penicillin against murderous endocarditis. They tested an arbitrary dose of it, 40,000 units daily; they did not know whether the dose was large or small. It sounded big with its digit plus four zeros. All victims, so treated, died. From the OSRD the word was broadcast—since penicillin is ineffective, there will be none available for subacute bacterial endocarditis.

Leo, the Brooklyn boy, had his own ideas. Giving patients 250,000 to many million units of penicillin daily by continuous intravenous drip, Loewe began by dragging twenty-five endocarditis victims—all doomed to die—back to life. Mr. John L. Smith, penicillin production genius at the Charles L. Pfizer Company, bootlegged for free all penicillin Leo needed in his seemingly wild experiment. The federal OSRD threatened Government proceedings against Jack Smith for his crime of disobedience that had saved those lives.

At this moment we were getting ready to write about Leo's discovery for the *Reader's Digest*. Suddenly we were warned by an emissary from the Government that Dr. Loewe "was at least potentially dishonest." But the *Digest* editors, trusting us, bet their blue chips on Leo and Jack Smith and published our story and in a few months Leo had cured so many incurable endocarditis victims that it would have caused a real stink if the OSRD hadn't released penicillin for subacute bacterial endocarditis. So they released it.

In the beginning of his battle against subacute bacterial endocarditis in 1940, Loewe had no penicillin, but only sulfadiazine. Leowe had begun his adventure with the aid of a chemical, heparin, so named from its having been first found in the liver. Heparin slowed up the clotting time of shed blood, and if he got just the right amounts of heparin into these sick people, maybe it would keep clots from forming in damaged blood vessels.

Heparin should really have discouraged Leo. It had to be obtained in finicky small yields from vast amounts of animal tissue and that made it fantastically expensive. Also, it was a two-edged sword. Certain doses did slow down the clotting time of blood; but just a bit more heparin could cause fatal hemorrhages. What exasperated Loewe was that he had to keep injecting it again and again to build up effective levels of it in the blood of his infected animals. It meant that Loewe and his colleagues had to keep going back to the laboratory at all hours of the night, to keep up the heparin levels.

Now Loewe happened on a hope—Dr. Ralph D. Shaner, a tall, swarthy Hoosier of Spanish descent, the medical director of the pharmaceutical firm of Roche-Organon, Nutley, New Jersey, makers of heparin. Wasn't there some way to prolong heparin's action so that he wouldn't have to make so many injections, particularly in the middle of the night? Loewe asked Shaner.

Certainly there was a way to prolong heparin action—mix it with Pitkin's Menstruum. Then Shaner told Loewe of one of his own special discoveries—the strange Dr. George Philo Pitkin, a surgeon and a stock-operating millionaire of Bergenfield, New Jersey, and an obscure authority on spinal anesthesia. After hours of Pitkin's almost unintelligible mumbling, it appeared that Roche-Organon might produce his Menstruum—patents applied for— composed of gelatin, glacial acetic acid, glucose, and water —according to Pitkin's cook-stove science.

Shaner tolerated Pitkin's eccentricities because his Menstruum greatly prolonged the pain-killing action of morphine. For morphine it really worked. Pitkin alleged—though without proof— that his Menstruum would retard the absorption and prolong the action of *any* water-soluble drug when the mixture was injected under the skin of human beings.

Heparin was water soluble. "Loewe and I were elated," said Shaner. This joy might have been premature, based as it was only on Shaner's belief in old Pitkin. So now our two optimists tried it and it worked wonderfully—just one shot of heparin/Pitkin was enough to build up levels safe and effective in the blood of a rabbit for as long as two to three days. Yet Loewe had no real cure for S.B.E. in rabbits when he tried heparin/Pitkin combined with sulfadiazine. All he could say was that when his rabbits died and he autopsied them, heparinized, the blood clots did seem less on their heart valves.

On this wisp of hope, Loewe tried heparin/Pitkin plus sulfadiazine on human beings doomed with S.B.E. Shaner, pleading with Roche-Organon technical men, got large batches of heparin/Pitkin (fabulously expensive) for free for Loewe. In the early summer of 1943, Loewe reckoned up its effect, with sulfadiazine, on his first seventeen human cases. Two of them had remained alive. "If we only had a better curative agent than sulfadiazine," said Loewe, always hoping.

To his help in the steamy Brooklyn summer of 1943 came

another collaborator, bearing the plain name of John L. Smith. He was executive vice president of the Charles Pfizer Company and together with his technical men he was trying to industrialize the still rare common mold, *Penicillium notatum.* Their prospects seemed dim. Jack Smith and his men were fumbling to cajole penicillium into pouring out a flood of golden penicillin, fermenting the mold in enormous vats. They were dreaming up deep fermentation of penicillin in 15,000-gallon vats, but, alas, the mold seemed to prefer to make its penicillin in thin layers on the surface of the soups that nourished it. The slightest invasion of air-borne contaminants stymied the timid mold's penicillin production when they tried to run it in big vats. In June, 1943, Loewe went to Jack Smith and begged that smallish, poker-faced Pfizer executive for some of his scanty penicillin to save the life of a doctor's little daughter who was dying from subacute bacterial endocarditis.

Loewe could hardly have come to Jack Smith at a worse moment. Pfizer was turning out pitiful smidgins of penicillin by surface fermentation. Jack Smith was a business tycoon with a rigid, exacting exterior, so Loewe then described him. Jack Smith coldly told Leo that medical authorities, under directives from the Government's National Research Council, were right then getting ready to report that penicillin, for all its magic, was disappointing when tried against subacute bacterial endocarditis.

Jack Smith's discouraging news did not budge Loewe. Look, this little girl was going to *die,* didn't Mr. Smith understand? "I'll come to see the patient," said Jack Smith, finally. Maybe Jack was moved by Leo's dogged effort to save this one little girl? Maybe this made Jack remember his own child, who had long ago died for lack of life-saving science? Whatever the reason, it seemed there was sentiment beneath his "rigid, exacting exterior of a business tycoon." He relented and, against Government orders, slipped penicillin to Loewe and this was in June, 1943.

By July 23 all traces of the little girl's apparently absolutely fatal infection had vanished. Her chart at Brooklyn Jewish Hospital was marked "Discharged for further observation at home."

From here on Jack Smith was more than Loewe's benefactor; he was his collaborator. Jack Smith told Loewe, who began to take steps beyond Government prohibitions, that "Your first departure from the orthodox and the official, that's the real beginning of any discovery."

Within a week after that little girl had gone home, Leo Loewe stood by the bed of a woman for whose life he had been fighting since May with heparin/Pitkin, plus many courses of giant doses of sulfadiazine, plus urea, plus vitamin C—complete lack of response. She was in the clutches of the invincible assassin, the streptococcus viridans, the green microbe of seeming low virulence that nevertheless gnawed at her heart and swarmed in her blood. Leo explained the special tragedy of the dying woman to Jack Smith. All the failures of the National Research Council's doctors had been made on a dosage schedule of 40,000 units of penicillin daily. Loewe asked Jack Smith, "*Why* did they stop with 40,000 units? That might sound big. It was really next to nothing. It meant only a wee bit of penicillin actually. Only 24 milligrams per dose, hardly a thousandth of an ounce." Why not shoot it into dying people, ad lib? An unorthodox hundred thousand units of penicillin daily cured the woman. It was in this very week that Jack Smith let Leo run wild with his big new doses of penicillin, starting treatment of two more close-to-dead S.B.E. victims toward the end of August.

If penicillin is not only harmless but curative in 100,000 daily units (as it had shown itself for that woman) and since another patient was now downhill on that dose and on the road to death, why not *two* hundred thousand units daily? And that day, August 27, on this big new dose the man began to live.

The next day, August 28, should remain forever a guffaw in medical annals. The *Journal of the American Medical Association* published the solemn report by the National Research Council as follows: On seventeen cases of S.B.E. treated with standard government doses of 40,000 units of penicillin, four were dead, ten had shown no appreciable improvement and bid fair to die;

and of three who at first had seemed to get a bit better, two re-lapsed soon after treatment was discontinued and were on the way to the mortician. In view of these disappointing results, the National Research Council, now our country's dictator in the use of all penicillin, announced that it had decided to terminate the S.B.E.-penicillin death fight for this reason. In short, on August 28, S.B.E. was declared out of bounds for treatment with penicillin.

On the day of the publication of the National Research Council's official thumbs down, a fifty-two-year-old woman was carried in coma into Brooklyn Jewish Hospital, dying. She had been given the last rites at another hospital and discharged, probably so that her death would not count in the hospital's mortality statistics. She was paralyzed by clots detaching from her heart valves and swirling through her blood to block vessels in her brain. She was blind from blood clots, embolisms lodging in her eyes, and the admitting physician marked her moribund.

That momentous day of the government edict against further use of penicillin for S.B.E., Leo Loewe and his men began to give this woman massive penicillin treatment plus heparin/Pitkin. The next day the woman was sitting up in bed, clear-headed, and talked rationally with Jack Smith, thanking him for the penicillin. A few weeks later she was back at her secretarial job, thanking them all at the office for helping her financially after her insurance had run out.

Then, still later, back at the Jewish Hospital for a checkup, she felt grand and proud to be one of the exhibits who might convince high Government authorities that Leo was now actually curing incurable S.B.E. She heard it said that while penicillin might be a remarkable drug, it couldn't raise people from the dead. "But *I* was," said the lady proudly. "I sat up in my coffin and I was resurrected!"

At this moment, by now, seven successive victims of S.B.E. seemed to be going to live though they had no right to. At this moment—I will never understand why—Jack Smith was informed by the National Research Council that he was to allot no more penicillin specifically to Leo Loewe.

In late October, 1943, Loewe had the honor of a visit from the National Research Council's arbiter of who gets penicillin, for what, and who does not. He examined all ex-victims, including the witty lady who said that Dr. Leo's medicine had made her sit up in her coffin. Smith and Loewe humbly told the investigator that they would suspend further investigations pending restudy of the S.B.E. problem by the National Research Council Committee. They all but begged the Councilman's pardon for saving these lives.

In December, the desperate husband of a forty-three-year-old woman who was fatally sick with S.B.E. broke Leo down—to the degree that he once more appealed to Jack Smith. Hadn't Smith stipulated he'd release penicillin for patients still under treatment? Granted, said Jack, but this one had not been under treatment by Leo Loewe. Yes, but, by God, protested Leo, she'd been under treatment with penicillin by another doctor; and she'd *almost* got better, again and again. Her blood had been temporarily sterilized of the evil green streptococcus, time and again! "Okay, Leo, you can have it," said Jack Smith; so the two of them now broke their promise to the National Research Council Committee man.

After twenty-one days of continuous treatment, her blood was completely clear of green streptococcus, and soon after she went home, cured. Her case was historic as the first one who would almost surely have died with moderate doses of penicillin alone. But she'd been cured by *massive* penicillin plus heparin/Pitkin.

For the Council penicillin man, this insubordination of Jack Smith's was a bit too much. He called a special meeting of his committee to discuss bringing up John L. Smith, executive vice president of the Pfizer Company, on charges. It is reported that this committee meeting was stormy. Jack Smith's allocating penicillin in defiance of Government regulations? It was reprehensible! But Jack Smith's helping to save a human life by *breaking* Government regulations, mightn't that conduct, when discovered, make banner headlines on newspaper front pages? So the committee at last considered it the better part of discretion *not* to bring Jack up on charges. After the meeting, one of Jack Smith's friends on the committee phoned him, warning him that, beginning on a definite date, he'd have to refrain from giving Leo Loewe any more penicillin at all. Jack promised.

That night Jack Smith phoned Loewe. How many S.B.E. patients did he have under treatment? For these, what would be his presumptive penicillin requirements? Would he please come over to Pfizer and pick up that much penicillin, personally, before Jack Smith's promise to the committee became effective? It was bootlegging to save life. It had a smack of the black market without profits, excepting life. It was like Loewe sneaking around to the back door of the Pfizer fermentation plant to draw off an illicit canful of penicillin in the dark of the moon.

These events of the summer, autumn, and winter of 1943 were epochal in the history of penicillin. Jack Smith made his rounds with Leo at the bedsides of those who were being rescued. As one after another came back from what before would have been a one-way trip across the River Styx, Jack went back with the news to the penicillin plant at Pfizer. "You boys have saved another life," he'd tell the engineers, fermentation men, mycologists, bacteriologists, organic chemists, mechanics, and floor sweepers at Pfizer.

Jack made them feel a bit beyond human. Deep, 15,000-gallon-vat fermentation, impracticable? Who said so? Now Jack Smith's boys teamed up to make a miracle of Paul Bunyan bacteriology on a 15,000-gallon scale. They kept the huge vats free from the faintest trace of bacterial contamination. Penicillin production zoomed from milligrams, to ounces, to pounds of the golden mercy.

Early in 1944, having officially restudied Loewe's first eight cured cases, the National Research Council reopened the project of penicillin treatment of subacute bacterial endocarditis—this time with Loewe's recommended doses. Jack Smith had a mild streak of irony. He comforted Leo for the way the Government penicillin men had abused him; at the same time he dished out praise to the Government committee. "The committee should be given credit for its negative results," said Jack. "Those people who died after the committee's little inadequate doses—those negative results were really a challenge to the bold investigator."

CHAPTER FIFTEEN

Rhea needed to be less and less my tamer now. It was 1945 and my age and shattering events combined to tame me. And my friend, Ralph Shaner, a Hoosier of Spanish blood, shook my faith in the so-called religion of science. "Science," said Shaner, "is a mixture of good and bad. And bad, evil? So many of us think it the mere absence of good. *I* believe evil is a positive force; and it may triumph over God and mankind."

I had to ask myself now what I thought of scientists, who in 1946 were trying to mitigate the murder at Hiroshima with promises of future good that may be hiding in their atom. Yet for the atom men other scientists had a grudging admiration. To bring their bomb about, hadn't they pulled off the most exquisitely interdigitated collaboration in human history? Talk about teamwork, talk about discipline, talk about the discretion that for years had kept the developing murder a secret from the entire mass of mankind. "Aren't our A-bomb wizards the portent of a new, scientific, Satanic brotherhood?" asked Ralph.

What got me down during this autumn of 1945 was a vision of the possible ghastly dawn of a new human era. The new science for death might defeat all science for life. The A-bomb explosions were a salute to a horrid morning.

It was a bad day when my old friend Henry Mencken taunted me. Mencken was proud when he said he had been born with no more public spirit than a cat. He pointed out to me that my own public spirit had got the hunt for truth and the fight for life mixed up together. "I hope you insert something about the atomic bomb in your book," said Mencken, who had always been worried about me as a do-gooder. "The atom bomb is, I believe, the greatest of American inventions, the greatest glory of Christianity since the hanging of Martin Luther." He added, "Please don't forget to say that our noble patriots, in their development of the bomb, have also devised an entirely new disease—galloping cancer."

But Mencken wasn't completely fair. Certain men of science did seem aghast at the explosions they'd set off over Hiroshima and Nagasaki. Professor Einstein, who'd used his great name to convince our late President about the need of launching the two-billion-dollar gamble that resulted in these stupid tragedies, was shocked and dismayed at the consequences. Einstein now urged the collection of more money to start an organization that might prevent the atom bomb from doing all of us in. Men of science seemed like so many clever monkeys in their confection of con-tradictions.

A trustee of the University of Chicago told a sorry tale of an obscure happening on the day of the sensational news from Hiro-shima. That afternoon, two eminent developers of atomic fission, taking a constitutional with their ladies, met on the university campus. In despond, the bomb instigators looked at each other. Then they sat down side-by-side on the curb in the quiet street. They had no words. They began to weep, like children.

It was a sunny day, exceptionally warm, in April, 1948, at Wake Robin. The ice floes had melted out of the lake so we could hear the surf again after the long silence of winter. There was a soft clear sky above the budding black oaks and maples and a haunting warble of bluebirds migrating north for nesting.

From far away on the lake we could hear the ventriloqual honking of Canada geese, resting on their way north for mating. It was one of those mysterious days. Dr. Sidney Garfield, Dr. Edna Schrick, Rhea, and I sat all day outside in the dream around our hexagonal table. Its legs were the stumps of a clump of cherry trees that Rhea and I had cut down years ago when we were young, clearing the woods on the lake shore so we could begin to build the shack that had grown into Wake Robin. And now we were how much older?

What Rhea and I remembered best about that day was the fiery eloquence of Dr. Edna. She was a small-town doctor from near-by Holland, Michigan. She was groping to give her dream to Dr. Sid Garfield from California—who was on the way to fame as the discoverer of how to bring modern medical care to ordinary people at a price that they could pay.

Dr. Edna, who ran her own individual little cure store—a private practice—was an admirer of Sid's group prepaid medicine, but she had something new to add to it. Both Edna and Sid were young, clean-cut, tough, with no malarkey and with the mark of competence stamped on them. You had to listen to them. Edna began really telling us. She had been thoroughly schooled in the speciality of pediatrics. She had wanted to make a career of building a new kind of child—superchildren. But she had been forced by a lack of group organization in medical practice to spend the bulk of her time as a plain family doctor. While the doctors of her city of 18,000 admired Edna highly, it seemed that there were not enough little patients around to support a full-time pediatrician.

She was trying to make the best of that disappointment. She was a blend of modern specialist and old-fashioned doctor—you don't find too many of them. She didn't mind at all making house calls. She was locally esteemed for coming out to her patients any time of the day or the night no matter the snow or the freezing rain. Edna had a tremendous practice and was working over capacity and got up every morning tired.

"What we docs ought to do is to teach people how to keep

away from the doctors," said Edna. Sid Garfield looked at her puzzled and a bit suspicious. I was stirred to hear family-doctor Edna leap out ahead of Sid Garfield, who directed a prepaid group medical care project of more than 100,000 people on the West Coast. "Of course I'm for your prepayment plan," she said to Sid. "It brings your patients to you early. It makes curative medicine a vanishing economy. But how much do you do to keep patients away from you altogether?"

"Is most of what we doctors do so difficult, so remarkable?" asked Edna. "Most of it could be done by any loving mother." She seemed to Rhea and to me to be a new kind of medical animal, a hybrid, a cross between a front-line family doctor and a healthman. She was teaching mothers to be assistant doctors so that they could do a lot of what's supposed to be pediatrician's work on youngsters up to adolescence. She was a strange type of medical professor; her medical college was only her crowded office; and most of the students, the mothers, hadn't gone beyond high school.

Her textbooks? There was Herman Bundesen's famous book *Our Babies*. And she urged all mothers filling her office with their bawling babies to get Dr. Spock's *Baby and Child Care* in its Pocket Book edition. If a mother couldn't afford it, Edna bought the book for her. "They tell me it's their *Bible*," said Edna. "It keeps many calls away from my office."

By the books and by personal talks Edna was beginning to turn mothers into medical assistants. They learned to modify the feeding of their youngsters as they grew older. They learned to spot signs of rickets that might mean bad bone structure and broken-down feet. They used vitamins to speed lagging growth and to boost antimicrobic resistance. They punctually brought their children for all preventive inoculations. They became psychologists to conquer fears and to teach sex mysteries openly to guard their kids against becoming problem children or juvenile delinquents.

Edna was gallant and she was tired. Look what she'd be free to do if all mothers were part-time doctors for their own youngsters. Then Edna could concentrate on the truly tough ones, on rheumatic heart disease, by preventing the respiratory troubles that triggered it. By practicing psychotherapy on early mental quirks that might be danger signals of schizophrenia. By drawing blood for chemical tests that might detect prediabetics. By finding out with chemistry and X-rays whether a high blood pressure was perilous. By drawing blood for liver function tests that might predict a later fatal breakdown in the brain or kidneys or the heart.

Almost forty years before, I'd listened to late great Dr. Victor C. Vaughan, Dean of the University of Michigan Medical School, pronounce that medicine was unique among all professions because it worked to destroy the reason for its own existence. Now at last I'd seen a plain practicing doctor trying to put Dean Vaughan's words into all-out action. Not long after that Dr. Edna Schrick joined Dr. Garfield's staff at the Permanente Hospital in Oakland, California.

In the early 1940's, led notably by doctors in California and Michigan, the medical profession was stirring, they actually offered citizens voluntary prepaid health insurance. They found it really rough economic going. Michigan physicians in the beginning went half a million dollars in the red. But now at the end of the 1940's, 2,600,000 citizens were budgeting for health in the Michigan Medical and Hospital Services. By the late 1940's, more than eighty million Americans were already covered by one or another type of voluntary prepaid health service. It was this popular wave that drove Mr. Truman's medical regimenters back into their holes after they'd tried to make medical robots of all of us—doctors and patients alike—by government medicine. Even then the medical powerhouse had not lost its kilowatts, so it seemed.

No wonder Dr. Fernald Foster, Secretary of the Michigan State Medical Society, asked me a troubled question. "Paul, why don't you tell us why doctors *individually* are pretty much 140,-000 tin gods to their patients—and at the same time are regarded by the Government as 140,000 connivers as a national organization?"

Presently, along with certain loyal medical friends, Fern Foster induced Michigan doctors to perpetrate an act of honesty. A conference was called, consisting of presidents of various state medical societies. The upshot? In June, 1949, the A.M.A. was deprived of its dispenser of political kilowatts. Upon the Prolocutor, Dr. Elmer Henderson of Louisville and Dr. John Cline of San Francisco led in the swinging of the ax. "You can't fire me," protested the Prolocutor, "I have an international reputation." "You're fired, just the same," said Elmer.

The realization of a great change to a north wind of honesty first hit me when two of the A.M.A. brass asked to come to see me at the Hotel Drake in Chicago. Dr. Elmer L. Henderson was then president-elect of the A.M.A. He came from the Abe Lincoln country in northern Kentucky where the soil must grow honest men. Dr. George Lull was the general manager of the A.M.A. He had convinced Elmer and the other trustees that he was a straight-shooter. When they came in my door Elmer introduced himself and George. "De Kreef," he said, "you'll find we're straight-shooters." The look in his eyes told me he didn't mean maybe.

Not long after, when we'd got to know each other, I asked Elmer a question: "What's really wrong with medicine?" "Not your Prolocutor. It's mainly one thing—professional jealousy," said Elmer.

"The Michigan State Medical Society wants me to do their 1952 Biddle Lecture. I'm supposed to tell them how we can have better medicine," I told Elmer. "You think I ought to?" He did.

So in 1952 I found myself on a big platform in a big room, before more than a thousand doctors and their friends. I praised the doctors for organizing the Michigan Foundation for Medical and Health Education. One of its aims was to search out and end medical negativity. Negativity? "It was an instinct"—and I quoted Boss Kettering—that meant "We didn't discover it so it can't be so." That was one of the roots of professional jealousy.

I grew bold and told my audience that this negativity lurks wherever there is that powerhouse—medical authority. Then I grew bolder and told how such an authority was trying right now to discredit science which, if adequately applied, might possibly check fatty degeneration of the arteries—atherosclerosis—a champ killer in mid-life and after. It was beginning to be surmised that excessively fatty livers may be at the bottom of this degeneration of the arteries.

It had been known for some time that the bodies of animals contained lipotropic—fat-moving—chemicals. Among these were the B vitamins, choline and inositol, and the amino acid, methionine. These were known to remove dangerous fat from the livers of dogs. Then too, my friends, Dr. Henry A. Rafsky of New York City, had seen the beneficial effects of injections of crude liver and a combination consisting of high animal protein and high vitamins plus the chemical, Methischol—lipotropic—on cirrhosis of the *human* liver.

The grave audience chuckled when I said this talk, tonight, could not have been given if Dr. Rafsky hadn't used this combination to chase the fat out of my own highly cirrhotic liver. I had no right to be alive. Or were they chuckling because I was a series of one case? I kept my brashness and told them it was Dr. Rafsky's hunch that we're really as old as our liver—not our arteries—and I was merely Exhibit A, an illustration of Henry's hope of reversing atherosclerosis, dangerous to liver, heart, and brain. Debatable. But not disproved.

What then was my dismay when my son, Dr. Hendrik de Kruif, not long after told me of a remark made by a high scientific authority at a round table conference at a recent A.M.A. meeting. "I trust nobody here is so bold," said this authority, "as to admit that he prescribes lipotropic substances to control atherosclerosis." Said Hendrik: "He kicked lipotropics out the window, just like that. Giving no evidence."

Envy may operate at the highest medical levels. In 1951, the great surgical investigator, Dr. Charles Huggins of the University of Chicago, was given a rising ovation at the end of the Ramon Guiteras lecture before the American Urological Association in

Atlantic City. Huggins had told them how his new operation, total adrenalectomy, had eased the pain, returned the strength, and was prolonging the lives of some—but by no means all—patients on whom he'd performed it.

These were victims of otherwise far-advanced inoperable cancers that had started in the breast or prostate. He made no claims of cure. He stressed it that this desperate operation was merely a last thing to try when all else had failed. This bold surgery had excited his audience, for how were any of these people to go on living at all—with no adrenals?

This chemical miracle shook the listeners. Deprived of their adrenal glands, certain of Huggins's patients went on living and felt fine—just by taking 50 milligrams of the adrenal hormone, cortisone, by mouth. Two little 25-milligram pills, twice daily. Huggins showed a movie of what should have been a dead or a moribund man, without adrenals, now back at work as a boiler-maker; and another movie of a cancerous lady who had been given up for dead, now looking lovely, working in her garden. He told of other cases where the adrenalectomy had failed. Yet the operation was technically safe in the hands of competent surgeons and hormone men.

Huggins admitted that the operation was only a last-ditch hope for some hopeless. He set me to wondering. What alert family doctor who'd really studied this work would turn down its slim chance for a dying patient? And how many poor wretches who were far gone with far advanced prostate or breast cancers and cachectic and in pain—wouldn't risk this new adrenalectomy?

This conservative little story had no sooner appeared in the A.M.A.'s *Today's Health* and in the *Reader's Digest* when there came a blast. From a man so high in authority that he was nick-named "Mr. Cancer," a Mount Everest of cancer science, the late Dr. C. P. Rhoads at the Sloan-Kettering Institute in New York. His blast was to the effect that Huggins was a fake and Rhoads wouldn't send a sick dog to Huggins. I pondered why such authorities do not themselves find remedies for ills over which they are authoritarian.

In one medical field there has been a sensational saving of life by doctors who have rid themselves of such childish paranoia. Chicago's doctors had pioneered it, by calling in, routinely, obstetric consultation they themselves believed was for cases of childbirth too tough for their own skill. They had put these particular fights for life ahead of their own personal vanity. And they've beaten maternal and newborn deaths down to an all-time low in Chicago.

The leaders of this battle were a queerly assorted pair and could not be called comrades at all. Dr. Joseph B. De Lee did not mind that his fight for life made many doctors detest him. He was tall and dark-eyed and aristocratically Jewish. His cofighter, Dr. Herman N. Bundesen, looked like Jimmy Cagney and was Chicago's health commissioner and the bulldozer of all the city's practicing physicians in De Lee's fight for infant and maternal life.

Bundesen—unlike Dr. Lee—had no profound technical knowledge. Bundesen had the simplest measure for better medicine. "My yardstick is simply cutting down those death rates," he proclaimed. And he had a prescription against professional jealousy, all of it, his own included. It took the form of a simple watchword: "You can get *anything* done, if you don't care who gets the credit for it." Consultations, when you're stuck with a tough case? "Goddamnit, they're a human right, just as in the law it's the right of all of us to courts of appeal," said Herman.

Bundesen worshiped De Lee and De Lee thought that Bundesen was foolish when he ran for Governor of Illinois. "If he wins, who'll be our health commissioner?"

Another new selfless teamwork by doctors has spread statewide in California. Its medical association, the C.M.A., has transformed the most precious of all medicines—human blood—from deadly scarcity to routine availability—for all who need it—whose lives may be saved by it. California's doctors have formed a blood brotherhood with citizens. It's a state-wide chain of community blood banks sponsored by the C.M.A.

If you ask a doctor, who's dying for lack of blood in your state? he can look you in the eye and say—*nobody*.

All through the talk I kept thinking of physicians as plain docs, the opposite of the cliché portrait of the gentle and dignified physician with the medical beard at the bedside of the dying child. Few docs any longer have beards and, these days, far fewer children die. At the same time you can flatter doctors when you think of them as medicine's white hopes. Even so they are in danger from their own miracles.

Now, when a patient has chest pains, coughs, and is feverish, it's easy for doctors to say: "No need to take him to the hospital, it's only pneumonia." Yet, a few years ago, that ill was nicknamed the captain of the men of death. Today, thank God for the antibiotics. But here's the danger: it's convenient for physicians not to have to take a patient's sputum to a laboratory for the verdict the little white mice can give in regard to a type of pneumonia. Why not give the patient a big shot of penicillin, or so many capsules of an all-purpose antibiotic? Here's the trouble. Such slapdash diagnosis might miss something more sinister—early lung cancer.

Medicine hasn't simplified itself into a quick shot in a patient's behind. Yet it's astounding what a doctor can now do in his office or in a patient's home. But how does a general practitioner know on what patient to try the hormones, cortisone or A.C.T.H.? There are ivory-tower doctors who seem to be more interested in how dangerous the hormones are, than in explaining how to use which of them to drag what people out of needless misery or keep them from dying.

Early in the hormone excitement in the first of the 1950's, Dr. Tom Spies at a conference in Birmingham, Alabama, showed a parade of fifty resurrected people to an audience of almost five hundred visiting doctors. The patients had all been so ill with disorders—from deadly lupus erythematosus to severe rheumatoid arthritis—that they'd lost their livelihoods. He had given them all cortisone or A.C.T.H.

He gave them short courses of these hormones at intervals. None stayed in hospital. All were treated at the clinic. Dr. Spies did not claim they were cured, but they were virtually free from pain and all of them were working and self-supporting. Rehabilitated. Remember, Tom Spies had the peculiar diagnostic savvy to know on whom to try the remedies.

Dr. John W. Cline, when he was president of the A.M.A., had warned our medical society about the prevalence of what he called "medical chiselers." "About five per cent of congenital medical chislers"—he meant dishonest and incompetent doctors—"constantly embarrass the decent ninety-five per cent of ethical physicians."

This is medical honesty at its top and its practice is all too rare. It's the antichiseling duty of local medical grievance committees to throw these rascals out of the practice of medicine. I went further and admitted that if the practice of medicine would throw all its chiselers out, all would not yet be sweetness and light between doctors and patients.

The California Medical Association was still finding that its doctors have far too many dissatisfied patients. The Alameda County Association's secretary, Mr. Rollen Waterson, launched a psychological inquiry. Its questions: What do patients think of their doctors? What do doctors think of their patients? What do doctors think of other doctors? And why?

The upshot of Waterson's inquiry was epochal and it resulted in what's called "the Alameda County plan." In the Alameda plan the general physician becomes a *personal* physician—a specialist in the whole human being. The general physician is the general manager of his patient's health. He guides them through the maze of modern medicine. A given doctor does all he can to diagnose and treat a given patient. If he fails, and if a specialist is needed, he tells the patient why. He confers with the specialist in the patient's presence. He finds out the probable cost of the consultation and subsequent treatment.

225

The personal physician follows through till the patient is cured or his illness over—for better or for worse. The personal physician guarantees his own services regardless of the patient's inability to pay. When we're sick, we're sometimes desperate for a friend who may really know the score. The personal physician is our friendly advocate before the court of medical appeal. He's our economic friend too, holding himself responsible if a specialist should try to soak us. He's our defender from the iniquitous five per cent of what John Cline calls chiselers. The personal physician does not look down his nose at his patients as "laymen." The Alameda plan recommends that "layman" be dropped from the medical vocabulary. The new type of doctor tells his patients all he knows about their illness and what its treatment is probably going to be like. He comes clean about what a patient may hope for. So, it comes about that the patient becomes an amateur doctor co-operating with his personal physician.

The know-how of the conscientious personal physician may often cut down our medical bills. He'll see to it that his patients are not needlessly given elaborate X-ray and laboratory diagnostic work in hospitals. He treats them as often as he can in his own office or at home.

"What you've done," said Rhea after I had outlined all this to my doctor friends, "is to tell them that honesty is the same as bravery."

CHAPTER SIXTEEN

THE romance of the thirty-five years of the marriage of Rhea and Paul came to its end at two in the morning of July 9, 1957, in Chicago. Was it that God saw fit to part us now that He was sure we were calm and happy?

This last day in Chicago was close to the anniversary of our best of all days. That anniversary, July 12, we had kept sacred over many years, calm and happy, or tragic and stormy. Just remembering it had sometimes turned bad days to good ones for both of us. The anniversary? It was that of the first day we had kissed in the night on the little wooden bridge over what we called our old millstream, near Ann Arbor. That moment was the first I'd realized the solemnity of a first kiss. Now this final day in Chicago was just three days short of thirty-eight years since that deepest of all our days together—July 12, 1919.

Etched in my memory is a birthday message Rhea gave me a little more than a year before this last desolate day in Chicago. Then I was about to be sixty-six. It was her wit to call me "old 666." On that day I remember her to have been so lovely— serene and just, like Portia, and strong and wise, like Diana.

Here was her birthday letter:

March 1st, 1956

Darling 666:

Happy birthday and my every wish for many, many more for you. Do you realize that we have spent half of all your years together?

Some of them have been rugged, but there have been many happy ones. For me, the last one has been by far the happiest of all.

I love you more and more and I shall try so hard to make the future years better for you and your work—which is you.

My dearest love,
Always.

The coming year, my sixty-seventh, was going to be still better for both of us. I had a feeling that we were just getting started. Never had we worked so closely, so happily, so boldly together.

So in the early spring of 1956 we began work on the story of a man and his lady. Its theme was the history of a strange original, Charles T. Ferguson and his wife, Mary. Just as Rhea had done for me, Mary's devotion alone had kept Ferg alive and working.

Ferg was a doctor, an M.D., brilliant but so unstable that he'd had to be locked up in mental hospitals, repeatedly—five times over a period of years. Ferg had been overwhelmed again and again by heavy barbiturate addictions. At last, with the help of Mary and three Indiana doctors, Ferg had thrown all his pills and capsules away. He finally fought his way up out of his last and deepest psychosis. He knew insanity inside out because he had been so deeply crazy himself.

Ferguson's *curriculum vitae,* which he had given us with no reservations, was hardly reassuring. Till a few years ago he had been the king of rolling stones. He had been a cinder snapper in the big steel mill at Gary, Indiana; he had been a locomotive fireman on the Monon railroad; he had been a brilliant bartender, a whisky peddler, and a highly successful insurance salesman and in between these vocations had done several stretches in mental institutions. It had taken him twenty years to struggle through to his M.D.

What kind of background was this for a physician who dared to explore the grim and sad frontiers of mental illness? When we met him, Ferguson was deep in doing that. For the past six years, coldly sane, he had been a resident physician in Michigan's Traverse City State Hospital.

Jack Ferguson fascinated us. I mean not for his present work, but as Ferguson. He was utterly out in the open. "If you're going to write about my work," he told Rhea and me, "you kids 'd better know and tell right out what's been bad about me." He narrated it all as if telling about another crazy man he had known. "The last time I went crazy, they carried me to the mental hospital, higher than a kite and dangerous," Ferg explained with a smile. "I'd tried to kill myself. I'd tried to kill Mary. And goofy? I had hallucinations in technicolor."

We told him that one of his oldest medical acquaintances had already warned us how crazy Ferg was. "He doesn't know the half of it about me," said Ferguson. "I was a really classic bastard," he said laughing. And to prove it he held Rhea and Mary and me at Wake Robin all of one long afternoon and into the evening while he told, low key, his life's history. During that narrative, a present significance of his turbulent past dawned on Rhea and me.

Here sat Jack, tranquil yet active in a state we could only call emotional solidity. This man must be ahead of all others in his present chemical battle against abnormal behavior. But as my editors couldn't see him as the subject of a *Reader's Digest* article, I decided to write a book about him.

Mind you, Ferguson was not the first observer of the new chemical magic of what he called "the behavior medicines." From other hospitals these remedies were beginning to parole psychotics. But there was a special trick about Ferg's method of using the medicines. When at last he had become respectable and got a resident's job at the Traverse City, Michigan, State Hospital, he proceeded to try for the recovery of only the incurable insane.

We asked him why he took on only these hopeless. Jack said that was simple. "You see, psychotics in the early stages of their illness often have spontaneous remissions. They recover temporarily without any medicines at all. But those poor doomed wretches in what we called the 'back' wards? If these hopeless ones behave better on our medicines—it's for sure the medicines are responsible."

Here's what he told us in a flash that's poetic rather than

scientific. Here inside the mental hospital Jack saw a weird world. The obstreperous, cantankerous, sullen, suspicious, silly, filthy, suicidal, homicidal bad behavior of my back-ward patients—what is it?

"It's only an exaggeration of abnormally behaved humanity, outside the hospital walls just not crazy enough to be committed." I thumbed through a great stack of case histories of tragedies. Why had they come? "She keeps tearing her clothes off her. . . . Or, we have to feed her every mouthful she eats. . . . Or, she doesn't know where the bathroom is. . . . Or, we try hard but we can't keep her clean. . . . Or, we're afraid she's going to set the house afire. . . . Or, she's constantly screaming and hollering. . . . Or, she's mean. . . . Or, she abuses us. . . . Or, she attacks us and we're afraid she may kill us. . . . "

"It's that simple," said Ferg. "It's their excessive *abnormal behavior* that brings them to us." There was no special big word for it.

What Jack wanted to do was to expand a small fact that Dr. William Lorenz—you remember?—had stumbled upon forty years ago; a little fact, yet far too deep for him to reason out in advance. That little event? It was only a sudden lucid interval in the life of an absolutely hopeless lunatic. It was as if, Lorenz had said, you saw a veil lifted—by chemistry—to reveal sanity that was hidden, latent. But sanity existing in a brain that was supposed, by all clinical experience, to be dead, to be gone. Here was Lorenz's insight. These lucid intervals, some of them lasted as long as eight hours, suggested that many mental illnesses might be chemically reversed, permanently.

In the middle 1930's there had begun a great searching for causes of insanity. Dr. Manfred Sakel, of Berlin and Vienna, announced an actual cure of victims deemed hopelessly demented. Not by the production of a merely lucid interval in their insanity —but its cure. His subjects were dope addicts, crazed as they came out of their addiction. What goes on in brain cells when they're deprived of their absolutely necessary food—sugar? He wanted to know. Sakel tried to answer that by bigger and bigger insulin injections. So he put one of these patients into heavy insulin shock, ending in a deep coma. The man seemed about to die. Sakel saved him by a quick big shot of sugar into his blood. And when that patient came back to consciousness, he was calm, he was quiet, he was sane. It seemed that their terrible ordeal of insulin shock did more than calm these agitated addicts. In some of them a character change appeared, a change for the better—permanent.

Manfred Sakel defended his experiments. After all, the lunacy of a hopeless dementia praecox victim is a desperate state and does that not suggest desperate chemical measures for their sick brain cells? Wasn't his insulin shock giving the sick insides of their brain cells a real housecleaning? If it did, then they might set up a new, clean chemical housekeeping. If only he didn't kill those brain cells by cleaning them! Sakel fancied himself to be presiding over a battle. In these people there seemed to be two selves—a sane and a crazed self struggling with each other. The sane self seemed to be fighting to throw out the crazed.

In his first therapy against insanity, Ferg tried to duplicate Sakel's work. Ferg found the catch was that insulin shocks aren't safe enough to be used, routinely. Then at last Ferg had the luck to try an absolutely new treatment, on his own. He had got hold of a lot of pills left at the hospital by a Ciba detail man. They were known to produce tranquillity among their other virtues. These Rauwolfia pills—derived from an Indian plant—went under the trade name of "Serpasil" as they were put out by Ciba in Summit, New Jersey.

At Traverse City in the autumn of 1954 he set himself up in business, testing the effect of Serpasil on the bad behavior of the worst and the longest and the most invincibly horribly behaved among the more than one thousand crazed ladies on his service.

At Traverse City State Hospital, medically, Ferg was alone. He hadn't a medical resident, doctor, or even an intern or any other kind of doc to help him. But he did have 107 nurse attendants. He explained that they were his hands and eyes and ears. They were really wonderful women, said Ferg. They had cared for this terrible type of psychotic for years before Ferg had come. They had loved them for years through thick and thin—hardly human, screaming, dirty, depressed, sad, wildly elated, or suddenly destructive, suicidal. And some of them deadly dangerous.

Pretty soon Dr. Frank Mohr from Ciba came up to Traverse to show Ferg and other members of the hospital staff a movie film depicting the antics of a crazy monkey. Dr. Mohr had had to handle his insane simian with long, biteproof, scratchproof gauntlets. But one shot of Serpasil into this dangerous devil, and within an hour he underwent what could only be called a transmogrification. The monkey was suddenly gentle, petted his attendant and, like a puppy, snuggled up to him. Ferguson was not completely impressed. Was this all there was to Dr. Mohr's monkey show? The catch in this wonder drug, Serpasil, was that it not only tranquilized certain patients but then sank them down deeper into the blues, into Parkinsonian shakes, into suicidal depressions. What had Ciba to offer against that?

So it came about that, in the late autumn of 1954, Ferg found himself co-operating with Ciba. They were sending him another new compound to try to tame Serpasil. It was Serpasil's opposite. It was a booster. It had the trade name Ritalin. It had a curious quality. People could be overdosed with barbiturates till they got so dopey they couldn't do simple additions and subtractions. Then Ritalin. And they became arithmeticians! Unfortunately that seemed to be all there was to Ritalin. Its boosting action was so gentle, medically, that Ciba scientists deemed it no great shakes, therapeutically.

Now at Traverse City Ferg proceeded to use it to make a minor miracle. Ritalin turned out to rouse human Serpasil zombies into activity without disturbing their tranquillity. Here's what Serpasil and Ritalin, acting together, made Ferg realize. Insanity is more than merely abnormal behavior. Insanity can be *overactive* abnormal behavior and Serpasil tranquilizes that. Or insanity can be *underactive* abnormal behavior and Ritalin boosts it back toward normal.

232

Insanity? It's only an exaggeration of the conduct of all of us who are not confined in asylums. Said Jack: "We on the outside don't carry a full head of steam all the time. And we don't have our dobbers down all the time. We're all of us creatures of moods —overactive, then underactive."

I listened to Jack attentively and felt sad. He could likely hope for no great scientific success because he looked at insanity so simply. Yet in regard to psychotics Jack had a curious insight. He showed me a woman, lying on the floor, seemingly utterly underactive. He touched her and she jerked violently. "You see, she's tense. Like a mainspring wound too tight." Jack kept insisting that abnormal behavior is almost always a mixture of over and underactive.

One of the great days in Jack's life came at the Midwest Research Conference of the American Psychiatric Association. Here he read a paper: "Improved Behavior Patterns in the Hospitalized Mentally Ill." What caused a mild scientific sensation was the type of the patients Jack was bringing back to sanity. It was the hopelessness of all his cases when he started treating them. In psychiatric slang they were the cats and the dogs in the bottom of the barrel. Without regard to their age, all of them many years in the hospital, all chronic, all resistant to insulin shock and electroshock treatment, all custodial, all residual, all waiting blankly for the black wagon to back up to the hospital to take them away for their last ride.

And his medicines? Serpasil—a tranquilizer but so mild in ordinary doses. And Ritalin, a booster, but so gentle. The rolypoly scientist told his learned audience in a low, level voice that, among all categories of their behavior profiles, their improvement was "impressive." Fighting and destruction had disappeared in seventy per cent; night wandering had stopped in seventy per cent; seventy-three per cent could now participate pleasantly in parties; seventy-four per cent were now industrious and good at occupational therapy.

Here was an off-beat result of his treatment; since he'd begun the Serpasil-Ritalin project, the hospital's beauticians were swamped with requests for permanent waves from stringy-haired, dilapidated ladies who for years had not given a damn how they looked. And he was pleased to report that the hospital now had more than 150 vacancies, more than one hundred empty beds since he'd started his treatment. This, in a three-thousand-bed hospital that had had a long waiting list for admissions.

The audience of psychiatric savants stayed awake. They all knew that, in the over-all discipline of the treatment of mental disease, there have been systematic lectures on psychotherapy; attempts to calm down victims with high pressure streams of cold water; putting wild patients into long heavy sleeps—German scientists called it *Dauerschlaf*—with barbiturates; confining them tightly in camisoles; dipping patients, manic but mummified, for a while in cold water; convulsing them with jolting shocks of electricity or with bangs of metrazol; or sending them into deep coma with insulin; or slashing their brains with lobotomies. All acts of violence.

Who in psychiatry's drab, stern discipline had devised a treatment consisting of a couple of mild chemicals, one tranquilizing, one boosting; plus tender loving care for all the patients—even for those too crazed to know what love was; plus a simple science of games and fun? This last was the invention of one of Jack's nurses, Donna Pillars. "This fun is wonderful for the patients, and our own morale," said Donna. "They play games like kids. The fun reinforces the new medicines."

"What am I, compared to my nurse attendants?" Jack asked me. "I'm nothing. All I've done is provide the new medicines for them to administer to their patients. There are far too many for me to treat personally. It's the nurses who regulate the doses and keep all the records. And then they give the patients the tender loving care without which the medicines would be nothing. That's their own medicine."

Why had these nurse attendants been plying their patients with loving care for years before Ferg came with these new medicines? Why did they lavish their love not only on early, possibly curable cases but equally on the completely regressed, the human vegetables, the invincibly insane? I asked Sara Downey, R.N.—supervisor Bertha Orcutt's assistant director of nursing. She couldn't explain it to me. She couldn't say why the nurse attendants had always knocked themselves out, loving these completely unlovable derelicts. Why hadn't they gone away to jobs less frustrating, less physically revolting and thankless? Sara did not know.

Or was it that, secretly, all of them were making some personal expiation, as I knew that Jack was making his atonement for his past?

On Ferguson's service at the hospital before he brought the new medicines, there were four "locked wards." They were full of violently disturbed patients. Now there is only one locked ward—Hall Eleven. There will always have to be one disturbed room to shelter the wild, the incorrigibles, the dangerous and derelict who come from other state hospitals that can't handle them or from the Neuropsychiatric Institute at the University of Michigan or from the Hospital for the Criminally Insane at Ionia—homicidals or suicidals who need maximum security.

"You should have seen Hall Eleven the way it was two years ago, to appreciate the way it is now," said one of Jack's nurses. In Hall Eleven there are lovely curtains and draperies now and it is rare for any patient to try to tear them down. There is a record player and the patients dance pleasantly to its music and a TV set to which they attentively look and listen. There is a piano and a couple of patients can play it well to an appreciative audience. There are books and they're read and not thrown at other patients.

Rhea looked around, wondering. "How do you keep it the way it is now?" she asked. "You still get the wild ones, the toughies, the smashers?" "Yes," said the nurse, "but now we have the new medicines they don't stay wild very long."

The patients told Rhea how much Jack was a part of it. "Don't forget, Dr. Ferguson is beloved in this hospital," one of them said, looking through and through Rhea and me out of her newly lucid gray eyes. "No, we'll not forget, don't worry," we said, and there were tears in our own eyes.

At the beginning of 1956 Mary Ferguson was proud of her Jack and happier than she'd been, ever. Superintendent Nickels, Bertha Orcutt, the supervisor of nurses, and her assistant, Sara Downey, had all told Mary and Jack that this was the nicest Christmas they'd ever had at the hospital. Jack said it was thanks to Mary. Rhea said she didn't believe Jack would have held on without his Mary. Jack had remained cool and level now for almost six years.

He'd been able to send more than 150 patients back to their home or family care—from among the nearly one thousand chronic, deteriorated ladies on his service. There were several hundred more of these patients ready for trial visits or parole or even discharge from the hospital.

As I worked at Jack's story, Rhea and I talked about Mary and Jack constantly. We wished we were as tightly linked as they were. I stewed and fussed and worried about Jack's being so alone in his work. He had only Mary and Miss Orcutt and Sara Downey and Donna Pillars and the other nurse attendants and the recovered patients to cheer him on. No outside audience. "Jack's being an outsider is his strength," said Rhea. She asked how could I be so stupid as to want Jack to get respectable and stuffy and not be an outsider. Didn't I remember my original heroes? What about Robert Koch, alone, trapping anthrax microbes in his kitchen? Even his devoted wife, Emmy, was fed up with his kitchen bacteriology. What about Fred Banting, who found insulin in a hot attic with only one medical student, Charlie Best, to help him, while both of them were bombarded with professorial sneers?

There were still subtle booby traps set for Jack in his one-man fight against insanity. He had been a stunning success curing chronic, far-advanced schizos. Would Jack believe his own publicity if it should boil up around him? But in the backwoods of Traverse City there was no publicity. That was surely one secret of his success.

Did Jack believe that their medicine of life plus chemicals would cure the ultimate deterioration of senile old people—a deterioration that was as sure as death itself, nearly? They were in the stage not of life but of that pitiful terminal existence that the doctors euphemize as "the senium." That makes it sound less horrible.

Jack's eyes flashed sparks. "I ask you in all sincerity, what're we gonna *do* to help the grandmaws and grandpaws and poor old Aunt Mary? In countless, maybe in close to a million homes from coast to coast there exist poor old gentlemen and poor old ladies, clearheaded one moment, foggy the next. Even in their lucid intervals they are afraid. They ask their sons and daughters, pitifully: 'You're not going to have to put me away?'

"The state's senile dementia cases are going up by leaps and jumps. People don't die the way they used to. It's the power of the antibiotics. So the poor old people are pouring in on us from their families, who can't stand their bad behavior. Then others are coming in from the county poorhouses. They're arriving from nursing homes that can't cope with their incorrigible conduct."

Jack said he'd wrestled for years with this mystery of senile insanity. He fought it when he could not sleep and he never did sleep much. Wide awake, he no longer reached for the bar-biturate bottle—indeed he'd thrown it away. He kept thinking and working and work was his only sedative. He had lost his fear. It is as if his having survived his stormy weather in his Hamlet practice and in all the locked wards of state hospitals, killing his fear, has let loose a surge of energy in him. Not turbulent but like the energy in a deep, fast-flowing river. It is notable that in men whose energy is strong under an unruffled surface, underneath there is usually an absence of fear.

Jack is bold and unorthodox in his use of research money. The pharmaceutical houses give him the medicines for free. Jack with their many grants buys record players, TV sets, and corn poppers for each of the wards on his service. Isn't this a dubious use of money meant for scientific research? What will the committees of eminent scientists, the "Study Groups" of the Public Health service, what will they all say about goldfish and apple pies as a part of his treatment for insanity? Jack plugged ahead, noting the tremendous therapeutic power of his nurse attendants beyond their point of routine duty. He saw their understanding and tenderness penetrating beneath the surface, the outward insanity of the patients. The attendants' love was digging down toward inner fear.

"But why do my grandmaws have no families to go home to? Why do their children, so many of them, no longer want them, normal though we show them they now are?" Jack finds no answer, only keeping on asking: "What are we going to do for grandmaw, grandpaw, and old Aunt Mary?"

In January, 1956, the *Journal of the American Medical Association* published a report by Drs. John T. Ferguson and William H. Funderburk on a now hopeful theme of the possible improvement of senile behavior. The scholarly editors of this greatest journal of our doctors ordered Jack to make over two hundred grammatical and stylistic changes in his seventeen-page, double-spaced manuscript. "Just the same, Dr. Austin Smith, *chief* editor, didn't query a single one of our facts or interpretations," said Jack with a grin. With Jack's permission Dr. Smith dictated the lead of the article: "The medical prevention and control of these abnormal behavior patterns in the elderly by those closest to them—the general practitioners—should be the starting point of the attack."

Jack agreed, but here is what gnawed him. "Can family doctors in general be induced to treat these poor old people in their homes—before they're committed—when they're just on the verge of having to be put away? If they'd do that, there'd be far less heartache, and far less of the economic burden of the aged insane." Would the plain docs believe that? But wouldn't that be too common sensible? To Jack it was just that simple. Maybe too simple? If the family physicians could do this, would they?

It would take a lot of time and in the routine of their practices they're awfully busy.

"There's a lot more to mental disease than this abnormal behavior we're fussing with here." Jack's words kept haunting Rhea and me all day and every night all through our year of digging into Jack's biography. Rhea said: "You say there's a lot more to mental illness than surface behavior. *We'll* say there is, oh yes, much more and how much more you don't know and God only knows and He's not telling."

In the face of the enigma of mental illness, what's Jack Ferguson? Only one insignificant man, almost like a G.I. infantryman, in today's brilliant biochemical battle to try to reach millions of minds sick, scarred, scared, and muddled. His modest goal is only to bring abnormally behaved dopes back close enough to normal to be able to live with themselves and others around them. Yet, in today's big brilliant biochemical battle against insanity, normal behavior is far from enough to attain as a victory.

Let's say Jack attains normal behavior for most of them. That leaves unexplained the chemical mystery beneath insanity. Of this mystery, Jack knows little. Normal behavior? That's merely a surface sanity. Among the seemingly sane there are those who will suddenly confide to you that they're Joan of Arc back from the dead or the Angel Gabriel come down to earth. One of the patients may have been paroled from the hospital in what seems a state of beatific tranquillity. On her own steam she'd got a job waiting table. She serves you cheerfully and with dexterity. Till one day she pours a dish of hot vegetable soup down your neck and bursts into wild laughter.

Can we have confidence in the solidity of the sanity of such unpredictable people? What astounded Rhea and me about Jack is that such failures did not unnerve him. He looks at us. He smiles. It is as if he is admitting, with regret, to have swept away only one surface layer in the insanity of this person. Yet isn't that something? What if it does leave a deeper, a stubborn layer of lunacy below it? Very well. Now he'll root out that next stratum of craziness with some hoped-for new chemical, of the structure of which he hasn't the faintest notion.

Chemical help came from the celebrated neurologist and psychiatrist, Dr. Howard D. Fabing of Cincinnati. Howard gave Jack his chance for a chemical attack upon delusions and hallucinations. Howard shares Jack's humility. "I've always been ready to try anything on a disorder of the nervous system that seems to carry with it a possible hope of success without probability of harm," explains Howard. "Abandoned concoctions and brews by the dozen litter my past."

Howard looks as if he'd come out of a Frans Hals painting. Howard is red and round-faced and burly, with shrewd, doubting, china-blue eyes. He acts every inch of him like a jolly country doctor (which he is) but beyond that he has a bit of knowledge of the terrifically complicated mechanism of the human brain. Above all, he has curiosity.

This led him to the new compound, Frenquel, that had no known chemical use; and to finding that it was an enemy to delusions and hallucinations. The day Fabing received his first tablets of Frenquel from the researchers of the W. S. Merrell Company, that day a university student—Fabing says she looked like a blond Juno—was admitted to Christ Hospital in Cincinnati in a storm of acute schizophrenia. She was loud. She was destructive. She was dissociated from reality. She tried to run out into the street in her panties and bra—she had no shame. She was hallucinated, suspicious, overactive, surly, confused, and deadly in her sarcasm.

Insulin and electroshock had not helped her. Immediately, Fabing began giving her Frenquel in more and more tablets by mouth and it was amazing the way they brought the crazy beautiful blond Juno out of her torment. Convalescing, she told Howard of her horrible hallucinations—of her having walked arm in arm with a corpse with worms crawling out of its cheeks; of her hearing beautiful music mixed up with shouts of voices calling her a slut and a whore. Now after Frenquel these horrors were quickly gone. Now she is lovely and sane again and working. She has to keep taking moderate doses of Frenquel. It is the first formidable medicine ("alpha (4 piperidyl) benzhydryl hydrochloride") against hallucinations.

Fabing reports that Frenquel is an in-and-outer—its average of improvement in his series of 115 schizophrenics is about forty per cent over-all. Though chronic schizophrenics don't do too well on Frenquel, Jack Ferguson, not having any acute ones, tried it on his chronics. Some of them had become just short of normally behaved on Serpasil plus Ritalin plus loving care. Then they'd relapse. Here was a lady who, while her general behavior was serene, was convinced that she was to be appointed the leader of Admiral Byrd's expedition to the South Pole and was also conducting negotiations on the location of the proposed jet aircraft base in northern Michigan. And she had plans ready to submit to state and federal authorities for the reorganization of the Traverse City State Hospital. Jack found that Frenquel tablets, many times, not only wiped out this mental overactivity but also convinced the patients that their activity had been foolish.

Frenquel struck home personally to Fabing. He was sitting in his father-in-law's hospital room forty-eight hours after that old gentleman had successfully undergone a prostate gland operation. Howard had just come downstairs from his lab where he had been observing one of his young student volunteers driven experimentally insane by imbibing the hallucinogen, mescaline. Now— it was a coincidence—as he sat at his father-in-law's bedside, he saw a peculiar change in the old gentleman's behavior. He suddenly began talking wildly. He did not know where he was and he was confused and frightened. It was not uncommon after prostate operations. "Postoperative confusion, we call it," muttered Howard.

"It suddenly flashed over me," said Howard, "that he was acting exactly like my mescaline volunteer upstairs. Why not try Frenquel on Dad? I gave the old gentleman 50 milligrams of the drug into a vein. His psychosis melted away during the next half hour. . . . "

Here, Frenquel had actually conquered what was a very early, acute attack of schizophrenia. Such was Howard's takeoff on an inquiry into an acute psychosis, postoperative. Fabing reports that Frenquel has been almost uniformly effective in relieving some seventy-five cases of this sudden, mysterious postsurgical dementia.

What did these poor wretches have, besides hallucinations and delusions? On his own service, Jack watched them. It boiled down to his old story: they had abnormal behavior. Some of them were violently overactive; others despondently underactive. "Keep on with Frenquel, even though some patients relapse under it," Jack told the discouraged nurse attendants. Then, as a lady began to show the sinister return of her hallucinations and delusions— *if she was overactive*—Jack had the nurses add Serpasil to Frenquel. And if they were underactive and depressed, Jack told them to add Ritalin.

It was really something to see. It was new, unprecedented. Ritalin added to the underactives and Serpasil added to the overactives—both tended to bring back and maintain the original control of Frenquel over those deeper layers of insanity—delusions and hallucinations.

When a bright chemical hope blows up in Jack's face, he corrects himself ruthlessly. So it was with the Serpasil analog, Harmonyl. Tested on wildly overactive ladies, Harmonyl calmed them down like so many millponds on a quiet day. "But then," said Jack, "though tranquil, they developed levity. They began to giggle and couldn't stop giggling, not even in church."

At the Traverse City State Hospital some of Jack's colleagues were not ready to accept the various types of treatment he advanced and there were some who were alert to snipe at him for his failures. Here to a staff meeting with all the hospital's physicians present, a catatonic patient is brought. He has had insulin, electroshock; he has had the works. Yet he remains as uncommunicative; dumb, a blank. Even Thorazine, a good tranquilizer, hasn't budged him. Jack speaks up. "This patient doesn't need a tranquilizer. Why not wake him up with Ritalin?"

One of the doctors says that he has had no luck with Ritalin in tablet form. He believes that Dr. Ferguson overrates this Ritalin.

"Gentlemen," Jack asks, "would you mind my showing you right here, right now, what Ritalin will do for this patient?" The doctors would be delighted.

An ampoule of Ritalin, 10 milligrams, injectible, intravenous is brought in. Within five minutes after Dr. Frank Linn, a young resident, has sent the Ritalin slowly into the catatonic's arm vein, this poor fellow who has been so dazed, so dumb, so blank, so mute for many months, is wide-awake, clear-eyed, and is answering questions.

"Ritalin, intravenously, in a few minutes may wake up a dumb catatonic, lying all out on the floor and drooling. Serpasil into an arm vein will quiet a manic; Ritalin into the vein of that manic's other arm will wake him up, active yet tranquil. In many of them, no matter how bad, how chronic," said Ferguson.

CHAPTER SEVENTEEN

Ferguson's story was more fun than anything Rhea and I had written. *A Man Against Insanity* was popular in book form. From its long condensation in the *Reader's Digest* more than ten thousand readers wrote personally to Ferguson. They begged him to tell them what to do, specifically, for the insanity of members of their families. Ferg answered them all as best he could.

The comments on the book made Rhea and me happy when it appeared in the spring of 1957. Said Dr. Austin Smith, editor of the *Journal of the American Medical Association:* "It offers hope and encouragement for those who wonder in moments of despair if there's a road back. . . . Equally challenging is the story of the man who knows his patients because he has lived through their experiences."

"The biography," wrote Dr. Howard Fabing " . . . is one of the most remarkable things I have ever seen. I don't know when I've encountered an actual living mortal so fully undressed down to his complete nakedness in the middle of his life, like this, anywhere in literature. The scientific material . . . is good . . . true. . . . It is tough as nails."

Rhea and I were walking on air because we had pulled our project off completely together. We talked excitedly of now writing stories of other original types, biographical, not necessarily medical.

"I love you more and more," wrote Rhea, "and I shall try so hard to make the future years better and better for you and for your work, which is you."

She was thrilled that I no longer was the turbulent, wild man I had been, but she did not know there were to be no future years better for me and my work, or for both of us together. And no future years, better for me alone. I looked at her proudly as we walked many miles along the Lake Michigan shore in the strong sun in the middle of June and I had never seen her so seemingly happy and so utterly lovely.

Then one day, coming home hand in hand from our walk, Rhea's face became twisted in pain, contorted, and it was all she could do to hobble home. Next morning we drove to Chicago to Saint Luke's Hospital and the pain was still with her. "Acute thrombophlebitis," said Dr. Ormond Julian, the best in Chicago. He was not only a skilled and amiable man but a kidder who gave us both confidence. "No surgery," said Julian, "but you're going to have to stay here on your back for a while." He was a joker.

"I don't like to have to take care of you, Mrs. de Kruif. It always seems I have bad luck with the wife of a medical man."

"But Paul isn't medical," said Rhea, laughing. "He's only an ex-microbe hunter."

But it was only the medicine of rest that Rhea needed, said Julian.

This was June 19 and Julian made us feel good, reassuring us we'd both be back home to celebrate our usual July 4—always our greatest of all days of the high summer at Wake Robin. In a few days it was marvelous how her pain had left her and all swelling had vanished from her leg. I was staying at the Hotel Drake, deep in writing a blood-bank story. Herman Bundesen's chauffeur, Larry Hurt, drove me to see Rhea again and again day after day. Rhea wouldn't let me stay with her long. "Get back on that blood story—it'll kick the worry out of you," said Rhea, trying to smile.

Worried, I asked Dr. Julian and the nurses every day, "How's my baby getting along?" More and more they were noncommittal because they were not going to kid me. "When are you going to let her sit up?" I asked them.

"I haven't any pain. I just get out of breath going from the bed to my chair," said Rhea.

She refused day nurses or night nurses or any kind of special nursing. "They're busy and I don't need anything special."

One day she lost her breath; it came in short fast gasps as she struggled from bed to her chair. And that was the day, early in July, when she wouldn't let me stay with her for more than fifteen minutes. "You've got a deadline on that blood story," she said sternly. "Don't bother about me."

One day while I was kneeling by her, my head on her bed, Dr. Julian came in cheerily and apologetically. Rhea's breath was coming with difficulty. "Poor darling, are you crying?" said Rhea, patting my head. "No, only praying for both of us," I said. "What are you kids talking about?" asked Julian as he came in smiling.

"We're trying to sum up what's been worth while in our life together," I said.

"May I know what it's been?" asked the doctor. Then Rhea managed to answer, though out of breath as if she'd been running hard along the lake shore.

"It's easy, Doctor. Just two seven-letter words is all. We've tried for honesty and courage." She smiled.

I recall these to have been her last words and her last smile.

As Julian and I went out of the room he said, "I may have to call you, Paul, tonight at the Drake. You'll be ready?"

When in answer to Julian's phone call I got to Rhea's room at the hospital, she lay in torture on her bed, amid silly complicated apparatus and the low clicking hum of activity of nurses, doctors, residents, and Dr. Julian. I said, "Hello, Rhea honey, you're going to be okay?"

She looked at me it seemed for a moment as if I were far, far away; but she really did not know me and at two that morning she drew her last breath.

Julian and I laid her poor tortured body straight on the disordered bed. I bent over her and kissed her forehead. How could God have allowed her to go away? The experts dismantled their futile apparatus. All of them left Rhea's room except Julian, who stayed with me, trying to console me.

"Will you be all right, Paul?" he asked.

"Thanks, Doctor, but I'm all right. You see, Rhea and I had a little joke between us. That's what has been holding me up."

It was the ninth beatitude.

"Blessed be they who expect nothing. For they shall not be disappointed," I said, and I did not cry.